Cultivating Curious and Creative Minds

The Role of Teachers and Teacher Educators: Part I

Teacher Education Yearbook XVIII

EDITED BY CHERYL J. CRAIG
AND LOUISE F. DERETCHIN

Published in partnership with the
Association of Teacher Educators
ROWMAN & LITTLEFIELD EDUCATION
Lanham, Maryland • Toronto • Plymouth, UK
2010

Published in partnership with the
Association of Teacher Educators

Published in the United States of America
by Rowman & Littlefield Education
A Division of Rowman & Littlefield Publishers, Inc.
A wholly owned subsidary of The Rowman & Littlefield Publishing Group, Inc.
4501 Forbes Boulevard, Suite 200, Lanham, Maryland 20706
www.rowmaneducation.com

Estover Road
Plymouth PL6 7PY
United Kingdom

ISSN: 1078-2265
ISBN: 978-1-60709-628-3 (cloth: alk. paper)
ISBN: 978-1-60709-629-0 (pbk.: alk. paper)
ISBN: 978-1-60709-580-4 (e-book)

∞™ The paper used in this publication meets the minimum requirements of American
National Standard for Information Sciences—Permanence of Paper for Printed Library
Materials, ANSI/NISO Z39.48-1992.
Manufactured in the United States of America.

Contents

List of Illustrations   vii

Foreword   ix
     Annette D. Digby

Introduction   xi
     Cheryl J. Craig, Louise F. Deretchin

Overview and Framework   1
     Cheryl J. Craig, Louise F. Deretchin

1   In Pursuit of Joy: Creativity, Pedagogy, and the Science of
     Well-Being   4
     Kevin Cloninger, Christina Mengert

2   Can We Teach for Surprise?   24
     Gadi Alexander

3   Jumping to Conclusions or Jumping for Joy? Reframing Teaching
     as the Art of Talent Development   66
     F. Richard Olenchak, John P. Gaa

4   Aesthetic Themes as Conduits to Creativity   99
     Christy M. Moroye, P. Bruce Uhrmacher

5   Child Study/Lesson Study: A Catalyst for Teacher Curiosity   115
     Herbert P. Ginsburg, Joan V. Mast, Merrie Snow

6   Nurturing a Creative Curiosity for K–2 Mathematics Teaching:
    Lessons from the Dreamkeepers   132
    Patricia L. Marshall, Allison W. McCulloch, Jessica T. DeCuir-Gunby
7   The Impact of Creativity within the Inquiry Process in
    Science Education   161
    Terri R. Hebert
8   Capturing Teacher Learning, Curiosity, and Creativity through
    Science Notebooks   178
    Carole G. Basile, Sharon Johnson
9   Freeing the Body to Build the Creative Mind   195
    JeongAe You
10 Teaching Creatively in-between Contested Contradictions and
    Complexities in the U.S. South   218
    Ming Fang He, Wynnetta Scott-Simmons, Angela McNeal Haynes,
    Derrick M. Tennial
11 On the Need for Curious and Creative Minds in Multicultural
    and Cross-Cultural Educational Settings: Narrative Possibilities 252
    Shijing Xu, F. Michael Connelly

Summary and Implications   267
    Cheryl J. Craig, Louise F. Deretchin

Afterword   271
    Cheryl J. Craig, Louise F. Deretchin

Illustrations

Tables

1.1   Characteristics of Creative People   10
1.2   Examples of Mnemonic Devices for Creativity   12
1.3   Creativity Expressed in Human Life   14
1.4   Creativity Framework for the Schools   16
7.1   Essential Features of Classroom Inquiry and Their Variations   164

Figures

3.1   Mary's Adapted Version of the Future Problem Solving Process   81
5.1   Children's Answers to Questions Proposed   123
7.1   Types of Inquiry   163
9.1   Five Educational Values of Physical Activities toward the
      Creative Mind   210
9.2   Creative Movements with Creative Minds   212

Foreword

Annette D. Digby
Lincoln University of Missouri

> Annette D. Digby, EdD, began serving as the vice president for
> academic affairs and provost and professor of education at Lincoln
> University of Missouri on August 1, 2007. Prior to her appointment
> at Lincoln, Dr. Digby was associate dean and then dean of the Divi-
> sion of Education and professor of middle and high school education
> at Lehman College/City University of New York in the Bronx, New
> York (2000–2007), and associate dean for undergraduate studies and
> student services and associate professor of secondary education in
> the College of Education and Health Professions at the University
> of Arkansas (1989–2000). Dr. Digby's scholarly work focuses on ac-
> creditation, faculty professional development, and school/university
> scholarships. She is also the 2009–10 president of the Association of
> Teacher Educators and has served in a variety of leadership roles since
> becoming a member of the association in 1992.

As the 2009–10 president of the Association of Teacher Educators (ATE), I am
pleased and honored to write the foreword for *Cultivating Curious and Creative
Minds: The Role of Teachers and Teacher Educators: Part I* (Teacher Education
Yearbook XVIII). As I perused the chapter titles and accompanying annotations,
I reflected on my own experiences as a high school English teacher in rural Mis-
sissippi and then as a teacher educator in two universities with distinctly different missions. A resource such as this yearbook would have served to enhance my
knowledge, skills, and overall effectiveness as an educator, at both the secondary
and collegiate levels.

As noted by the Center for International Studies in Creativity, "Creativity is
an effective resource that resides in all people and within all organizations . . . that
can be nurtured and enhanced through the use of deliberate tools, techniques and
strategies" (http://www.buffalostate.edu/creativity/). This yearbook, the first of
a two-part series, combines discussions of theoretical frameworks with practical
recommendations for nurturing and encouraging creativity. This volume focuses
on the role of P–12 teachers in fostering their students' creativity through the

education of the whole child while making recommendations for organizational structures within the P–12 setting (e.g., professional learning communities) that support and promote the teachers' abilities to fulfill these roles.

Part II of this volume will be Teacher Education Yearbook XIX and will follow in 2011. It will contain two divisions, the first of which, *Teacher Education*, will focus on components of programs that prepare teachers to successfully and confidently fulfill the roles as discussed in the first division. Highlighted is the challenge for teacher educators to engage in critical and creative thinking while using techniques such as observation and narratives to encourage creativity in teacher candidates. The second division, *Students*, will present the results of selected research studies during which students' creativity and curiosity were enhanced through a variety of activities, including writing poetry and completing collaborative assignments and projects.

Editors Cheryl J. Craig and Louise F. Deretchin have brought together authors from Canada and Korea, from urban and rural America, and from P–12 and university settings. The authors also represent diverse academic backgrounds and professional expertise, including mathematics, the sciences, aesthetic education, and democratic education within multicultural settings. Amid the diversity of backgrounds and ideas, however, is one unifying theme: restoring joy in and passion for teaching through curiosity and creative thought.

As a novice teacher in the 1970s, I would have found this volume on creativity to be invaluable as I developed lesson plans to promote my students' creativity, critical thinking, and curiosity. Perhaps I, too, would have been challenged to expand my own creativity and curiosity in a greater way. Editors Craig and Deretchin are to be commended for engaging a topic that emerged decades ago (Guilford, 1950) but continues to be at the forefront of today's professional discussions. Their foresight, coupled with the expertise and thought-provoking findings of the contributors, has resulted in a much-needed resource for teachers, teacher educators, parents, and anyone else interested in promoting and developing creativity and advancing the field of education in productive ways.

References

Guilford, J. P. (1950). Creativity. *American Psychologist, 5*, 444–54.

International Center for Studies in Creativity. (n.d.). Retrieved June 25, 2009, from http://www.buffalostate.edu/creativity/

Introduction

Cheryl J. Craig
Educational Consultant

Louise F. Deretchin
Educational Consultant

Cheryl J. Craig is a professor at the University of Houston, where she serves as the coordinator of teaching and teacher education program area and director of elementary education. She was recently elected secretary of the International Study Association of Teachers and Teaching. Cheryl Craig's scholarship is published in such journals as *Teachers College Record, Teaching and Teacher Education, American Educational Research Journal*, and *Journal of Curriculum Studies*. Her book, *Narrative Inquiries of School Reform: Storied Lives, Storied Landscapes, Storied Metaphors*, was published in 2003 by Information Age Publishing.

Louise F. Deretchin, PhD, is an educational consultant, former director of higher education for the Houston A+ Challenge (formerly the Houston Annenberg Challenge), former director of the Medical Informatics Education Center at Baylor College of Medicine, a fellow in the Association of Teacher Educators Leadership Academy, founding member of the Texas Higher Education Coordinating Board Houston P–16+ Council, and cofounder of the *Regional Faculty*, whose purpose is to take a regional approach to directing the growth of educational systems. She has been coeditor of the *Association of Teacher Educators Yearbook* since 2006. Her work focuses on creating collaborations among colleges, the business community, and school districts to improve teacher education, teaching, and learning.

When we began our four-year term as coeditors of the *ATE Yearbook*, we knew from the beginning that one of our theme issues would be curiosity and creativity. However, we had some other topics that demanded attention first: namely, accountability from the teacher's perspective (*ATE Yearbook XV*), imagining a renaissance in teacher education (*ATE Yearbook XVI*), and teacher learning in small-group settings (*ATE Yearbook XVII*). Finally, the time for *Cultivating Curious and Creative Minds: The Role of Teachers and Teacher Educators* arrived. Little did we know, however, that the response to the call would be so overwhelming that we would end up with two volumes. In *ATE Yearbook XVIII, Part I*, we present the K–12 teaching theme. In *ATE Yearbook XIX, Part 2*, to be published in 2011, we follow the teaching chapters with those dealing with teacher education and students/programs/schools. In essence, our "curious and creative minds" ballooned and morphed into two yearbook issues.

   Cultivating Curious and Creative Minds: The Role of Teachers and Teacher Educators, Parts 1 and 2 present a plethora of approaches to developing human potential in areas not conventionally addressed. This international collection of essays provides viable educational alternatives to those currently holding sway in this era of high-stakes accountability. We feel certain that readers will find the essays presented in the two volumes a refreshing change to the typical approaches that have dominated how students are characteristically taught in schools and colleges of education.

ONE MORE WORD (Cheryl Craig)

With these two volumes (XVIII in 2010 and XIX in 2011), Louise Deretchin concludes her editorship of the *ATE Yearbook*, a task she has undertaken with diligence and grace. I am certain our membership will join me in recognizing Louise's outstanding contributions to the development of the 2007–11 installments of the *Teacher Education Yearbook* and in wishing her a happy and fulfilling retirement.

Overview and Framework

Cheryl J. Craig

Louise F. Deretchin

Cultivating Curious and Creative Minds: The Role of Teachers and Teacher Educators is a theme addressed over a two-volume Yearbook set. This first volume addresses teaching, whereas the second volume takes up the topics of teacher education and students/programs/schools. We begin with the teaching theme, which comprises eleven chapters presented in this first volume.

Chapter 1, authored by Kevin Cloninger and Christina Mengert, kicks off this first volume and the teaching theme. Titled "In Pursuit of Joy: Creativity, Pedagogy, and the Science of Well-Being," the work offers a comprehensive view of creativity, which is, in turn, linked to the science of well-being, a well-respected line of inquiry in the fields of psychology, neuroscience, and medicine. Connections are forged between creativity and the five overarching domains of human life: sexual, material, emotional, cultural/intellectual, and spiritual.

Written by Gadi Alexander, Chapter 2, "Can We Teach for Surprise?" discusses creativity and imagination, not as luxuries at our disposal but as imperatives foundational to understanding the increasing diversity and complexities embedded in the postmodern world. The work begins with definitional issues, follows with dilemmas associated with imagination and creativity, and ends with five case studies that depict imaginative teaching and learning.

Chapter 3, "Jumping to Conclusions or Jumping for Joy?: Reframing Teaching as the Art Talent Development," contributed by Richard Olenchak and John Gaa, provides a cautionary tale concerning what happens when teachers—the only individuals who meet students face-to-face in classrooms—find their talents sapped. Moreover, the negative and reciprocal influences of underachievement on learners, teachers, and educational milieu are brought to the fore for discussion.

In Chapter 4, "Aesthetic Themes as Conduits to Creativity," Christy Moroye and Bruce Uhrmacher center on teacher professional development and aesthetic experiences that develop both the capacities of teachers and the students taught by them. Six themes related to teacher-artist activities—imagination, sensory

1

experience, risk taking, perceptivity, connections, and active engagement—are addressed.

Herbert Ginsburg, Joan Mast, and Merrie Snow take up the topic of developing curious and creative minds within the mathematics content area in Chapter 5, "Child Study/Lesson Study: A Catalyst for Teacher Curiosity." Through the use of vignettes, Ginsburg, Mast, and Snow show how access to clinical interviews with children assists teachers in refining their teaching practices and aids them in more deeply understanding how individual students learn mathematical concepts.

In Chapter 6, "Nurturing a Creative Curiosity for K–12 Mathematics Teaching: Lessons from the Dreamkeepers," Patricia Marshall, Allison McCulloch, and Jessica DeCuir-Gunby explore how a critical constructivist perspective assists teachers in early mathematics teaching and learning. The deep understanding of early number concepts through culturally relevant pedagogy constitutes the focus of their research attention.

Chapters 7 and 8 turn the focus from the teaching and learning of mathematics to the teaching and learning of science. Terri Hebert examines "The Impact of Creativity within the Inquiry Process in Science Education" in Chapter 7. She makes the case that inquiry-based strategies are closely aligned with creativity, focusing on professional development activities made available through the Institute for Scientific Literacy.

Meanwhile, Carole Basile and Sharon Johnson, in Chapter 8, discuss "Capturing Teacher Learning, Curiosity, and Creativity through Science Notebooks." In addition to science notebooks holding and expressing teachers' knowledge of science content, such notebooks, in Basile and Johnson's estimation, reveal teachers' sense making of dispositions as well—with the key disposition being curiosity.

"Freeing the Body to Build the Creative Mind," Chapter 9, is authored by JeongAe You. The work centers on two cases in which the creative mind was developed within the context of physical education teaching and learning. The chapter confronts deeply held stereotypes concerning the relevance and contributions of physical education as a school subject.

The last two chapters in this Yearbook issue have to do with inquiry, creativity, and teaching and learning about diversity in cross-cultural contexts. In Chapter 10, "Teaching Creatively in-between Contested Contradictions and Complexities in the U.S. South," Ming Fang He, Wynnetta Scott-Simmons, Angela Haynes, and Derrick Tennial inform us of how both history and biography have prompted a group of educators to teach creatively at the boundaries of what has conventionally defined race relations in the American South.

Finally, Chapter 11, "On the Need for Curious and Creative Minds in Multicultural and Cross-Cultural Educational Settings: Narrative Possibilities," contributed by Shijing Xu and Michael Connelly, urges us to inquire into the nature of human difference and not to automatically regard those desiring to learn English as experientially deficit. Xu and Connelly conjure up the image of the bridge, a most helpful phenomenon for imagining two-way cultural and linguistic exchange in an increasingly global world.

Taken together, the chapters in *Cultivating Curious and Creative Minds: The Role of Teachers and Teacher Educators, Part I* provide a sampling of what the cultivation of curious and creative minds entails. The works sheds light on how curiosity and creativity can be approached in the teaching domain and provide specific ideas concerning how it plays out in particular situations and contexts.

CHAPTER 1

In Pursuit of Joy
CREATIVITY, PEDAGOGY, AND THE SCIENCE OF WELL-BEING

Kevin Cloninger
University of Denver

Christina Mengert
University of Colorado–Boulder

Kevin M. Cloninger, PhD, is the president of Anthropedia, a non-profit educational foundation dedicated to helping people live healthier and happier lives. After teaching high school science for some years, Dr. Cloninger taught in the Teacher Education Program at the University of Denver. He has also lectured and given workshops on well-being and education in the United States and England.

Christina Mengert, PhD, MFA, is the author of *As We Are Sung*, forthcoming from Burning Deck Press. Dr. Mengert is also coeditor of the poetry anthology *12 x 12: Conversations in 21ˢᵗ-Century Poetry and Poetics* (University of Iowa Press) and was anthologized in *Best New Poets 2006*. She teaches creative writing at the University of Colorado at Boulder and for UCLA's Writers' Extension Program.

ABSTRACT

Using the science of well-being as a lens, this chapter explores the concept of creativity in human development, learning, and teaching in order to identify strategies that might lead to increased creativity and joy. We offer a framework to help teachers explore the concept of creativity; however, rather than being offered a systematic technique, teachers are encouraged to deeply reflect upon the function of creativity in each of the five overarching domains of human life: sexual, material, emotional, cultural/intellectual, and spiritual. The chapter further calls for contemplation of the nature and cultivation of creativity in the teacher, student, classroom, and administration. It is argued that the development of creativity is of paramount importance for our society and the world in the twenty-first century and that education needs to play a key role in its cultivation.

Our attempts to understand the limits of human potential are frequently stifled by our own limitations. Like a young child stretching her neck to see what's happening at a dinner table taller than she is, we are sometimes frustrated in our attempts to see beyond our own shortcomings. Perhaps it is for this reason that much of the research in psychology has attempted to understand health as the absence of disease (C. R. Cloninger, 2004; Csikszentmihalyi, 2000; Goleman, 1995; Herrman, Saxena, & Moodie, 2005; Huppert, Baylis, & Keverne, 2005; Seligman & Csikszentmihalyi, 2000); it is easier to look at things that do not surpass us. As a consequence of such approaches, we have equated psychological health with being "normal" (C. R. Cloninger, 2004; Herrman, et al., 2005). A number of questions arise once the situation is framed in this way. Is health simply the absence of disease? Is maturity only the lack of immaturity? How do we define normal? This last question is perhaps most troubling. Biases coming from our culture, gender, ethnicity, or class may influence our conceptions of normality. Moreover, when trying to find firm definitions of what is "normal," we are sometimes swayed by our own preconceptions, leading to rigidity and inflexibility in the face of characteristics which conflict with our predetermined images. As if filtered, our perceptions of human development may be incomplete and partial due to our perceptual limitations. Whether we are psychologists or teachers, the problems are the same. Inadequate models of human development can prevent us from being sensitive to the unique characteristics and potential of individuals.

Fortunately, recent advances in the fields of psychology, neuroscience, and medicine have led to the emergence of a new theory, the science of well-being (C. R. Cloninger, 2004; K. Cloninger, 2005), which looks at human development and learning from the perspective of healthy functioning, not simply dysfunction and disease. Well-being, in popular vernacular, conjures images of spas, health food co-ops, new-age bookstores, and yogis.[1] We do not use the term in the popular sense. Instead, we employ the word in much the same way it is currently being used in the field of medicine.[2] Using the science of well-being as a lens, this chapter will explore the concept of creativity in human development, learning, and teaching in order to identify practices and strategies that might lead to increased creativity and joy. It will be argued that the development of creativity is of paramount importance for our society and the world in the twenty-first century and that education needs to play a key role in its cultivation.

It goes without saying that some of the most exceptional people in history have been anything but normal. Great works of art, giftedness of all orders, scientific invention and discovery—these are all facets of human development and consciousness that are not simply born from the absence of problems (C. R. Cloninger, 2004; K. Cloninger, 2005; Csikszentmihalyi, 2000; Deci & Ryan, 2008; Diener & Suh, 2000; Gardner, 1983, 1994; Spinoza, 1994; Whitehead, 1967). The brain and the body must function in ways that are not "normal" to produce the *Mona Lisa*, to write Shakespeare's sonnets, or to discover Einstein's theory of relativity. Whether it be polymaths like Leonardo da Vinci, musicians like Mozart or Beethoven, writers like Jane Austen or Petrarch, or orators like Martin Luther King Jr. or Cicero, extremely gifted individuals defy convention and standards—instead they push the limits of what society deems acceptable. By studying individuals who experience extreme states of health and well-being, we can understand something quite different about human psychology from what we understand when we study disease (C. R. Cloninger, 2004; Gardner, 1983; Seligman & Csikszentmihalyi, 2000). In fact, there are principles and laws which govern healthy development that may have nothing to do with why we become ill. The science of well-being is dedicated to studying these principles of healthy development and works from the premise that within every person is a spontaneous need for happiness, understanding, and love (C. R. Cloninger, 2004; K. Cloninger, 2008; Herrman, et al., 2005). Everyone wants to know how he or she can have greater happiness and reduce suffering. By understanding healthy development, growth in self-awareness, and the development of well-being, we can begin to address the root causes of the problems which we face as a planet. And of all the members of society who must have an understanding of well-being, teachers are among the most important because they profoundly impact the development of children.

As research on intelligence, creativity, and cognition has advanced, defini-tions have enlarged to encompass more than just strict intellectual gifts; they now include an ever-broadening set of abilities and talents (Gardner, 1983, 1993, 1999; Sternberg, 2003; Winner, 1996). In his theory of multiple intel-ligences, Gardner proposes eight discrete forms of intelligence: linguistic, logi-cal-mathematical, spatial, bodily-kinesthetic, musical, naturalist, interpersonal, and intrapersonal (Gardner, 1983, 1999). By looking in a pluralistic fashion at intelligence, Gardner helps widen the view of giftedness from something purely academic or intellectual. Likewise, Sternberg's work on defining giftedness has broadened definitions of giftedness to include wisdom, creativity, and intel-ligence, something he has since termed the WICS model: wisdom, intelligence, creativity, synthesized (Sternberg, 2003). In his words, the WICS model contends that "wisdom, intelligence and creativity are sine qua non for the gifted leaders of the future. Without a synthesis of these three attributes, someone can be a decent contributor to society, and perhaps even a good one, but never a great one" (Sternberg, 2003, p. 112). It is, perhaps, a failure of this synthesis that leads many to associate creativity with madness—creativity without wisdom, intelligence, and the self-awareness implied in both can look like insanity, when in fact it is just disproportionate maturity.

On the Relationship between Creativity and Happiness

For thousands of years, through cultural, scientific, and artistic advances, humans have been seeking to understand the development of their full potential. The science of well-being recognizes that creativity, love, and the search for meaning beyond the self are fundamental to the development of this human potential. Anthropologists and scientists who study the origin of human beings cite tool use, artistic creation, and spiritual behavior as distinguishing features of Homo sapiens (C. R. Cloninger, 2004; Gowlett & Knopf, 1993; White, 2003). With regard to human development, it is essential, therefore, that we consider these distinguishing characteristics.

Taking a step back and looking at the various domains of human life, be it our sexual life, our emotional life, our intellectual life, and so forth, it seems clear that *the activities that bring us joy are essentially creative*. Take the very simple example of trying to please a loved one—we often search for unique and innovative ways to give someone a gift (for example, buying a violinist tickets to hear Itzhak Perlman play Brahms' Violin Concerto in D and hiding the tickets in his or her violin case). But we could equally speak about cooking—if we become bored with the food we eat, we become quickly dissatisfied and will search for new recipes. So in each of the domains of our life (C. R. Cloninger, 2004)—sexual, material, emotional, cultural, spiritual—it is our creative experiences that bring us joy, that allow us to feel fully human and uniquely alive. The science of well-being shows us that well-being and creativity are inextricably linked—that creativity leads to well-being and that the cultivation of well-being, on the other side, opens a door to creativity.

At present, schools tend to ignore the fundamental human needs of love, creativity, and self-transcendence. Often, when we think about the cultivation of creativity in schools, we think about art class, theatre, or music, but creativity is part of every discipline, just as it is involved in all aspects of our lives: in scientific innovation, in reading and writing, in the imagination of history and social vision of politics. Creativity is present in our daily social interactions with teachers, students, and administrators as it is present in all of our emotional and social relationships. More importantly, creativity fundamentally leads to a concrete experience of joy in our lives. So then, what are the consequences of neglecting creativity and/or well-being? Are some of our schools joyless places where children work only for the promise of future experiences of joy? How then do we cultivate conditions for creativity in the classroom?

A CHRONIC CASE OF MNEMONOPHILIA

To tackle this issue, various curriculum theorists, psychologists, and teacher educators have asked four broad questions: What is creativity? What are creative people like? How do we measure it? And how do we encourage it? (Amabile, 1989; Cramond, 2005; Csikszentmihalyi, 1996; Eisner, 2005; Esquivel & Houtz, 2000; Guilford, 1970; Hennessey & Amabile, 1998; Maslow, 1968; Piirto, 2004; Robinson, 2001; Rogers, 1970; Shallcross, 1985; Simonton, 1994; Starko, 2005; Sternberg, 2008; Torrance, 1979). In this section, we will briefly review each of these four major questions, culminating in our suggestions for cultivation and encouragement of creativity in the classroom.

WHAT IS CREATIVITY?

Most major thinkers in the field of creativity studies have attempted some defini-tion of creativity (i.e., Hennessey & Amabile, 1998; Robinson, 2001; Sternberg, 2008; Torrance, 1979), often giving operational definitions with an eye toward cultivation—that is, "conditions" of creativity like internal motivation, freedom, and domain-relevant skills (Hennessey & Amabile, 1998; Plucker & Renzulli, 1999; Sternberg, 1988, 2008).[3] At the root of the word, we find the notion of making (the English word "create" is derived from the Latin *creatus* and *creare*, meaning "to make or produce") and newness or novelty, both of which fre-quently find their way into working definitions (Piirto, 2004, p. 3).

Creativity is, furthermore, frequently linked to imagination, though with the caveat that creativity should produce something useful, adaptive, or valu-able. One such definition, by way of example, is Ken Robinson's "imaginative processes with outcomes that are original and of value" (2001, p. 118). Robinson distinguishes between imaginative and *imaginal*—the former being the recom-bination of memories to imagine something never seen (like a green polar bear), the latter being a mental image of something real (which works like recollection). Creativity, in Robinson's view, is applied imagination to the end of some recognizable good.

Though we understand and appreciate that Robinson offers clear examples of how we can understand and see creativity in our daily lives, our view is that creativity is deeper than imaginative processes and often transcends them. Such definitions, while helpful, cannot account for all aspects of creativity, as its role in human psychology and human development is profound. Starko even asks "whether any single theory, or even any conception of creativity, can encompass the multiple creative activities of human beings across many cultures" (2005, p. 85). While these questions are interesting, this paper will not specifically focus on trying to find an adequate definition of creativity. Schwab (1969, 1971, 1973) notes that all theories of education are partial, and in that spirit, we acknowledge the lack of a single, codified definition and will instead suggest reflection on the part of educators to develop their own definitions through classroom practice.

WHAT CHARACTERISTICS DISTINGUISH CREATIVE PEOPLE?

This is also a vast discussion. Distinguishing traits are often separated into three categories: cognitive characteristics, personality characteristics, and domain-related qualities (K. Cloninger, 2005; Csikszentmihalyi, 1996; Esquivel & Houtz, 2000; Feldman & Goldsmith, 1991; Vernon, 1970; Winner, 1996). The following illustrative table (table 1.1), compiled from the research of Piirto, Csikszentmihalyi, Winner, and Simonton, gives a sense of the types of characteristics researchers have attempted to identify in highly creative individuals.[4]

The hope, implied in this research, is that by identifying the characteristics of highly creative individuals, we can understand how to help others learn to be more creative. If we look at this list of cognitive and personality characteristics, we notice a series of largely positive descriptors; as we pointed out earlier in the chapter, well-being leads to creativity, so it is not surprising to see the characteristics of highly creative people are positive. We do not mean to suggest that highly creative people never have difficulties in life or experience a lack of joy, but rather, the traits that they possess that lead them to be highly creative are healthy, functional, and positive traits. Mozart provides us with a compelling example of this. Not famous for being a paragon of well-being, his descriptions of creative moments show the inner state that precedes and accompanies his most fulfilling production:

> When I am, as it were, completely myself, entirely alone, and of good
> cheer—say, traveling in a carriage, or walking after a good meal, or

during the night when I cannot sleep; it is on such occasions that my ideas flow best and most abundantly. *Whence* and *how* they flow I know not; nor can I force them. . . . What a delight is this I cannot tell! All this inventing, this producing, takes place in a pleasing lively dream. Still the actual hearing of the *tout ensemble* is after all the best. What has been thus produced I do not easily forget, and this is perhaps the best gift I have my Divine Master to thank for. (Vernon, 1970, p. 55)

The work of humanistic psychologists like Carl Rogers, Clark Moustakas, and Rollo May supports this view. They maintain that "the creative life is a healthy life" (Piirto, 2004, p. 24). Maslow argues that "self-actualized" creativity "stresses first the personality rather than its achievements" and is "synonymous with health itself" (ibid.). So we can see that the development of well-being is not antithetical to creativity but, indeed, is evident in cognitive and personality traits.

As teachers, we rarely look at the personalities of our students as indicative of the success of our teaching practices. As humanist psychologists have argued, this is especially important when attempting to foster creativity in our students.

Table 1.1   Characteristics of Creative People

Cognitive Characteristics	Personality Characteristics	Domain-Related Qualities/Qualities of Young Writers (Examples)
Metaphorical thinking	Willingness to take risks	Playfulness with words
Flexibility in skill and decision-making	(novelty-seeking)	Sense of humor
Independence in judgment	Perseverance, drive, commitment (persistence)	Ear for sounds of language
Coping well with novelty	Curiosity	Use of figures of speech:
Logical thinking skills	Openness to experience	metaphorical/ rhetorical ability
Visualization	Tolerance for ambiguity (negative capability)	Early readers
Finding order in chaos	Broad interests	High conceptual verbal intelligence
Escaping entrenchment	Valuing originality	Non-conforming and like to be alone
	Intuition and deep emotions (self-transcendence)	Value self-expression
	Introspective	Productive
		Driven and can take rejection
		Like to work alone

Simply put, the more aware we are of who our students are, the more we can help them to be creative.

HOW DO WE MEASURE IT?

It is important to consider the role of measuring creativity because of the emphasis of accountability and standardized testing in today's schools. Mayer (1999) points out that there are many different methodologies to examine the measurement of creativity, including both quantitative and qualitative techniques. Guilford (1970) had a tremendous impact on the field of creativity studies. He pointed out that most tests of intelligence and achievement focused on convergent thinking; in other words, what is the "right answer"? But when considering creativity, it's important to think of multiple solutions to one problem (i.e., divergent thinking). Torrance (1974) took Guilford's work on measures of creativity and adapted and expanded them, leading to the Torrance Test of Creative Thinking (TTCT).

What is interesting to consider for schools today is that we have once again placed the emphasis on the "outcome measures" of schooling, on convergent thinking; this has deep ramifications for curriculum, pedagogy, and administration in schools and is probably the biggest obstacle to the development of creativity in the classroom. We echo the sentiments of Robinson:

> I am not arguing against academic standards in themselves nor would I celebrate a decline in them. *My concern is with the preoccupation with these standards to the exclusion of everything else.* I am not arguing against formal instruction. I am not appealing for a wider use of so-called progressive teaching methods. Both have an important place in teaching. Some of these methods do put a strong emphasis on creativity: some do not. Some of this work is excellent: some is not. A common failing is the tendency to misunderstand the nature of creative activity not only in education but more generally. Too often what passes for creativity has been an undisciplined and undemanding process. (2001, p. 200; italics added)

As Robinson eloquently states in this passage, we need to find the just balance between standardization, accountability, and creativity.

HOW DO WE ENCOURAGE IT?

It is interesting to observe that most of the approaches to fostering creativity in schools have focused on systematic techniques, resulting in an acute case of mnemonophilia, or the education equivalent of alphabet soup. Table 1.2 summarizes some of the techniques and strategies developed in answer to this overarching question. There are certainly other techniques and methods that have been outlined by curricularists, teacher educators, and psychologists (Piirto, 2004; Cramond, 2005; Robinson, 2001; Sternberg, 2008; Torrance, 1979; Starko, 2005; Csikszentmihalyi, 1996; Esquivel & Houtz, 2000; Eisner, 2005) that do not rely on mnemonic devices, but they still often seek systematic techniques like those we've just noted.

Table 1.2 Examples of Mnemonic Devices for Creativity

Name of Researcher	Acronym or Mnemonic Device (Method)	What Does It Stand For?	Description
Rhodes, Crammond	The 4 Ps	Person, Process, Product, Press (i.e., Environment)	Helps teachers examine the components of creativity
Piirto	The 7 Is	Inspiration, Imagery, Imagination, Intuition, Insight, Incubation, Improvisation (and Playfulness)	Helping students understand the creative process
Eberle	SCAMPER	Substitute, Combine, Adapt, Magnify or Minify, Put to other uses, Eliminate, Reverse or Rearrange	Ideation technique (brainstorming)
De Bono	EBS	Examine Both Sides	Develops lateral thinking skills
	PMI	Plus, Minus, Interesting	
	OPV	Other People's Views	
	AGO	Aims, Goals, Objectives	
	C&S	Consequences and Sequel	

We decided to take a different tact based on the science of well-being to try to understand the dimensions of the classroom that the teacher and/or administrators must attend to in order to help foster creativity in children. We will offer a framework to help teachers to reflect on their own teaching, to consider their classroom, their curriculum, their students, and themselves, and their relationships to creativity and joy. This framework will be useful for teacher educators, teachers, and administrators. It is an experimental approach that does not rely on a simple formula, though there are principles to contemplate and try to understand. Understanding these dimensions does not give rough and ready rules or a specific formula for teachers to use; instead, it insists upon the need for teachers to reflect deeply on their own practice, their own classrooms, and their own students. It gives teachers freedom and leaves room for creativity in their own teaching practice. It is less of a definitive structure and more of an approach or strategy to help teachers engage in reflective practice (i.e., Schön, 1991).

There are many different ways that one can approach the concept of creativity. First, we can approach it as a philosophical idea; for example, what is the nature of creativity? How do we define it? What is its role in society? One can also approach the concept of creativity by examining specific outcomes: How is creativity involved in our work? How does creativity produce art or technical innovation? One can also approach creativity by examining its function in human life. The literature explored above frequently uses all three approaches simultaneously. For our purposes, we will focus on the function of creativity within the human being, using a framework adapted from the science of well-being (C. R. Cloninger, 2004; K. Cloninger, 2005, 2006a, 2006b, 2008).[5]

We can easily observe that each of us has a sexual life, a material and corporeal life, an emotional life, an intellectual and cultural life, and a spiritual life.[6] Previously, in this chapter, we discussed how creativity exists in each of the domains of our existence and leads to joy in each specific domain. It may seem a bold claim that all human experience is expressed in these five domains, but these five domains are completely and intrinsically intertwined. For example, our sexual experiences may have emotional components, cultural components, spiritual components, and vice versa. Thus, while it may seem limiting to speak about five domains, the interdependence of these domains leads to thousands, if not millions, of possible permutations.

So what, then, does creativity look like in each of these five domains? We know that creativity is expressing itself in every aspect of our lives; therefore, we can use this domain structure to help us to begin to tease apart *how* this important capacity is expressed in the classroom, in the students, in the teacher, and in the school. Before considering the relevance for the classroom, we will consider how creativity expresses itself in each domain of human life. Table 1.3 offers a summary of the descriptions that follow.

Table 1.3 Creativity Expressed in Human Life

Domain of Human Life	Descriptions of Creativity
Sexual	Drive, passion, play, curiosity, delight
Material/corporeal	Craft, ingenuity, innovation, moving beyond prescribed forms (finding a medium)
Emotional	Discovery, receptivity, originality, exhilaration
Intellectual/cultural	Inspiration, imagination, artistry, novelty, meaning
Spiritual	Revelation, self-transcendence, self-transformation

It may seem strange to consider the *sexual* domain of life with regard to creativity, but we see philosophers and writers linking eros to creativity as far back as Plato's *Symposium*, when Diotima links eros to reproduction and the impetus to create (Hyland, 2008). Plato's *Phaedrus* likewise explicitly links inspiration and eros, which is "given us by the gods to ensure our greatest good fortune" (245b). Furthermore, contemporary curriculum theorists, like Joseph Schwab, have discussed links between eros and teaching, arguing that eros inspires in us a "capacity for feeling and action" (Pinar, 1997; Schwab, 1978).

Creativity in this domain involves drive, passion, play, curiosity, and delight. In other words, it involves those impulses and fervors that lead us to *want to make something*. We also recognize, here, that creativity in this domain (or any domain for that matter) may be social. It often involves another person, or group of people, in its function. Shared passion may magnify passion; shared delight may magnify delight. It is easy to see how the classroom can become a site for this shared passion, desire to understand the world, as well as the creation of something contributive to it. Parents, for instance, often express how their children are their greatest "creation" and an immense source of joy in their lives. All of these are examples of how creativity is expressed in the sexual domain of life.

When we work creatively, we work with forms, materials, mediums, and domain-specific knowledge. These things are often *material* in nature (a book, a canvas, a tuba, the body). The creative work is to be innovative with such structures, to move beyond prescribed forms into the realm of ingenuity, where one cultivates their craft. We can also consider the material aspects of the classroom, the "shape" or arc of a given lesson, the broad forms that our courses take. Earlier, we referred to the ingenuity involved in finding a new recipe; creativity in this domain of life involves moving beyond the confines of the structures and knowledge that we're given or are working within. But it also includes knowledge of those forms.

In the nineteenth century, Romantic poets made the argument that the social importance of art was rooted in empathy—that is, the ability to project oneself into the situation of another, which requires an act of *emotional* imagination (Campbell, 1987). We have chosen the broader word "receptivity," by which we mean a state of openness and sensitivity to the world and to others, which potentially allows new discoveries (inside and outside of the classroom). Furthermore, when we convey those things we are being receptive to, there is a bit of us (our personality, our character) in that expression, which leads to originality. We could say, in other words, that originality is an expression of the self in a state of receptivity. Again, to refer to Mozart:

> When I proceed to write down my ideas, I take out of the bag of my memory, if I may use that phrase, what has been previously collected into it in the way I have mentioned. For this reason the committing to paper is done quickly enough, for everything is, as I have said before, already finished; and it rarely differs on paper from what it was in my imagination. . . . But why my productions take from my hand that particular form and style that makes them *Mozartish*, and different from the works of other composers, is probably owing to the same cause which renders my nose so large or so aquiline, or, in short, makes it Mozart's and different from those of other people. For I really do not study or aim at any originality. (Vernon, 1970, p. 54)

We can see, then, that originality is not a goal but rather a natural by-product of receptivity (the state of "flow" he described in the previously cited paragraph and the natural "Mozartness" of his expression) or that particular filter of the self.

The *intellectual/cultural* domain is the domain that we classically associate with creativity, insofar as it involves artistry, imagination, inspiration, and novelty. The role of art in society has often catalyzed new developments in culture, changed the way individuals related to their societies, and helped people to find personal meaning. Indeed, some of the greatest minds, musicians, and artists have helped human civilization to understand itself by reflecting on the state of society in art and culture. And since education is concerned with the cultivation of these great minds, it is unfortunate that the arts are frequently considered peripheral to education. The creative mind is frequently, although not exclusively, an artistic mind, and it is important that our schools help exercise it.

If the cultural features of creativity are frequently considered, the *spiritual* aspects are often neglected (in the classroom as well as in popular discourse). Yet, the spiritual domain of human life is part of our unique human constitution (C. R. Cloninger, 2004; C. R. Cloninger, D. M. Svrakic, and T. R. Przybeck, 1993; K. Cloninger, 2006b; Gowlett & Knopf, 1993; Maslow, 1968; Noddings, 1992; White, 2003). So it is no surprise that some of our earliest notions of art were born from the spiritual domain: inspiration, genius, vision. Here we are dealing with all the facets of our life that lead us to look beyond and within ourselves. Creativity in this domain of our life helps us to reinvent ourselves, to move beyond our self-imposed limitations, and to slowly discover what it is to be human. Such revelations, self-transcendence, and self-transformation help us to live a healthy and happy life.

Getting to Work

Having considered the expression of creativity in the human being, we can now focus specifically on helping teachers work on creativity in the schools. The domains of creativity discussed above provide a framework to aid teachers, teacher educators, and administrators to engage in deep reflection on the subject of creativity in the classroom. As we began to expand on the expression of creativity in each of the domains of human life, it quickly became apparent that there were many ramifications for teachers, students, the curriculum, the pedagogy, and the school program as a whole (table 1.4). There is a temptation to try to spell out a "how to" program for cultivating creativity in the schools, but such techniques will always fall short. This is because creativity has profound ramifications in each of the domains of our life, so to attempt to limit the cultivation of creativity to a checklist or a simple technique would only prove to be a shallow treatment of what is undeniably a very deep function of the human being. Moreover, a definitive structure would not leave room for the creativity of each individual.

Table 1.4   Creativity Framework for the Schools

Domain of Human Life	Descriptions of Creativity	Level of Analysis
Sexual	Drive, passion, play, curiosity, delight	
		Teacher/classroom
Material/corporeal	Craft, ingenuity, innovation, moving beyond prescribed forms (finding a medium)	**Student**
Emotional	Discovery, receptivity, originality, exhilaration	
		Curriculum/pedagogy
Intellectual/cultural	Inspiration, imagination, artistry, novelty, meaning	
		School/district
Spiritual	Revelation, self-transcendence, self-transformation	

What we need is for teachers, administrators, or teacher educators to consider for themselves the ramifications of this framework in their own classrooms or schools, and more *importantly in their students and their own practice.* Take, therefore, table 1.4, and make it your own. Sit with it, contemplate it, challenge it, wrestle with it, and see where it leads you. We have done the same and will now offer you some of the themes that have emerged for us.

Considering the various expressions of creativity in the domains of human life is a means of gauging the creativity of our students. Are they working with drive and passion? Are they playful or curious? Have they demonstrated innovative work, an understanding of craft, or ingenuity? In each of the domains of human life, we can look at students and have a sense of the expression of creativity. This can be done over a number of different time periods: during a single class, a unit, a semester, a school year, or during an entire period of study (i.e., high school or middle school). The period of time over which we look for the expression of creativity depends on our needs, but the framework can be incredibly helpful to anyone interested in understanding the creativity of his or her students. Students need encouragement, clarity, and awareness concerning the importance of creativity in life and in school. One way of accomplishing this is to ask them to consider the expression of creativity in the world and in their life, and this framework could be of great utility in such endeavor.

There are also many considerations teachers must make in their own lives and in their instruction in order to help students express creativity in the classroom. First, the teacher himself must take time to consider how creativity is expressed in his own life. We need to embody creativity, so we can model it to our students and see it within them. If a teacher is unaware of creativity in his or her own life, it is difficult if not impossible for the classroom to be conducive to a student's growing creativity. Of course, students may find their own way to work on their creativity despite the level of awareness of the teacher, but a teacher may overlook the intelligence or creativity of a student if she lacks such awareness.

This leads us to our next point, that teachers must cultivate humility and examine their own expectations in the classroom. If we, as teachers, are unwilling to learn from our students or keep an open mind about how they respond to our questions or assignments, then we may inadvertently be stomping out creative impulses. By working on humility, care, and receptivity to our students, we can create classrooms that are safe and secure (K. Cloninger, 2008). This safety and security gives students the freedom to hear the muses—to explore, discover, play, find inspiration, discuss their discoveries with others, and hopefully work on their own improvement and self-transformation.

This framework also touches on evaluation in the classroom, the school, and the district. In some circumstances, at least those in which we are seeking to cultivate creativity, evaluation must be tailored to individuals; this could be through differentiation of assignments or tests or through individualization and will depend on the specific context in which the teachers and students are working. Whether at the district level, the school level, or in individual classrooms, we are currently placing a high premium on specialization in specific subject-matter disciplines and declarative knowledge. Our systems of accountability, standards, and high-stakes testing are only reinforcing this trend.

Hyper-specialization and a focus on the "right answers" may cripple the creativity of our teachers and our students. Furthermore, much of the high-stakes testing cannot account for a diversity of responses or solutions to problems. Testing and evaluation of this nature is only one measure of achievement, especially if we are interested in helping students develop creativity. *Do not hear us to say that we need to loosen standards or dispense with rigorous academic curriculum.* Of course, there is a place for this in schools but not at the expense of creativity, divergent thinking, and the well-being of the students.

There are certainly many other implications and ramifications that can be pulled from this framework. Undoubtedly, the intelligence and creativity of each person may find other connections that we have not touched on here or that we might not have even thought of. Our goal was not to be exhaustive but rather to empower teachers, teacher educators, and administrators with a framework to consider the questions for themselves. We would encourage those of you who read this chapter to share your deductions and classroom experiences with us if you so desire.

Conclusion: An Exhortation to Act

As teachers, administrators, and parents in the twenty-first century, we must resist the temptation to simply follow formulas, recipes, "do-it-yourself" manuals, alphabet soups, and codified techniques. Our reliance on the vision of various authorities is necessarily limited because the authorities we rely upon have a limited vision. Furthermore, the needs of each student, classroom, and school will differ, and we must be sensitive to this diversity.

For the sake of our students and our children, we must dare to contemplate our pedagogical approaches to creativity with our own imagination and intelligence—all the while understanding that creativity in thinking is a tall order. As Spinoza once quipped, "All things excellent are as difficult as they are rare." To excel in creativity is not an easy task; it requires us to rethink our preexisting conceptions and biases. It requires us to consider each of the domains of our life in new ways—to understand them in light of the challenges we face in the new millennium. This chapter offers one means to help teachers begin to do this work of reflection, but the work is yours to accomplish.

In a seriously challenging and challenged world, it seems important to prepare our students for the difficulties and complexities they will face as fully grown members of the global community. A blunt, unblinking approach might seem the only responsible one—yet sometimes focusing too narrowly on our problems can lead to despair (which is an emotional clamp on our creative drive).

So while we might focus specifically on ecological, economic, and social crises (and there certainly are teachers who could manage these titanic issues in the classroom with a spirit of hope), *what is essential* is that we focus on creating the kind of mind that can face such challenges—and that mind is creative. We have endeavored in this chapter, deliberately, not to be prescriptive. We respect the intelligence of teachers more than that. It is in our hands to act and to actively reflect on what it will require to help students be creative.

There is no magic bullet or panacea. Each one of us has to do the work of reflection. It may be overwhelming to face up to this fact in light of all the pressures teachers face today in the classroom (school accountability, standards-based education, and school rankings, to name a few). Nonetheless, if we truly have little time to do this most essential work, it is important that we take action to change these short-sighted policies for the sake of our children and their futures. In the words of Gandhi, we must "be the change we wish to see in the world." So then, let our classrooms be the change we want to see in the system.

We live in a challenging time—some challenges are unique, like our profound ecological crisis or the peaceful integration of a global, multicultural society—some are variations on a familiar theme, like our troubled economy, wars, and the threat of wars. It will require a unique and creative generation, the children we are educating today, to meet and overcome these challenges and those we have perhaps not yet imagined. In point of fact, we are using early twentieth century pedagogy and curriculum theory to address the needs of the twenty-first century. It may be a nostalgia for simpler times that causes us to look backward for our models of education when the complexity of the twenty-first century actually calls for us to radically transform our patterns of thought.

As we discussed in the introduction, we often react with rigidity and inflexibility in the face of characteristics that conflict with our preconceptions. Because our future is so uncertain, it is imperative that we generate new ideas to address these challenges. Creativity is, therefore, indispensable to this endeavor. Furthermore, since we know that there is no escaping the problems and challenges we will collectively face, we may as well resolve to face them with serenity and well-being. This will require the cultivation of a new mind that is fluid, flexible, and able to meet and embrace uncertainty with creativity; this will, in turn, bring us joy, which will again, in turn, help us meet new challenges. It is a healthy, generative, and necessary cycle for the uncertain world we face in this new century. Let us hope, then, that we have the wisdom and humility to help our children face this new world.

Notes

1. For this reason, the concept of "well-being" has image problems among serious researchers in all fields of study. Those unfamiliar with the concept may well be ignorant of the advances made in the scientific understanding of the development of well-being (Argyle, 2001; C. R. Cloninger, 2000, 2004, 2006; K. Cloninger, 2005; Deci & Ryan, 2008; Diener & Seligman, 2004; Diener & Suh, 2000; Diener, Suh, Lucas, & Smith, 1999; Felce, 1997; Fry, 2006; Herrman, et al., 2005; Hird, 2003; Huppert, et al., 2005; Ickovics & Park, 1998; Ryan & Deci, 2001; Ryan, Huta, & Deci, 2008; C. Ryff, 1989; C. Ryff & Singer, 2008; Schalock, 2004; Seligman, 2002; Seligman & Csikszentmihalyi, 2000; Servan-Schreiber, 2004; Veenhoven, 2007).

2. Moreover, the concept of well-being in medicine is very similar to the conceptions of well-being in ancient Greek philosophy and other ancient philosophic traditions.

3. "Domain-relevant skills" refers to skills/knowledge particular to one field or domain (e.g., to write a novel, one must have acquired sufficient literacy; to build an algorithm, one must have a basic understanding of mathematics).

4. We will use Piirto's "qualities of young writers" to show characteristics of one possible domain.

5. The relevance of the science of well-being in the classroom has been previously explored. The same approach is being used in developing a framework for understanding intuition in the classroom (K. Cloninger, 2006), a model of giftedness (K. Cloninger, 2005), and an understanding of love in the classroom (K. Cloninger, 2008).

6. Cloninger (2004) refers to these various dimensions of life in his quantum description of human thought and relationship in his book on the science of well-being.

References

Amabile, T. (1989). *Growing up creative: Nurturing a lifetime of creativity.* New York: Crown.

Argyle, M. (2001). *The psychology of happiness* (2nd ed.). New York: Taylor & Francis.

Campbell, C. (1987). *The romantic ethic and the spirit of modern consumerism.* Oxford, UK: Blackwell.

Cloninger, C. R. (2000). A practical way to diagnose personality disorder: A proposal. *Journal of Personality Disorder, 14*(2), 99–108.

Cloninger, C. R. (2004). *Feeling good: The science of well-being.* New York: Oxford University Press.

Cloninger, C. R. (2006). The science of well-being: An integrated approach to mental health and its disorders. *World Psychiatry, 5*(2), 71–76.

Cloninger, C. R., Svrakic, D. M., & Przybeck, T. R. (1993). A psychobiological model of temperament and character. *Archives of General Psychiatry, 50*, 975–990.

Cloninger, K. (2005). The science of well-being: A new way to understand the gifted. In N. L. Hafenstein, B. Kutrumbos, & J. Delisle (Eds.), *Perspectives in gifted education: Complexities of emotional development, spirituality and hope* (Vol. 3, pp. 76–115), Denver: Institute for the Development of Gifted Education, Ricks Center for Gifted Children.

Cloninger, K. (2006a). *Helping students become self-aware.* Paper presented at the American Association for Teaching and Curriculum.

Cloninger, K. (2006b). Making intuition practical: A new theoretical framework for education. *Curriculum and Teaching Dialogue, 8*(1), 15–28.

Cloninger, K. (2008). Giving beyond care: An exploration of love in the classroom. *Curriculum and Teaching Dialogue, 10*(1 & 2), 193–211.

Cramond, P. D. (2005). *Fostering creativity in gifted students.* Waco, TX: Prufrock Press.

Csikszentmihalyi, M. (1996). *Creativity: Flow and the psychology of discovery and invention.* New York: Harper Perennial.

Csikszentmihalyi, M. (2000). Positive psychology: The emerging paradigm. *North American Montessori Teachers' Association Journal, 25*(2), 4–25.

Deci, E., & Ryan, R. (2008). Hedonia, eudaimonia, and well-being: An introduction. *Journal of Happiness Studies, 9*(1), 1–11.

Diener, E., & Seligman, M. E. P. (2004). Beyond money: Toward an economy of well-being. *Psychological Science in the Public Interest, 5*(1), 1–31.

Diener, E., & Suh, E. M. (2000). *Subjective well-being across cultures.* Cambridge, MA: MIT Press.

Diener, E., Suh, E. M., Lucas, R., & Smith, H. E. (1999). Subjective well-being: Three decades of progress. *Psychological Bulletin, 125*, 276–302.

Eisner, E. (2005). *Reimagining schools: The selected works of Elliot W. Eisner.* New York: Routledge.

Esquivel, G. B., & Houtz, J. C. (Eds.). (2000). *Creativity and giftedness in culturally diverse students.* Cresskill, NJ: Hampton Press.

Felce, D. (1997). Defining and applying the concept of quality of life. *Journal of Intellectual Disability Research, 41*(2), 126–135.

Feldman, D. H., & Goldsmith, L. T. (1991). *Nature's gambit: Child prodigies and the development of human potential.* New York: Teachers College Press.

Fry, D. P. (2006). *The human potential for peace.* Oxford: Oxford University Press.

Gardner, H. (1983). *Frames of mind: A theory of multiple intelligences.* New York: Basic Books.

Gardner, H. (1993). *Creating minds: An anatomy of creativity seen through the lives of Freud, Einstein, Picasso, Stravinsky, Eliot, Graham, and Gandhi.* New York: Basic Books.

Gardner, H. (1994). *The arts and human development.* New York: Basic Books.

Gardner, H. (1999). *Intelligence reframed: Multiple intelligences for the 21st century.* New York: Basic Books.

Goleman, D. (1995). *Emotional intelligence: Why it can matter more than IQ.* New York: Bantam Books.

Gowlett, J., & Knopf, A. (1993). *Ascent to civilization.* New York: McGraw-Hill.

Guilford, J. P. (1970). Creativity: Retrospect and prospect. *Journal of Creative Behavior, 4*, 149–163.

Hennessey, B. A., & Amabile, T. (1998). Reward, intrinsic motivation, and creativity. *American Psychologist, 53*(6), 674.

Herrman, H., Saxena, S., & Moodie, R. (2005). *Promoting mental health: Concepts, emerging evidence, practice.* Geneva: World Health Organization.

Hird, S. (2003). *Individual well-being: A report for the Scottish Executive and Scottish neighbourhood statistics.* Glasgow, UK: NHS Health.

Huppert, F. A., Baylis, N., & Keverne, B. (2005). *The science of well-being.* New York: Oxford University Press.

Hyland, D. (2008). *Plato and the question of beauty.* Bloomington, IN: Indiana University Press.

Ickovics, J., & Park, C. (1998). Paradigm shift: Why a focus on health is important. *Journal of Social Issues, 54*(2), 237–244.

Maslow, A. H. (1968). *Toward a psychology of being.* Princeton, NJ: Van Nostrand Reinhold.

Mayer, R. E. (1999). Fifty years of creativity research. In R. Sternberg (Ed.), *The handbook of creativity* (pp. 449–460). New York: Cambridge University Press.

Noddings, N. (1992). *The challenge to care in schools: An alternative approach to education.* New York: Teachers College Press.

Piirto, J. (2004). *Understanding creativity.* Scottsdale, AZ: Great Potential Press.

Pinar, W. (1997). Regimes of reason and the male narrative voice. In W. G. Tierney & Y. S. Lincoln (Eds.), *Representation and the text* (pp. 81–113). Albany, NY: SUNY Press.

Plucker, J. A., & Renzulli, J. S. (1999). Psychometric approaches to the study of human creativity. In R. Sternberg (Ed.), *The handbook of creativity* (pp. 35–61). New York: Cambridge University Press.

Robinson, K. (2001). *Out of our minds: Learning to be creative.* West Sussex, UK: Capstone.

Rogers, C. (1970). Toward a theory of creativity. In P. E. Vernon (Ed.), *Creativity* (pp. 137–151). Middlesex, UK: Penguin Books.

Ryan, R., & Deci, E. (2001). On happiness and human potentials: A review of research on hedonic and eudaimonic wellbeing. *Annual Review of Psychology, 52*, 141–166.

Ryan, R., Huta, V., & Deci, E. (2008). Living well: A self-determination theory perspective on eudaimonia. *Journal of Happiness Studies, 9*, 139–170.

Ryff, C. (1989). Happiness is everything or is it? Explorations of the meaning of psychological well-being. *Journal of Personality and Social Psychology, 57*, 1069–1081.

Ryff, C., & Singer, B. (2008). Know thyself and become what you are: A eudaimonic approach to psychological well-being. *Journal of Happiness Studies, 9*(1), 13–19.

Schalock, R. L. (2004). The concept of quality of life: What we know and do not know. *Journal of Intellectual Disability Research, 48*(3), 203–216.

Schön, D. A. (1991). *The reflective turn: Case studies in and on educational practice.* New York: Teachers College Press.

Schwab, J. J. (1969). The practical: A language for curriculum. *The School Review, 78*(1), 1–23.

Schwab, J. J. (1971). The practical: Arts of eclectic. *The School Review, 79*(4), 493–542.

Schwab, J. J. (1973). The practical 3: Translation into curriculum. *The School Review, 81*(4), 501–522.

Schwab, J. J. (1978). Eros and education. In I. Westbury & N. J. Wilkof (Eds.), *Science, Curriculum, and Liberal Education: Selected Essays* (pp. 105–132). Chicago: University of Chicago Press.

Seligman, M. E. P. (2002). *Authentic happiness: Using the new positive psychology to realize your lasting fulfillment.* New York: Simon and Schuster.

Seligman, M. E. P., & Csikszentmihalyi, M. (2000). Positive psychology: An introduction. *American Psychologist, 55,* 5–14.

Servan-Schreiber, D. (2004). *Healing without Freud or Prozac.* New York: Rodale International.

Shallcross, D. J. (1985). *Teaching creative behavior: How to evoke creativity in children of all ages.* Buffalo: Bearly.

Simonton, D. K. (1994). *Greatness: Who makes history and why.* New York: The Guilford Press.

Spinoza, B. de. (1994). The *ethics.* In E. Curley (Ed. & Trans.), *A Spinoza reader: The ethics and other works* (pp. 85–265). Princeton, NJ: Princeton University Press.

Starko, A. J. (2005). *Creativity in the classroom: Schools of curious delight.* Mahwah, NJ: Lawrence Erlbaum Associates.

Sternberg, R. J. (Ed.). (1988). *The nature of creativity: Contemporary psychological perspectives.* New York: Cambridge University Press.

Sternberg, R. J. (2003). WICS as a model of giftedness. *High Ability Studies, 14*(2), 109–137.

Sternberg, R. J. (Ed.). (2008). *Handbook of creativity.* New York: Cambridge University Press.

Torrance, E. P. (1974). *The Torrance tests of creative thinking.* Bensenville, IL: Scholastic Testing Service.

Torrance, E. P. (1979). *The search for Satori and creativity.* Buffalo, NY: Creative Education Foundation.

Veenhoven, R. (2007). *World database of happiness.* Retrieved June 18, 2007, from http://worlddatabaseofhappiness.eur.nl/

Vernon, P. E. (Ed.). (1970). *Creativity.* Middlesex, UK: Penguin Books.

White, R. (2003). *Prehistoric art: The symbolic journey of humankind.* New York: Abrams.

Whitehead, A. N. (1967). *Aims of education and other essays.* New York: The Free Press.

Winner, E. (1996). *Gifted children: Myths and realities.* New York: Basic Books.

CHAPTER 2

Can We Teach for Surprise?

Gadi Alexander
Ben-Gurion University

Gadi Alexander, PhD, completed his BA and MA (summa cum laude) at the Hebrew University in Jerusalem and his doctoral studies as a Fulbright graduate exchange student at the University of California, Los Angeles. Since then, he has been a member of the department of education at Ben-Gurion University in Be'er-Sheva, Israel. A former head of the teacher education program, Gadi Alexander currently serves as the head of the graduate program in curriculum and instruction. Besides specializing in the cultivation of creative thinking and educational technology, he has worked as head of product development in a high-tech company, producing educational courseware for middle schools in the US. He co-headed several innovative projects promoting creative thinking and the use of technology. Gadi Alexander also initiated a nine-program series on creative thinking in collaboration with an educational television network.

> Everything is foreseen, yet freedom of choice is given . . .
>
> —Pirkei Avot 3:18

ABSTRACT

This chapter explores the possibility of nurturing creative thinking in schools and looks at ways to encourage teachers to engage their own imaginations and those of their students in order to make it a viable part of the curriculum and their learning experiences.

The first half of the chapter explains why a theoretical understanding is essential to any effort to engage the imagination and foster creative abilities in the classroom. Included is a short comparison of different approaches to defining the key concepts and understanding the implications of each theoretical standpoint on the educational strategy to be used. This theoretical examination is based on the assumption that although the imagination and creativity have a strong cognitive bias, their successful integration into learning tasks and kinds of understanding depends on the affective involvement and the social and cultural context in which the learning takes place. The second part of the chapter spotlights five exemplary case studies of teacher education programs or in-service innovations in which the author has been involved. These cases are then analyzed in an effort to find differences and commonalities in their conceptual under-standing and related educational strategies. The chapter culminates with descriptions of change in teaching and learning reported by teachers who made spontaneous efforts to engage in imaginative education and relied on their own pedagogical creativity and that of their students.

Introduction

What do we mean when we say that we are "engaging the imagination of the students" (Egan, 1992, 1997)? And how can such an engagement relate to the nurturing of creative thinking (Torrance, 1976; Treffinger, Isaksen, & Dorval, 1992; Cropley, 2001; Craft, 2005)? There is obviously no single answer to these rather ambiguous questions. And the number of theories and practical approaches that attempt to contribute to our understanding may be close to the number of scholars who could guide us through this perplexing terrain.

On the surface, it seems that the answers to these questions do not have to be complicated. There are obviously many ways to spark the imagination, and it makes sense to suppose that all of them are needed in order to nurture this ability in schools and to link the fancies and thoughts of learners with some valuable educational purpose.

A similar direction of thinking can lead us to the conclusion that it should be easy enough to adopt one of the many approaches and techniques available in the flood of practical and commercial books on creative thinking and harness it to teach a specific curriculum unit.

This type of conventional wisdom can tempt a teacher to introduce, for instance, techniques like Osborn's (1948) brainstorming, de Bono's (1985) six hats, or Buzan's (North & Buzan, 2001) mind map. Each of these tools and ap-proaches has some potential for encouraging students to think in a different and more flexible way, and this ability can be linked to specific school-related prob-lems. In addition, many of these approaches contain a promise to overcome the ruts of habitual thinking and even increase the odds for a small or large discovery (at least in the eyes of its beholder). However, these approaches, with all their charm, cannot be easily adapted as the "bread and butter" of our educational practice for several reasons. First, their relationship to school-related disciplinary content is, in many cases, artificial. Second, they do not seem to promote the basic skills and kinds of knowledge that is appreciated in most schools. A third reason for the poor match between these methods and the curricular content is that the common introduction of one or several of these techniques to the classroom usually reflects a piecemeal effort to use a given technique. A single use of a technique may be suitable for a specific instructional unit, but it will probably not transfer to other learning assignments. Only rarely are these sporadic creative techniques grounded in a comprehensive and systematic educational approach or a broad conception of how a theory of human development can be connected to the aims of education. Consequently, many of these techniques are used by teachers merely as enrichment materials or as a single demonstration of what can be done with creative thinking or, even worse, as triggers for the generation of ideas for special occasions and for school festivities and not as integral parts of daily classroom practice.

The problem with some of these approaches—from an educational and curricular standpoint, at least—is that many of them were originally designed to facilitate creative thinking in industrial or organizational settings or in fields that have no direct relationship to the disciplines that are taught in schools or to acceptable educational objectives. Consequently, these techniques, if and when they are used in a mindful way, can supposedly increase the chance that their users will "think outside the box," and even generate some interesting and original ideas, but they will not necessarily guarantee that the topics and skills learned in school will gain depth or will be internalized in a more meaningful way.

What Is Meant by Imagination and Creativity, and What Difference Does It Make?

Researchers and theoreticians disagree about the need for a good operational definition of imagination and creativity as a precondition to the ability to foster them in the classroom. A formal definition can sometimes be a burden and not an asset, especially if it is based on a tautological fallacy (like Boring's [1923] definition of intelligence that sees it as "what the test is measuring"). Additionally, in many cases, teaching practices are not directed by a precise definition but rather by an intuitive grasp of what is being sought. It could, of course, be argued that most teachers will recognize a creative answer when they come across it or that they will be able to tell when an idea represents an act of imagination.

The downside of refraining from a formal clarification of terms is that the educator can easily get carried away and move from one possible meaning and implication of the construct to another, and this may not be the best foundation for good teaching. In some instances, the teacher may face two contradicting or competing senses of the same definition. How is she going to judge, for example, a work of a student that does not appear to be too original but, nevertheless, reflects an expressive urge and a serious investment of effort and time? Or, if she is not so sure what is required in an act of imagination, will she insist like Nigel Thomas (1997) that the student use rich verbal or visual images? I have seen this theoretical confusion in my work on school campuses. In one case, the school had decided to use Gardner's multiple intelligences as a leading construct. However, when the theory was to be implemented by a number of teachers, it soon became clear that they had only a faint idea of what was representative of each of Gardner's intelligences and when each should be exercised. The result was a very superficial enactment that looked like a caricature of the original idea. A deliberation of the constructs and what they might imply could have eliminated this kind of misapplication.

It seems, therefore, that some kind of a formal definition or, better yet, "a working definition" is unavoidable. It can hopefully provide the teacher with a clearer conception about the specific behaviors that match the theory and help develop criteria or standards that will enable her to detect good examples of the use of imagination and creativity.

A related issue that can be clarified through the teacher's adoption of a specific definition is the possible relationship that apparently exists between imagination and creativity. It will allow her to determine whether these terms should be treated as synonymous or even as interchangeable constructs and if they are covering exactly the same terrains or are only partly related. Part of the theoretical controversy may very well deal with the more general issue of how important it is to distinguish between these two constructs.

A possible way to deal with the difference between the two constructs is to examine the semantic coverage of the terms *imagination* and *creativity*. For example, the first can be perceived as the engine that ignites thinking and creative thought and the latter as the locomotive that pulls the imaginative wagons and turns them into finished and elaborated products. The British physicist and thinker David Bohm (1998) adopted a similar strategy to explain the difference between the two constructs, but he added to this a further distinction that is based on Coleridge's (1817, 1983) differentiation between primary imagination and fancy. The first kind of imagination (Bohm prefers to call it "imaginative insight") refers to the creative perception that is not based on direct sensual data. "These images are fresh and original rather than derived from memory," states Bohm (1998, p. 41). At the other extreme, one can find what Coleridge has called "fancy" (which actually derives from the word *fantasy*). It includes constructions that are based on a combination of separate and distinct images already available from the memory.

According to Bohm (1998), Coleridge meant it to include not only images generated through associations but also a wide range of more intelligent modes of thinking, starting from the simple everyday arrangement of things that are first planned in our mind and going on to composition, design, and possibly invention. Bohm's analysis is based on the work of distinguished men and women in fields such as literature, arts, and science.

In Coleridge's view, there are not necessarily two mutually exclusive modes but rather two extreme poles of thought. He sees the tension between these two poles as generating the energy and the movement that yields primary insights and hypotheses. Bohm prefers to call the second pole in which a new paradigm has to be justified—"constructivist imagination." An example he uses from Newton's discovery of the force of gravitation can help to distinguish between the two types of imagination. Newton's insights in the first phase of imagination triggered him to move from the commonplace belief in his times that the moon is essentially different from the earth because it is made of celestial and not earthy material. This assumption, which was based on his generation's funded knowledge, explains why the moon stays in its orbit and does not fall on the earth. When Newton introduced a new paradigm—that is, maintaining that all objects are made of the same kinds of matter and that all objects are attracted by the same force of gravitation—the old explanation of why the moon is not falling upon the earth became invalid. His challenge was to come up with an alternative expectation. The new hypothesis also created a problem—namely, if materials that the moon is made of are not lighter than those on Earth and if gravitation has the same effect on all matter, one has to find another explanation why the moon is not pulled toward the center of Earth. For our purposes, it may not be necessary to continue to describe Newton's solution to this problem, but those who are interested can read about it in Bohm's (1998) book.

I would like to concentrate on the ways in which this example demonstrates the difference between the two kinds of imagination. According to Bohm, the first phase in which Newton had the insight about the earthy substance of the moon is representing what he calls an *imaginary insight*, while the second pole in which Newton had to solve the conflict between his new hypotheses and his observations of the moon, Bohm (1998) defines as the pole *constructive imagination* (pp. 41–46). Although Bohm calls his book *On Creativity* and focuses on the process of creative thinking and the use of the imagination by outstanding scientists and artists, I believe that his analysis and distinctions between different types of imagination can be applicable to more mundane situations and to education. It can even explain what happens in the classroom when a student attempts to understand a new concept or explain a natural or artistic phenomenon.

However, not all theoreticians, including those who are aware of Coleridge's two kinds of imagination, rely on this distinction as a means to understand what is meant by imagination. Kieran Egan, for example, who devoted many books and articles to clarifying the role of the imagination in teaching and learning

(1992, 1997, 2005) and founded the Imaginative Education Research Group (IERG) in Vancouver, Canada, prefers to adopt White's (1990, p. 184) definition: "To imagine something is to think of it as possibly being so" (as cited in Egan, 1992, p. 36). This deceptively simple definition has several advantages as a working definition. First, it does not require differentiation between different poles or kinds of imagination. Egan is aware of Coleridge's distinction between the two poles of imagination and refers to it in his comprehensive historical survey of the development of the concept of imagination in philosophy, psychology, and Western thinking (Egan, 1992). Nevertheless, when he chooses to select only one definition, he prefers to stick to White's definition, which is reminiscent of the idea that the imagination generates hypothetical "what if" ideas. This quality of producing alternative hypotheses forms the gist of Coleridge and Bohm's theory about the two poles of the imagination. Secondly, the choice of White's definition rather than the one of Coleridge and Bohm (which has some mystical undertones) suggests that Egan wishes to strip the imagination of some of its mystical and romantic connotations. This fits his theory that connects the imagination to the use of cognitive tools and the development of types of understanding during one's lifetime (1997).

It is important to emphasize that in contrast to a number of philosophers who wrote about the place of imagination in our thinking and cognitive psychologists who researched creativity, Egan does not see the imagination as confined to the cognitive domain. He emphasizes in many of his writings that without an affective and motivational attachment, it is impossible or even futile to engage the imagination. The very use of the word *engagement* in his writing proves it, and his advice to a teacher that it is necessary to have a feeling toward punctuation before being able to teach it is just one example of the place for the affect in the imagination (Egan, 2005).

Following in the footsteps of Vygotsky, Egan adds another important dimension to our understanding of what is implied in the use of imagination, and that is the socio-cultural and the historical meaning of the construct. In the chapter omitted from his book *The Educated Mind* (1997), he explained the role of the imagination in the cultural and social history of civilization and especially in affording the progress and development of humankind.

To sum up, then, imagination has an important role in maintaining our curiosity and eagerness, and it drives our desire to discover new and exciting terrains. This is part of its motivational power. But it is also embedded in the socio-cultural fabric of the context in which learning occurs. Imagination is thus perceived not as a purely psychological entity but one that has historical roots and many social and cultural implications.

Vygotsky's heritage can be recognized elsewhere in Egan's use of the term *cognitive tools*; although, he seems not to be entirely happy with the construct.

The tools that he suggests are not only cognitive in the narrow sense of the term but also mediated by social and cultural conventions and by the use of language and other cultural artifacts.

We will conclude this description of Egan's comprehensive perception of the imagination by quoting from the role that Egan and Nadaner (1988) reserve for the imagination in the school:

> Imagination is not some desirable frill . . . It is the heart of any truly educational experience; it is not something split off from "the basics," or disciplined thought or rational inquiry, but is the quality that can give them life and meaning; it is not something that is belonging properly to the arts, but it is the pragmatic centre of all effective human thinking. Our concern is not to promote imagination at the expense of something else—say rational inquiry or the foundational "3r's"; rather, it is to show that any conception of rational inquiry or the foundations of education that depreciates imagination is impoverished and sure to be a practical failure. Stimulating the imagination is not an alternative educational activity to be argued for in competition with other claims; it is a prerequisite to making any educational activity (cited in Egan, 2005, p. 212).

Interestingly enough, a British group led by Anna Craft and her colleagues (Craft, 2005) preferred to use the term *creativity* as their leading construct. But they color (or colour, according to the British spelling) in very similar shades to those found in White's definition. Craft uses the term *possibility thinking* as a close synonym to the term *creativity*. Thus, in spite of their different theoretical backgrounds and the fact that the Imaginative Education Research Group led by Kieran Egan chose the imagination as their main construct while the British group talks about creativity, they both highlight the need and affordances of generating alternative thinking scenarios that will enrich our ideas about the existing reality. In Craft's case, as well as in Egan's theory, the formal definition is used only as a way of offering some kind of a hook that hides a much more complex theory.

In the British example, we can find an unstated dialogue with the vast literature on creativity, and it is echoed in the distinction that Craft (in Craft, Jeffrey, & Leibling, 2001) makes between Creativity with a big "C"—that is, the Creativity of the great scientists or distinguished artists—and the one she calls little "c" creativity, the kind of creativity experienced by almost everyone and that can be fostered in the classroom.

Craft's writings fill some of the gaps that will allow teachers to add "possibility thinking" to their teaching repertoire and turn it into an essential part of learning. The practical suggestions she offers are based on her work with teachers and are backed with the political work she has done with her colleagues to promote the concern for creativity in the British school system and include it in a respectful list of preferred objectives (a detailed documentation of this political and pedagogical act can be found in the National Advisory Committee on Creative and Cultural Education [NACCCE] 1999 document).

However, although the recognition that this approach has gained is very impressive, a teacher who is interested in crystallizing for herself what is entailed in creativity and creative thinking does not have to restrict herself to the definitions used in the British intervention. But since the research on creativity is presented in numerous volumes, it may make sense to focus on several controversies that have also various educational implications. (Those who feel that it is difficult to see the forest for the trees can consult an article that I wrote with my colleague Yakir Shoshani [Alexander & Shoshani, 2008] that maps the different approaches to creativity and recommends the adoption of a dialectic definition of the term.)

I conclude this definitional section with a quote from a researcher (Esquivel, 1995) who summarized the research evidence on creativity by saying: "Although creativity is a complex and multifaceted construct, for which there is no agreed-upon definition, it is viewed as a critical process involved in the generation of new ideas, the solution of problems, or the self-actualization of individuals, according to whichever theoretical perspective is espoused" (p. 186).

Before we transition to how these theoretical ideas can be enacted in the realm of teaching and learning and in the development of teachers, it may be helpful to summarize some of the major controversies present in the literature about creativity and, to a lesser degree, in the one dealing with the imagination.

Controversy 1: The Relationship between Knowledge, Creativity, and the Imagination

One of the main disputes has to do with the place of knowledge in creative thinking and the possible interaction or partial overlap between critical thinking and creative thinking. Robert Weisberg (1999) is one of the most vocal spokesmen who pushes to recognize the importance of previous knowledge and understanding in creative work. In his view, there is a tendency to overestimate the importance of what he calls "the tension view on the role of knowledge in creativity" (p. 226).

The view that Weisberg opposes is the idea that creative thinking deals with different kinds of problems and phenomena from the ones addressed by critical thinking. It is well represented in the term "divergent thinking," an expression coined by the pioneering researcher of creativity Joy Paul Guilford (1950). This type of thinking assumes that the thinker will have a better chance of producing new ideas "by breaking away, or diverging from previously established ideas" (Weisberg, 1999, p. 228). It is led by the presupposition that excessive information may be harmful to the ability to generate new insights or hypotheses. This belief shapes many articles and commercial publications on creativity that advise us to first clear the existing liquids from our cup in order to be ready for it to be filled up with new wisdom and insights. This is also roughly what is meant when we suggest someone "think outside the box." In this view, creative thinking is perceived as being distinct from other forms of thinking and knowledge.

Another well known advocate of this view is Edward de Bono (1968). In his writing, the diversion from the "King's road of rational thinking" is called "lateral thinking." It contradicts what he calls vertical thinking, which typically resorts to automatic patterns and habitual schemes of thinking. De Bono maintains that our mind is pre-programmed, and one of the evolutionary explanations for it is that it enables us to make the right decision in life-threatening situations. In order to arrive at unconventional insights or at new kinds of knowledge, we need to actively search for detours from the King's road of the vertical thinking and move sideways toward lateral thinking.

According to de Bono, such a move is actualized when we are stuck with the regular way of thinking or when we encounter a provocation (for which he invented the acronym *PO*) or a springboard that can afford new opportunities or allow us to examine an existing problem from a different perspective.

Weisberg obviously does not concur with this view and argues, rather, that many so-called innovations and revelations are much more dependent on regular types of thinking and previous knowledge and expertise than the creator or his advocates would be willing to admit. He explains that we tend to see some revelations as breakthroughs or unexpected combinations of familiar things because we are unaware of the database and previous knowledge that the thinker had access to and we did not.

POSSIBLE EDUCATIONAL IMPLICATIONS
OF THIS CONTROVERSY

This theoretical and, in part, empirical controversy has, of course, many educational implications. Weisberg's position may sound as good news to the ears of educators who fear that the cultivation of creative thinking or the imagination will undermine the knowledge base that every learner should master. Weisberg offers that "the relationship between creativity and knowledge is much more straightforward than theories of creativity typically assume" (p. 249). This means that in the train of insights that is pulled by the locomotive of imagination, there must be plenty of room for previous information. It also implies that creative products do not require a deviation from existing knowledge or to think "outside the box" or with thinking that is different in kind as many theorists of creativity assume. Weisberg assumes that it is necessary to "understand creative knowledge by determining the knowledge that the creative thinker brings to the situation that he or she is facing" (p. 249).

This is reminiscent of Nadaner and Egan's conviction that the imagination "is not something split off from 'the basics,' or disciplined thought or rational inquiry" (Egan, 2005, p. 212). It can also explain Weisberg's (1999) conclusion that "we do not need to have special theories to explain creative thinking. Rather, we simply need a complete theory of thinking" (p. 249).

To summarize this controversy: We can differentiate between a *harmonious view* of the potential relationship between (school) knowledge and creativity or knowledge and imagination that recognizes that there is no conflict and even an amelioration in substantiating the imagination on the grounds of knowledge and a *conflictual view* that advocates that knowledge or, at least, too much information can stand in the way of the imaginative thinker. The first view is voiced by Egan and his collaborators, who argue that the nurturing of the imagination should not be viewed "as an alternative educational activity to be argued for in competition with other claims" or by Weisberg, who is trying to persuade us that there is no place for the tension view between knowledge and creativity. The second view is supported by Guilford, Torrance, Bohm, and many other researchers of creativity who believe that the creative urge and the processes that lead great artists, writers, and scientists to their innovations and discoveries are fed by a different kind of thinking freed from the load of previous conventions and paradigms.

Obviously this dispute between the integrative and the conflictual view about the relationship between imagination or creativity and knowledge is not restricted to philosophical or theoretical discussions. It is, rather, a dispute that will determine the direction of the strategy that educators will have to adopt in their teaching for these ends. And, as will be evident in the latter section of this chapter, that presents several beliefs that teachers hold about creativity, the assumption that creative thinking is just another form of "good thinking" (or "the Mind's best work" as David Perkins [1981] prefers to call it) and, therefore, creative teaching is no more than "good teaching" and is shared by a substantial number of teachers.

A last remark on the tension between knowledge and creativity refers to the possibility that these conflicts can be expressed in ways that are not always explicit. There may be a tension between what teachers preach and what they practice. They may intend the learning to be very creative but are impatient when a student raises many questions or looks for her own ways to cope with the learning task. Unstated expectations and apprenticeship learning can easily override other more explicit directions or good intentions.

Controversy 2: The Possible Tension between Advanced Planning and Unexpected Outcomes

Even if we do not concur with the romantic view that portrays the creative thought as depending on an unexpected revelation in which the creator meets a muse or has a sudden sense of illumination, we will have to test whether creative ideas have a different nature than those that are typically handled in a critical thinking process. They tend to surprise their beholders and those that are exposed to them for the first time. "How come I did not think of this before?" is a typical reaction to a creative idea, and this reaction entails that at least those who encounter it for the first time are not prepared for many of its implications that require fresh and different paradigms or frames of reference.

The surprise is seen as unwanted interference by some theoreticians and as a blessing or even as a preferable way of learning by others. A number of theoreticians refuse to see a blind coincidence as a creative act (Perkins, 1981; Weisberg, 1999; Finke, Ward, & Smith, 1992). They insist that a creative product has to be accompanied by a previously stated intention. Others adopt a more permissive view and realize that the creative process can be a serendipitous adventure in which one can look for the donkeys and receive a kingdom (or vice versa in a worst case scenario). If we believe that some of the insights that students come up with and substantiate will lead to their ability to understand the learning assignment from a new and personal perspective, the question is: why should we not encourage it?

But surprises should not only be reacted to but rather be part of our planning. A classroom that encourages creative thinking and the engagement of the imagination needs to have the transitional space that will allow students to experience mistakes that are not harmful and play with speculations and turn possibilities into realities.

Although several cognitive psychologists make serious attempts to tame the creative beast and subsume a large part of creative thinking under the wide umbrella of critical thinking, they still recognize that creative thinking may call for some kind of "mental leap" that cannot be explained in terms of rigorous critical thinking (Perkins, 1981).

I have mentioned the desire of Weisberg and others to collapse the difference in kind between creative and critical thinking. The associated inference is that the thinking process will be transparent and controllable.

In contrast to this view, we can find historians of ideas and researchers of great discoveries arguing that most innovations are not so much the result of an intention and control but rather of luck and the maturation of certain historical or technological conditions. The thesis suggests that the evolution of ideas behaves similarly to the Darwinian theory of the evolution of the species. The thesis assumes that it is very difficult to preplan the creative product, and great discoveries and breakthroughs need a blind and lucky coincidence. Such a view obviously runs against the grain of the former assumption.

For Weisberg (1993), a new discovery is no more than a restatement of existing knowledge or a reshuffling of existing elements. For example, even the great works of Mozart, according to Weisberg, are no more than mere repetition of musical ideas that Mozart had been exposed to. This provocative and extreme view is seconded by researchers who identify the same kind of pattern in regular subjects who are asked to respond to creativity tests. All that they do is combine existing knowledge and make connections between elements that they were exposed to in the past (Finke, Ward, & Smith, 1992).

The dispute rests, therefore, on two different divisions. The first centers on the ability or inability to produce *something really new*. While Weisberg and those who adhere to the "nothing new" thesis seem to be reciting Kohelet's "There is nothing new under the sun," there are two other camps that believe otherwise and are convinced that new ideas and products can be generated. However, this camp is split in half as well between those who see the new insight and hypothesis as depending on the aims and intentions of the thinker and those who see the human creation as a result of a coincidence and the maturation of certain conditions.

Nevertheless, even the rationalists and cognitive psychologists who believe that creative thinking is just another case of good thinking will admit that in many cases the conclusion or solution does not follow logically and directly from the statement of the problem or from the original difficulty with which the thinker was faced. And in these cases, there is a need to explain how this is possible or readjust the original supposition.

For instance, in many books on creativity we are presented with so-called insight problems in which the nine dots problem is one of the most popular ones. The reader is asked to connect nine dots (which form a square of three by three) with four straight lines. This has to be done without removing the pen from the page. The solution to this problem is unexpected since it requires a change in an unpronounced restriction that we willingly impose on ourselves. We keep trying to draw the lines within the imaginary square that the dots are forming; although, nobody has instructed us to do so. The expression of "thinking outside the box" fits here perfectly since any other effort to solve the problem while thinking inside the contours of this box will fail. And the metaphor of inside or outside a box implies also that what is inside can be predicted and controlled while everything that is outside meets the danger of facing the unknown or, for the optimist, discovery of a new kind of understanding.

There are many similar insight problems. For most of them, one has to stop and think and redefine in one way or another what the problem really requires. In many cases, in order to succeed, one needs to rise above the level of operation and habit to the level of meta-cognitive thought and the selection of a new and unfamiliar strategy. When a thinker or a student is of full control and understanding, the solution can be seen as deriving from a systematic reasoning. In cases in which the problem solver uses trial and error or relies on intuitions and not on an explicit theory, we can talk about surprise or unexpected outcome. In many cases that call for insight, it is difficult or even impossible to plan our exact moves ahead of time. In other words, there will be moments and instances that will look in hindsight as "a mental leap" to the student who was working on the problem or to her peers and teacher, and the theoretical conception will frame these instances as unintended "surprises," or as a "remix" of familiar knowledge.

From a pedagogical point of view and from the standpoint of a politician who wishes to assure his community and parents that their children will get the best kind of education, surprises and unexpected outcomes can be perceived as a threat or a hassle. Nobody seems to want to "plan on miracles," as Groucho Marx mockingly suggested. On the other hand, some gaps between a declared educational plan and the learning experience that the students partake in will always exist (Goodlad, 1979). Goodlad sees such a gap as a problem and believes that it has to be narrowed as much as possible, but such a gap can also be perceived as a golden opportunity for both the student's and the teacher's agency. Thinking about it as someone who is interested in a change process or as an advisor or trainer of teachers, the gap between what is planned and what is experienced provides the educator with the degree of freedom that will make her profession more autonomous and less bound to external commitments. Such a gap, when seen as the half of a full glass, can enable the creation of a transitional space in which the student has a chance to practice her agency and develop her personal understanding. This leaves room, of course, for the imagination as an intervening entity. The student's play with ideas that is enabled in such a space can result in the formation of alternative hypotheses to a given problem.

The theoretical perspective to which the teacher subscribes can determine how she will react when the learner tells her about a new insight or belief he has reached. A teacher who is inclined to encourage experimentation can see the efforts to come up with even some erroneous interpretations to be part of a desirable process of exploration. Another much more goal-oriented teacher may fear that the student will be misled and arrive at a "misconception." A possible response would be to quickly correct the "mistake" that the student has made.

The implied paradox in the notion of teaching for surprise can be resolved by reducing the odds that such surprises will happen or, alternatively, by the inclusion of "surprises" as natural components in the design of the teaching unit. This will make certain that unexpected behaviors and hypotheses of the student are a legitimate way of exploration and learning. The second choice obviously needs more careful consideration since we are taking a risk of losing some control and encouraging indirect outcomes and a range of possibilities that cannot be fully monitored or predicted.

Controversy 3: Imagination in the Head and in the Public Sphere

Another dilemma that occupies the minds of those who discuss the issue of teacher's control versus the student's freedom of choice and agency stems from the built-in tension between personal and communicable thoughts. This dilemma tends to be even more acute when we perceive the imagination as part of our inner speech and its fancies as something private, not always communicable and translatable to the shared language of a learning group (Alexander, 2006). In principle, there should be no reason why ideas that are generated by an individual person are not to be ready for distribution in a group. There is documentation of the ways in which children were able to collaborate in building imaginary worlds. These worlds were shared by several children or two siblings, and the richness of the rules and the actions in this world benefited from the mutual contributions of each of the partners. Carl Bereiter (Bereiter & Scardamalia, 2003) goes even a step further and suggests that the new creativity needed today has to be based on the ability to communicate and elaborate it in a collaborative group, and ideas that remain in the heads of people have less value than many educators would assume.

Although the foundations of Osborn's brainstorming method are familiar to most readers, I would like to use the method as an example of the ability to alternate between a controlled process and the generation of unpredictable ideas or solutions and the ability to alternate between individual and group thinking. It is based on an assumption that some researchers find hard to share, that a permissive atmosphere will encourage its members to present half-baked ideas or work together on finding alternative solutions to a given problem (Treffinger, Isaksen, & Dorval, 1992). The process is designed to allow the group to alternate between phases in which associations, speculations, or strange suggestions are welcomed and a next step in which the group moves to the selection of the best ideas and engages in critical evaluation. The unstated assumption behind the collaboration in the process is that possibility thinking has to be generated within the mind of the thinker. While a deeper analysis of the relative roles of the individual members and the responsibilities of the group may not serve the discussion here, I am mentioning brainstorming here to make a point about the possible power of surprise and risk taking. Personal contributions that may look strange, unfamiliar, or even irrelevant at first can morph into very fruitful suggestions as the result of collective deliberation.

The New Roles of the Teacher in Engaging the Imagination and Creativity

The teacher is a key agent in any effort to change priorities in the classroom. Without her genuine belief that the change is needed, her commitment to the roles that have to be fulfilled, and her expertise in solving problems that the new strategy can raise, the reform will not be launched. My own experience in working with teachers in pre-service and in-service programs has taught me that such a change is possible, although its lasting effect depends on the sustainable support that the teacher will be able to get from external sources. In addition, I have learned that although instances in which creative thinking and the imagination are celebrated behind classroom doors are pretty rare, teachers can be instructed to increase the number of such activities, even in the most traditional classrooms. In discussing the new roles that the teacher will have to undertake, it will become apparent that she cannot remain confined to the role of technician.

Involvement in the process calls for a search for new venues in which the teacher will be able to stimulate her own imagination, be active in selecting appropriate learning experiences, be able to find innovative ways to turn on the imagination of her students, and be sensitive enough to catch spontaneous learning opportunities that seemingly appear out of the blue. All these tasks have to be carried out without sacrificing the need to use critical and analytical thinking by both students and the teacher as a tool of evaluation and reflection (Who has claimed teachers do not have to be angels?). This looks like a respectable list of assignments, and without the insistence and the genuine devotion of a teacher who is willing to fulfill these roles, it will be difficult, if not impossible, to fulfill this mission.

Five Cases

Before arriving at some generalizations concerning the new roles that imaginative and creative teaching call for and before commenting on the pedagogical strategies that have been selected to deal with some of the obstacles that were mentioned, I would like to introduce several cases in which I have been personally involved. Each highlights some of the theoretical and practical dilemmas that the transition to imaginative education can bring about. The cases represent different contexts and settings, and I hope to be able to draw from them a number of generalizations that hold some possibility of transferability to similar contexts.

Just prior to presenting my experiences, though, I would like to say a bit about myself and the background from which I make sense of the cases. My personal romance with creativity and reflecting on ways to cultivate it began at least four decades ago during my bachelor's studies; although, the seed of my interest in creativity had been planted in a much earlier period of my childhood. As a son of a composer who had (and still has, at 94) a very fruitful and creative career, my first memories are linked to new works of music frequently performed and celebrated in our house or in the concert halls that I attended almost from the time I remember myself. One natural consequence of this exposure could be discovered in my early and unripe efforts to write my own pieces of music or produce other forms of art. Many students have experienced some kind of exposure to creativity before they enter school, but only rarely do they get an opportunity to exercise and use their imagination or present their creative talents in the regular classroom. Fortunately, my own encounters with the different forms of schooling have not infringed upon the excitement that I still feel toward the mysterious process in which raw thinking scenarios turn into new and original products. I tend to remember my elementary and even my secondary years of schooling as enriching the desire to learn more about the creative process and the limits or affordances of the imagination.

My interest in creativity as a theoretical and practical field found new venues during my graduate studies in mid-1960s. There, I was able to meet several prominent professors who knew how to stimulate the creative urge in their students and made a point to highlight the creative process and the ingenuity of exceptional scientists, artists, writers, and philosophers who helped advance our culture and changed the way we perceive the world. I now introduce my cases.

CASE 1: CREATIVE THINKING AS PART OF A TEACHER TRAINING PROGRAM FOR OPEN EDUCATION

The first academic figure who introduced me to the accumulated knowledge about creativity in psychological and educational research was Professor Moshe Caspi from Hebrew University. He was, back in the 1970s (and still is today), one of the most prominent theoreticians of creative thinking in my country. The quest for creative thinking is a leading theme in his personal life and his academic career. His interest and devotion to the topic had an impact on many students and educational practitioners who followed his lead and started the open education movement in Israel. Part of the socialization process that I went through was related to the need to prepare teachers to work in the newly opened school established in Jerusalem at that time. Caspi's method, which he labeled as CASE (creative approach to self-education, Caspi, 1985), had five objectives (1985, p. 12):

1. To assist in mapping, organizing, and personally using the data, questions, considerations, and methods available for CASE
2. Creating a spatial embodiment of creative processes, real and imagined—spaces of sensing-planning, fantasizing, elaborating, and transforming "anti spaces" (difficulties) to "super spaces" (challenges) in which each of the spaces contains a variety of 3-D models, interactive exhibits, games, tools, guides, and creating opportunities to suit different types of persons
3. A set of some basic kinds of learning—working-playing experiences (e.g., "orientation events," "instrumental activities," and "feedback episodes") that take place in the "spaces" and elsewhere
4. Some diagnostic tools for self-assessing a range of awareness and levels of functioning at different "stages" of CASE
5. Verbal and nonverbal personal means for realizing CASE (i.e., self-instruction concerning starting, continuing, and concluding actions; cues of originating meta-procedures; etc.)

Caspi's short shrift may sound a little strange to those who are not part of his school of thought. But it will be sufficient here to highlight two innovations in his educational approach. The first is his insistence on the importance of self-awareness—of both the teacher and the student. The other is the creation of "everywhere," a new type of educational space and time allocation that consists of subspaces in which one or more of the functions of creative thinking can be practiced. Examples are a "fantasy room" in which learners are asked to change assumptions, challenge constraints, see the forest for the trees, produce crazy connections, separate the wheat from the chaff, and so forth (Caspi, 1985, p. 293) or an "elaboration room" that offers five modes of elaboration: a seed growing to a tree (nature's elaboration), letters growing into ideas (thinking), a recipe becoming a cake (a plan-guiding practice), a piece of coal becoming a diamond (technical—or rather, chemical), and a reflective elaboration as demonstrated in a photograph or a videotape recording of a learning sequence.

The teacher education program for this open school was based on the assumption that the ideal teacher in such a school would be somebody who "has not been contaminated" by the regular teacher training institution or by the "conditioning of the teaching experience" in a regular school. Since the major educational goal is to educate oneself, the main thrust in the program was to create sample spaces and opportunities in which such self-awareness will develop. This meant that the selection of candidates for the program excluded the ones that were "contaminated" by "too much pedagogical indoctrination." The positive virtues that the program leaders were seeking in the prospective teachers were, besides the willingness to explore who they are, a genuine interest in open education and an expertise in a given field of study. This had to be proved by presenting a bachelor's degree in one of the disciplines taught in school.

This approach was based on the supposition that without revolutionizing the foundations of the common type of school, it would be difficult or nearly impossible to establish a different ideology or to change stubborn routines and preferences in order to allow the creative approach to self-education to take place. Also, like many other alternative movements, the open school movement resented the common modes of teaching and learning in the traditional schools. These were perceived as promoting a cherished kind of knowledge and, as intended, to follow external standards. The usual resistance was to the ethos of productivity or effectiveness that is embedded in the current system and that does not scaffold individual talents or experimentation that may not lead to standardized performance.

The decision to turn the existing system on its head, start afresh, and turn the "anti space" of the existing school into a "super space" is part of the conviction that the evolutionary slow reform will not work. The need to change the teacher's conceptual framework and transform her dispositions and practices begins with a vital change of emphasis in which self-knowledge and self-education are the first targets. Starting to learn a whole system from scratch allows the teacher educator to focus all her efforts on the design of an ideal type of schooling without having to waste energy or time convincing the disbelievers or having to transform deeply rooted regularities.

And as one might expect, the curriculum in the teacher education seminar for open schools (where I have been a member of the staff) consisted of many courses that were primarily intended to increase and improve self-awareness and the abilities to collaborate in a group. The one-year, teacher training program included unconventional lessons not usually offered in teacher training institutions. Topics such as martial arts, yoga, and biofeedback were embedded in the program, and many of the workshops culminated in a "happening" in which guests and friends were invited to share the insights and products that had been planned by the student teachers. Another important facet of this training was, of course, the work on the ideological convictions of the participants and their conception of creative self-education. They were asked to read the open education literature that was very popular at that time, and part of their reeducation process consisted of fostering their ability to teach differently from how they had been taught.

CASE 2: MINDING THE GAP

The previous research that I conducted as part of my PhD dissertation, which was mentored by John Goodlad at the University of California, Los Angeles, helped me develop a kind of distance from the revolutionary claims of the open education movement. I learned that in addition to the theoretical ambiguities in the particular philosophy, there is a large gap between the declarations of open school educators in California and the decisions that they make in their daily work in the classroom. My findings were that although the revolutionary spirit of the open education movement was alive and kicking on the declarative level, its translation to decisions and commitments of teachers presented many potential flaws and incoherencies. One important consideration had to do with the excessive amount of freedom given to both teachers and the students in the Summerhilian-type of schools studied. Many of the teachers were perplexed when they had to make a pedagogical decision. The gap between the beliefs that crystallized in staff meetings in the afternoons and the actions that were taken the next morning was overwhelming for both the teachers and students. This insight calls for a second thought on the place that routines and regularities may have in the regular school, a thought that will be elaborated later.

A description of one typical instance can demonstrate the dilemma of choosing between freedom and license. This kind of choice is encountered by teachers on a daily basis. In one of the many observations that I videotaped in one of the schools, it was possible to witness the following sequence of events:

> A biology teacher told me she was planning to teach a lesson on frogs and brought with her several living frogs in a terrarium. However, a group of four children requested to spend the time of the biology lesson in decorating and painting drinking mugs. One of the students showed her the crayons that he had come with and a couple of blank mugs. Such an event can be seen as a test case of the decision making process in this kind of Summerhilian school: Will the teacher abandon her original plans to let the students follow their initiatives (a decision that could be seen as a case of exercising their autonomy and letting them follow their interests)? Or will she, rather, insist that they will first take part in the well-prepared activity that she planned for the biology lesson? In other words, what are the limits of flexibility and personal choice that the teacher is expected to allow? Can the encountering of such a surprise on behalf of the teacher be transformed

into an educational opportunity? The dichotomous decision between two extreme options that she faced called for a deeper understanding of what such a freedom of choice entails. In this particular lesson, I was surprised to see that the teacher did not even hesitate. The students were allowed to take over with their activity, and the frogs were soon forgotten, waiting, perhaps, for a better opportunity to become a topic of inquiry. In a later interview with the teacher, she stated that she did not feel that there was anything problematic in letting the students follow their hearts and fulfill their real and authentic interests. The frogs could wait because everything that students are not ready for in this school should not be forced on them (and this includes the mastery of basic skills such as reading and writing).

This example reminds me of the classical article by Madeline Lampert (1985) in which she is not able to start her math lesson because the boys and the girls in her classroom do not talk to each other and are seated in different ends of the room. While Lampert used the vignette to show that teaching is the art of managing impossible contradictions, the example I shared earlier shows how attending to the "natural readiness" of students can lead to absurd situations in which the creative urge of the student is seen as an excuse to abandon every other end. And it is not even clear that the free decoration of the mugs had any creative or artistic value beyond being an expressive act. In other words, in calculating the odds of allowing students to follow their interests, it is necessary to weigh the expected gains or the chance that such an activity will lead to a creative result against the probable waste of time and the option that the activity will lead nowhere.

This extreme case proves also that an interest in an activity can be a very short-lived capricious event, and it has to have other components in order to increase the chance for a creative activity. It clarifies also why several scholars prefer to talk about the engagement of the imagination and to avoid getting into the turbulent waters of when and how it is possible to assure that the learning experience will lead to a valuable and original outcome.

Another issue that deserves our attention is that this teacher in case 2 knew that she would get the backing for her decision from her principal and the larger school community. In other words, this kind of impossible management of conflicting possibilities, as Lampert (1985) describes it, seems easier to handle in an institution willing to take some risks and provide a lot of space for the autonomy of the teacher, even if the end result could be a failure to engage the students in a new topic. The acknowledgement that nobody will be made accountable for the gaps in knowledge that the students might have, in addition to the fact that the teacher is not confined by clear rules or expectations, produces a problem in my eyes. It creates a risk that the space in which the spontaneous and momentary interest of the child overrules an opportunity to harness the imagination to a discussion on the life of the frog and misses an opportunity to arrive at a deeper understanding of a new curricular topic.

Returning to the pre-service program for the open school in Jerusalem that I described earlier, readers may be interested to know that some modified versions of the teacher training program and open school still exist, but my personal impression is that much of the revolutionary spirit and many of the foci have changed tremendously over the years. In this case, some of the changes had to do with the replacement of faculty and the people who promoted the philosophy, and some resulted from different environmental conditions and changes in policy that affected the mission of both the training program and the open school. It may be useful to generalize beyond this specific case by noting that some of the changes can be attributed to the attrition and fatigue of the staff, in addition to the school, and the training program having to bend to pressures exerted by parents and the Ministry of Education, which was the funding agency. Another partial explanation has to do with the competition with the many other kinds of alternative programs that were opened later on—that is, democratic and Waldorf schools and campuses with other fashionable titles and philosophies.

The reason that the open school still exists and new teachers are still trained can be found in the permissive attitude toward many kinds of education programs, which result from the public's disappointment with the traditional public school system. However, in the remaining part of the article, I would like to argue that it is possible to educate in ways that will integrate the imagination and creative thinking without having to revolutionize the whole institution or to submit to the capricious whims of students. Additionally, case 3 will show that efforts to nurture creative thinking do not have to be limited to open schools or private or alternative institutions.

CASE 3: INFUSING CREATIVE THINKING THROUGH IN-SERVICE TRAINING

Two projects that I led with the help of several of my colleagues in the following years convinced me that there are many ways to fuse the imagination and think outside the box or differently within the same box and that this can be practiced not only in alternative schools but also in public school classrooms.

The first project took place in the late 1970s, and the second, which can be seen as a sequel to the first, began twenty years later in the 1990s. The two interventions show the importance of the teacher who is convinced that it is worthwhile to engage the imagination of her students and the many pathways she can take in order to do so. Moreover, although I will devote attention to the possible contribution of institutional support and that of an external agent, there are documented instances in which such initiation is carried out by a single teacher or by a small group of collaborating teachers. And, in many cases, we can witness a teacher who is directing such a move against all odds—that is, while defying instructional pressures and/or the disbelief of other members of the professional staff. This kind of lonely adventure will be described at the end of this chapter.

Let me first describe a more organized venture in which a university team was assigned by a local district to join forces with ten elementary schools in the southern region of Israel. Their joint mission was to introduce creative teaching and learning to the mandated curriculum. In this project, my colleague Amos Goor and I (with many other coworkers) taught elementary school teachers what creative thinking is all about for two semesters. The course combined a theoretical background and was interspersed with a number of specific methods or techniques intended to stimulate the imagination of the students and to allow them to come up with creative ideas in relation to the topics that had been studied. Our assumption was that small changes in the instruction or in the assignments that are given to the students can encourage students to think about the core subject matters from a fresh and original perspective.

The organization of the project reflected the know-how from research findings about successful change projects in the past. For example, the project was not forced upon the teachers in a top-down manner, and they were consulted before the school agreed to take part in the innovation. Campuses where the teachers were reluctant to participate were not asked to join the project. In addition, the project started with a flexible program that could be enriched and elaborated through the active contribution of the participants.

We met with the teachers on a regular basis in a weekly morning session that took place in each school. While the full-time teachers participated in the training sessions, substitute teachers taught in their classrooms. The university team was also allowed to visit the classrooms and help the teachers in the implementation of the techniques of the project (Alexander & Goor, 1980).

In this project, the teachers were not asked to change essential elements in the organization of the classroom or in the prescribed curriculum. Contrary to the fashionable organizational changes that were based on a move to open spaces, on team teaching, or on learning in small groups, we asked the teachers and the students to stay where they were. Our belief was, rather, that a teacher could stimulate creative thinking by starting the lesson in an unconventional way or by bringing to the fore, in an appropriate moment, a thinking challenge that would increase the students' curiosity, present different possibilities to understand a given topic, or reflect on what had been learned. A specific example can help to clarify the way in which this has been done.

On one occasion, we brought to the planning session a technique that we called "questioning about facts," which required the asking of as many questions as possible about a given statement. The idea was to encourage the students, rather than the teacher, to reflect on the information that was contained in a text or a unit that had been learned. In one history lesson that I was invited to attend, the students were asked to read a chapter in the textbook dealing with the restrictions and limitations that Jews were asked to abide by in the time of King Antioch. In the preceding teachers' preparation session, many of the participants commented that there is nothing new in the idea that the students will be instructed to ask questions since "this is what we are doing anyway in nearly every lesson." But when we attended this history lesson and other classes in the same school, it soon became evident that the learners had no experience in starting a discussion by asking questions. In most cases, the teacher had been the one who was asking most of the questions. This, of course, is not a real surprise to those who have read Goodlad's (1974) *Looking Behind the Classroom Door* and other similar reports. In our case, we found that in the rare instances in which a question had been raised by a student, it was often treated as a nuisance and not as a preferred way to study a new topic.

The next step after the questions were listed on the blackboard was to ask the students for possible answers to the questions and problems that they had generated. This led to a lively discussion and to disputes about the meaning of key ideas in the chapter. In this specific history lesson, the teacher conducting the lesson was able to deal with most of the objectives of the lesson simply by elaborating upon many of the questions posed by the students.

In other instances, we have elaborated the technique by introducing a critical thinking phase in which the students were asked to classify the questions and relate them to categories and prioritize them according to the ones that seem most futile or interesting to discuss. During the in-service training session that preceded this event, we suggested adding a second technique called "problem solution problem." The gist of this sequence is that, in most cases, a suggested solution raises new kinds of problems. This technique focuses on the possible difficulties that can result from a solution to a certain problem. For example, when a historical problem of the Jews has been that they were not allowed to keep their traditions, one of the solutions was to find ways to keep them in secret. However, this raised the additional challenge of tighter restrictions and sanctions being placed on Jews and their activities.

The sequence of stating a problem, attempting to find a suitable solution for it, and identifying another problem in the solution was not meant to discourage students from the possibility of reaching an agreed-upon solution. Its purpose was, rather, to demonstrate the built-in paradox that many promising resolutions are caught in. With technological progress and new inventions come troubling side effects and undesired consequences. Part of the process is being able to see the drawbacks of some of our customs and pleasures and finding ways to reduce the damage that we are causing. Humans invented cars to solve their transportation problems, but this has caused many environmental problems and a life toll in accidents, which calls for creative ways to overcome the negative impacts of the invention.

These short examples demonstrate how simple changes in the instructional sequence can turn a learning practice on its head and bring about more involvement and meaningful contribution among the students. After gaining some experience in using these techniques, the teachers were able to mix and match different techniques, and the students, who learned to recognize each technique by its title, suggested new ways of using them when they recognized an opportunity for such a thinking exercise to be incorporated in the curriculum. In other words, part of the success in such an intervention depends on the ability to create a need for and give permission to use these modes of thinking. Another element of the project, which was common to many other similar projects, was the development of a mutual language or jargon that allowed both the students and their teachers to refer to a specific technique or a sequence of instructional events or evaluate the originality and value of certain responses.

One interesting revelation of this project was that a change could be sensed not only in the involvement of the students in the issues and the thinking challenges but also in the modification in the attitudes and openness of the teachers. Many of the teachers commented in interviews that the project made sense to them, and they were especially delighted to realize that they were free to fit the strategies of the project to their own instructional needs. They were not asked to implement the techniques "as is" but rather to modify and adapt them to their student population and to the curricular demands of their field of expertise. The project started with a series of fifteen techniques that were introduced as the initial database, but the number grew to thirty techniques and more before we finally left the schools.

Unfortunately, these optimistic implications did not last for long. The lasting effect of the project was limited, and after the university team left, only a few teachers continued to use the techniques on a permanent basis. Although we could find some traces of the original methods that were developed, the impression was that the pressures of accountability and the requirement to "teach more, faster" forced most of the teachers to return to their old teaching habits, which reserve only a minimal place for creative ideas or the engagement of the imagination.

What are some of the lessons that can be learned from such an intervention? First of all, the good news is that it is possible to change some of the regularities in the teaching-learning process even in the public school next door.

An in-service training program can be more effective in this respect than a pre-service program because it contains several facilitating and supporting elements that can be missing when a student teacher leaves the teacher education program and starts her professional career. It seems easier to reorganize and reshuffle some of the teaching routines when there is an external agent that is supporting the process and when there is leadership in the school that is convinced in the direction of the project. Many of the teachers who at first showed resistance were persuaded and empowered by the collaborating school principals. This internal support tended to be sustained in cases in which the school principal remained in her position.

A more difficult dilemma is how to maintain the momentum in cases in which the school leadership changes hands. There is no simple panacea to the sustainability problem, which is reported in many articles on school reform (Hargreaves, 2009; Cuban & Tyack, 1997). From the literature on reform, we learn that in some projects, this problem finds a better solution than in others. My hunch, which is backed by evidence from a master's thesis that I have been advising, is that projects that are initiated by teachers, by so-called "champions" (teachers who have an idea and convince others to join them), may have longer prospects to survive (Joseph-Hassidim, 2007). In several national projects in the US, the finding is that in addition to the initiation of the single teacher and the instructional advice that is provided by an external agent, the perseverance in the project is supported by a network in which schools are helping each other out.

There is no satisfying solution to this conundrum. Turning an instructional experiment into a long-lasting practice that will result in serious changes requires changing some of the routines and daily practices in the school. If, for example, students are not used to asking questions as a rule, one or two experiences will not change their attitudes or the regularities in their classroom. And our experience shows that there is a need to act in several dimensions at once: it is not enough to be knowledgeable about the possible place that the imagination and creativity may have in our lives. It is not even enough to acquire certain techniques that will change the thinking directions in the classroom. The theoretical clarification and the ability to translate it to concrete practices are both required but may not provide the necessary conditions for the change to happen.

The third condition is much harder to implement, and it has to do with the climate that is built in the classroom. Is there a space for the student to play with possibilities? Is there permission to make mistakes or experiment with ideas? How are some of the institutional pressures for performance and achievement handled? These three dimensions of operation need further elaboration, especially because each of the dimensions contains a garden variety of options that are not always considered. But before we devote space to that, let me shortly describe how the four-year project ended and how it was revived in another form twenty years later.

This creative thinking project was terminated (like many of the externally funded projects) four years after it had begun, but it succeeded in demonstrating to the teachers and to those of us who initiated it that creative thinking could be incorporated in the regular school curriculum and change the direction of the work of the teacher and the students even if the lasting effects of these changes were found to be limited.

CASE 4: FLIGHTS OF FANCY—A TELEVISED INTERVENTION

Twenty years later, I was asked to produce a national television series devoted to creative thinking. The production was funded by the educational television station. We called the series "Flights of Fancies," and it was aired on the local station from 1999 onward. The ideas of the series were based on the insights that were gained from our project with the elementary schools that had been terminated in 1980.

Disseminating an instructional idea via the medium of television entails modes of operation that are very different from the ones that can be used in a direct face-to-face interaction. We designed broadcasts for the students in middle school but had in mind the adults, parents, or teachers who could use the content and form of the broadcast to trigger the activities of the young spectators. The programs were presented to interested teams of teachers in a biweekly in-service training program that had been offered by the television station. We supplemented the broadcast with a detailed teacher guide that included a description of the broadcasts and suggestions for further activities in science, in the arts, and in literature, which contributed to the theme of each program. The program titles were "Repetition and Change," "Parts and Wholes," "Points of View," "Contradictions that Live Together," "What If," "Translations from One Medium to Another," "Modification and Development," "Ambiguities," and "Everybody Can."

Each program contained many examples of problems and situations that demonstrated the main theme of the program. The series used all possible artistic forms that could be shown on TV, including animation, drama, interviews, and nature clips. The small vignettes were interpreted and reflected upon by a dreamy figure of a medieval fool who is puzzled about nearly everything that he discovers.

Here, again, an example could be helpful. In the program devoted to parts and the whole, for instance, the fool is trying to assemble a jigsaw puzzle of the river Seine. The puzzle is based on a famous picture by the painter Seurat. After laying the last piece in the puzzle, he wonders if he has gotten the whole picture. He asks himself: Is the puzzle a whole now or just an extract of a much larger scene in which the river Seine, Paris, and even the world are the larger entities? Can a part be a whole in a different setting?

These quasi-philosophical deliberations were only the beginning of a program that is full of examples of parts that can be combined to a whole in many ways. One example was based on the story of Cinderella, which was dramatized with a slight twist. In the broadcast, Cinderella wondered if the prince was just interested in her foot and its match to the lost shoe. She provoked the prince by asking if he was not interested in some other spiritual qualities that she might have. And the prince, after a moment of embarrassment, quickly responded that he realized that their relationship is only in its beginning phase and that they both needed to know more about each other and nurture their relationship.

Theoretically, this program was based on Koestler's (1964) idea of creating something new through the process of "bisociation," that is, the combining of elements that belong to unrelated fields to arrive at a new entity (a complete work of art or a new partnership). However, the broadcast allowed the spectator to put in action many other aesthetic and content-related elements. For example, many details in the story of Cinderella appeared as parts that are related to each other. Even the fingers of the pianist who is accompanying the wedding ceremony are dressed in gloves that looked like keys on a keyboard. Another example of parts of wholes was taken from archeology.

The setting of the archeological excavations in Caesarea served as a demonstration of the ability of the archeologist to build a theory about a culture that was based on few remnants. The archeologist tried to explain to the audience and the fool how one piece of a cooking pot that she excavated can lay the groundwork for a theory about a whole material culture. In this case, it was a remnant of a cooking pot that served as a clue for the reconstruction of the whole material culture of the Roman colony. David Perkins (1992) remarked: "If a pedagogy of understanding means anything, it means understanding the piece in the context of the whole and the whole in the mosaic of its pieces" (p. 75). We can, furthermore, add: if the ability to think in creative ways means anything, it means making meaningful connections between unrelated pieces or between pieces that are only connected in our mind in a fixed way.

In the in-service training programs that accompanied the implementation of the television series, the teachers watched the programs and were asked to bring examples of their reactions to the broadcasts and classroom products that were influenced by the TV programs. These examples were exhibited and discussed in the first half of the following training session.

The first meeting of the in-service training began with a short introduction on the nature of creativity and creative thinking. It was followed by nine meetings in which each of the nine programs was presented and discussed. The programs were originally designed for middle school students, but we found that teachers were using them in lower and higher grades as well. There are, of course, many disadvantages to this type of mediated program being openly transmitted without an ability to evaluate to what kind of use they are put. In the teams of volunteering teachers that we guided, there was much enthusiasm, and we were able to trace some of the activities in their schools. However, the main complaint was that the broadcast had an interdisciplinary orientation, and this made it difficult for them to find an appropriate niche in the mandated content-driven curriculum.

CASE 5: IMAGINATIVE EDUCATION—THE IERG VERSION

The last and most recent encounter with efforts to engage the imagination has to be credited to the dynamic group developing the idea of IERG at Simon Fraser University in Vancouver, Canada. The IERG group has been active for the last seven to eight years, and is headed by Kieran Egan. My first acquaintance with this multinational effort to engage the imagination of students began in 2004 when I first met Kieran Egan and his colleagues at a summer conference in Vancouver. I came to the conference after being exposed to Egan's books, which was a very refreshing experience. I found the IERG approach intriguing and, as a result, started to distribute the ideas that the group had developed to many teachers and teacher educators in institutions in Israel.

There are many differences between the various methods that I have used to introduce creative thinking in the schools and the practices developed by the IERG group. As I will show in the remaining parts of this chapter, some of the differences between the projects can be explained by their different theoretical roots. For example, imagination is a term that is mostly handled by philosophers, and it fits the methods of inquiry that resonate with that field. Creativity, on the other hand, turned out to be a popular object of study in both psychological research and organizational theory. This is one way to differentiate between the terms. However, in daily conversations, we do not always make the distinction, and the terms can be used interchangeably or in a single breath. The familiarity with the terms can help teachers feel comfortable with them, but the imprecise or even conflicting manners in which the terms are understood can be a hindrance to the cultivation of the imagination or of creative thinking. Therefore, the first obligation is to clarify what kinds of imagination or creativity we are seeking before linking them with other activities in the classroom.

A Number of Generalizations from These Experiences

Although I have never thought about the possible relationship between these separate experiences in which I participated in different phases of my career, the writing of this chapter afforded an apt opportunity to compare and contrast the projects and to check whether there is a common theme implied in these comparisons that can be shared with teachers and teacher educators.

THE CONTEXT AND STUDENT POPULATION

One main concern that seems to underlie many educational interventions is the nature of the student population involved in each of the projects. While the first open education program focused on a select population that had shown an interest in the open education philosophy, and the school attracted students from all parts of Jerusalem, a precondition for the government recognition and funding included opening the gates of the school to children from lower socio-economic backgrounds who lived near the school. This forced the founders to adopt a curriculum that could cater to a heterogeneous group of students in order to prove that the open education philosophy could be adapted to a wide range of backgrounds and needs.

In my experience, this forced move did not change the somewhat elitist tone of this school, and one of its hallmarks has been the pressure placed on the families and the school community to conform to the accepted ideology of the school. This meant that, among the families who lived near the schools, there was a natural preference to accept students whose families were ready to concur with the innovative ideas of the school. This makes sense in a school that wishes to deviate from the routines and beliefs of the public schools but has several implications regarding the necessary precondition for such a change. Some of these preconditions will be discussed later in this chapter.

In the next project, in which ten schools in the southern region of Israel took part, the condition for the funding was that the project would involve regular schools in low income neighborhoods. When the project continued, several religious schools were added in an effort to demonstrate that the ideas of the project could be implemented in a variety of settings and that many types of stakeholders can contribute to and enrich the teaching methods that the project offers. This tendency to widen the outreach of the project and implement the ideas in as many kinds of schools as possible was the foundation of the translation of the methods and contents of the project to the medium of television.

The educational television authorities, funded by the Ministry of Education, hoped that the ideas promoted in the series would reach the widest audience possible, and the in-service training that accompanied the programs was offered in remote parts of the country to allow teachers to participate in the project. Since a television broadcast is one-way communication, we have used the responses of the students that were brought in by the participants, together with the results of a survey administered by an external evaluation team, as a measure of the project's impact and the outreach span of its ideas.

The findings were problematic in part since they highlighted the fact that the same kind of program can have a different impact in different types of population. It soon became obvious that students from strong backgrounds find it easier to relate to the ideas of the project and to elaborate them in their own way. The series served as a springboard for these students, which allowed them to free their imaginations and come up with original and surprising ideas.

In schools peopled by children who were not socioeconomically advantaged, we saw efforts to develop some of the ideas mentioned in the broadcast and to come up with their own original additions. But, in many cases, these were duplications of the examples that had been shown in the program and not efforts to implement the principles learned in a new context. For example, in the "Parts and Wholes" program, one could see how an old clock is disassembled and the parts were used to create new products. The examples that the students suggested were based on disassembling another machine, but there was hardly any effort put into looking at the parts in a new way (redefining them) or to think how the newly assembled whole would be very different from the original piece of equipment. We also found that in many cases, students in these schools were allowed to free their fantasies without later having to substantiate and explain how their innovations related to the principles highlighted in the program. In other words, we saw a slippage to excessive uncontrolled fantasy or to a recitation and duplication of the examples in the program.

WHAT LEVELS OF EDUCATION ARE ADDRESSED?

The natural tendency of so-called change agents is to locate these projects in middle schools or in the lower grades of the high school. One reason for this preference is the developmental stage in which students find themselves. Another explanation has to do with the institutional qualities of schools for students of ages eight to twelve. It depends on which theory one uses in describing the typical characteristics of this age.

Piagetian theory could be a good source for those who believe that because children at this stage are in the transitional phase between sensory-motor perception and formal thinking, there remains a possibility to generate possibilities and hypotheses that are not completely governed and constrained by formal criticism. On the other hand, Egan (1997) prefers to see this age through the lens of his theory that describes the different stages in the development of one's understanding and highlights, for example, the need to fit the curriculum materials to the culturally bound natural interests and cognitive abilities in middle school to the romantic interests of students at that particular age. For example, students at that age will be attracted to heroes and the extremes of reality and will easily get excited about the wonders in our world without spoiling it with over-criticism and excessive cynicism. Egan also prefers to replace the Piagetian view with a Vygotskian one that perceives the learning group as being influenced by the socio-cultural context in which learning occurs and in which the zone of proximal development of each individual learner can be shaped and mediated by the learning group, the language used, and the distributed knowledge built into the group.

Without knowing about the IERG philosophy and implementation efforts, the projects that I have been involved in focused on interventions in elementary schools starting from age six or seven and ending at twelve or thirteen. The most meaningful examples could be observed in the middle, third, fourth, and fifth grades of these schools, and this can be explained on the basis of the ability of students to learn specific knowledge in the discipline, on their literary skills, and on their self-assurance in their ability to follow their hearts and interests in directions that engage the imagination (Egan, 1992, 1997). The institutional qualities that make the middle school a preferred location for such an intervention have to do with the expectations that in these years the students will be already treated as grownups, while many of the pressures to compete and excel in standardized tests or other performance measures can be delayed until high school.

PRE-SERVICE OR IN-SERVICE EDUCATION?

In a paradigm that conceives teacher education as a continuous process, the choice between the two periods in one's training can be seen as dichotomous since the compromise of mixing the two forms of training comes as a reasonable solution. However, pre-service training, especially when it is provided in a sheltered ideological glasshouse of an alternative program, can have many benefits. The proof of the pudding is in the eating, and many enthusiastic student teachers who join a school and attempt to implement the innovative approach that they have been exposed to receive cold shoulders in the staff room or from their supervisors.

The cons of a program that is designed to convince mid-career teachers, on the other hand, are that these teachers have developed routines and methods of teaching that are difficult to disturb, and there is a natural tendency to continue in the old ways of teaching while only changing the titles or the rationale for what is being done. A good example of this phenomenon is the abundance of interdisciplinary programs that are only multidisciplinary or, at best, a mechanical combination of familiar topics previously taught in separate disciplines. Only when these seemingly separate perspectives can be compared and taught in ways that will add depth to the key concepts or when the meaning of a fertile concept like "interdependence" (which is Perkins's example) is tested in different domains and fields of study will the interdisciplinary examination afford a more sophisticated kind of learning.

The dilemma of where to start the revolution or present an alternative approach to teach creative thinking is embedded in each of the projects I have described here and in many other approaches that have been developed by other educators and researchers (Williams, 1972; Treffinger, 1995; Nadler, Hibino, & Farrell, 1995, 1999). In most cases, it is easier to address practicing teachers than to base a whole new student teacher program on creative thinking skills. But this has been the payoff of having to combat established preferences and the threat that the delicate equilibrium maintained in most institutions will be endangered. This leads to the need to consider other elements in this equation, for example, the existence of an innovative landscape in the institution or a personal interest of the principal or the leading group in the school in the reform. A model that is rare solves the problem of discontinuity between teacher training and praxis by creating collaborations between the teacher training institution and an experimental school. This model requires substantial investments on the part of both partners, and its drawback lies in the difficulty to spread the fruits of the intervention to other institutions and in the energy that is required to sustain it.

TO INFUSE OR NOT TO INFUSE

Sternberg and Lubart (1999) divide the different approaches to the study of creativity in seven categories: mystical approaches, pragmatic approaches, psychodynamic approaches, cognitive approaches, social personality approaches, and confluence approaches. The last category assumes that there are multiple components that must converge for creativity to occur (Sternberg and Lubart, 1999). In other words, it is unlikely that creative initiations and an abundance of insights and open hypotheses will fill the air of the classroom if many separate preconditions are not met. We should not disillusion ourselves into thinking that a television program in itself will cause a change in the learners' attitudes or in their actual ability to think about possibilities not considered in the past. It takes more than involving students in a sequence of instruction when we intend to engage their imaginations in meaningful ways. One dilemma tied to this multiple component view concerns the ability to teach creative thinking within a separate "thinking program" or infuse creative thinking and imagination in the regular curriculum.

The "Flight of Fancy" television series was used by many teachers as an enrichment program or as additional "nice to have" activity adjacent to their regular teaching. In the ten schools intervention program, the project team taught what we called a list of "pure techniques." I worked with the teachers to search for intersections where these techniques could be fused with a given curricular topic. The parts and wholes exercise, for example, starts with a list of random words beginning with the same letter and continues with the instruction to combine all the words in one paragraph that looks like a news item. The notion was adopted by teachers to fit various curricular topics. In history, the words were taken from slogans of the French revolution, and the whole was a supposed news report on the victory of the freedom fighters while in the sciences, the parts could be elements of an electrical circuit, and the whole could be a functioning music instrument or light system.

Another pure technique offered a move from analysis to synthesis and back to analysis. One simple example, as foreshadowed earlier, is disassembling a clock or a mechanical toy made of Lego bricks and reassembling the pieces in a way that will yield a new toy or instrument. In the arts, the parts could be pieces that can be combined to form a collage. In science, teachers have tried to teach a lesson in which the students had to speculate about a given culture by amalgamating partial pieces of evidence.

In another lesson, we have used the format that was used in the 1970s in the learning by discovery units. For example: how do ants find the way to their food? Our parts here are pieces of evidence that are observed and compared to validate one of many possible hypotheses. Are the ants driven by the sight of the food or by the leadership of one of them? Are they led by the smell of the food or by following a certain map that they have in "their heads"? Another example originated in a constructivist lesson that Seymour Papert developed in his experimental school. The parts there were different types of sensors in a room full of remote controlled buggies. The whole was the classification principle that the students had to discover in order to group all buggies with the same sensors sensitive to light magnets or sound in the right place of the room where a speaker, a light, and a magnet have been placed. Since several of the buggies were equipped with more than one sensor, the students had to decide how to cope with this problem in a one-dimensional classification system.

In other words, in this project, we used techniques not as a list of skills to be blindly followed by the teachers or students but rather as guiding principles that represent one way of engaging the imagination and which could result in a creative solution or surprising revelation that, among other things, could have the potential to contribute to a deeper understanding of a certain problem or phenomenon rooted in disciplinary knowledge.

THREE DIFFERENT LAYERS OF OPERATION

The approach suggested in this article consists of three different layers or dimensions that have to be operated by the teacher simultaneously. The first dimension has to do with the teacher's ability to crystallize a clear conception about what the imagination and creativity entail and what are the possible ways in which the imagination can be harnessed to enrich one's thoughts and behaviors. The second dimension may be the most difficult one to materialize. It deals with the ability to translate the ideal of imaginative thinking process into techniques and guides for action. I hopefully have shown that this dimension is divided into many subroutines and roles.

Curriculum topics and learning opportunities have to be identified, the class environment has to be prepared in the physical sense and in the sense of creating the right climate for the required changes, and, in addition, the teacher is required to think how she will evaluate instances in which students have come up with new ideas. There is also a need to encourage them to explore the meaning of their findings. The third dimension originates from the emotional support that one needs to delve into creative endeavors. Nearly every method for the cultivation of creative thinking starts with an attitude of change toward the change involved. What does it take to follow a poorly developed hypothesis? What kind of a tolerance to ambiguities and risk-taking behavior has to be reinforced?

We have, hopefully, seen each of these dimensions as requiring the ability to select and choose among many options. Although there may be a wide agreement that creative thinking is a valuable asset, there is much less agreement on the operational definition of creativity and imagination. One can move from a mystical view, looking for moments of inspiration and rare moments of revelation and "aha effect" (Koestler, 1964, 1989), to a much more restricted view of creativity, which is seeing it as a subset of critical thinking or as an outcome of the mastery and connoisseurship in a given domain (Weisberg, 1993). The same flexibility can be found in the methods or strategy that can be adopted. We are betwixt and between projects that believe in a list of techniques and cookbook instructions that are religiously followed by teachers (what Esquivel [1995] calls the molecular level) to approaches in which a general attitude (the so-called molar level) and permissive legitimization to think differently are the essence. And in the third dimension that attacks the attitude change that is required, we can observe many degrees of flexibility as well. Some gurus will advocate the need to forget the old dictums and free heads from any previous convictions, while others will strive for a more moderate transformation in which learners will be gradually scaffolded in their efforts to go beyond the given and the familiar.

Before developing this multidimensional scheme, I would like to share with the readers several experiences of which this scheme is a result. I hope that this personal deviation will be patiently followed since it introduces the wider context in which these interventions happen and the ways that teachers can become partners in such a reform.

In all the aforementioned projects, the first step in convincing teachers and students to change some of their thinking habits is based on a *theoretical clarification*. It is necessary to clarify what one means by creativity and imagination and how it is possible to enhance its manifestation in different educational settings. The second dimension is the one in which appropriate *teaching strategies* are selected. A desire to see creative thinking processes happening in the classroom will not in itself produce this type of thinking. I have shown that there are various ways to move toward these objectives. The selection of the right curriculum materials and experience in promoting the necessary discourse in the classroom are only two examples of the importance of this dimension. And the third dimension focuses on the necessary *change in attitudes* and the ability to plan for a *transitional space* in which students will feel safe to look for creative and original ideas. The interplay with the imagination involves some risks and does not always lead the thinker to a safe ground. The road to the promised land of a new revelation can pass through the desert of frustration and questions about the mission. This requires the teacher to create a climate in which learners are allowed to make mistakes, play around with ideas, and arrive, now and then, at wrong conclusions and misconceptions. This can become part of the learning process when we allow students to learn from their own experiences.

These three layers of operation are interrelated and activated at the same time. Each of the layers calls for decisions on the part of teachers regarding what to put at center stage and what to ignore. For example, in adopting a working definition of the terms *imagination* and *creativity*, one has to select from a spectrum of meaning that ranges from the mystical and romantic to the critical and analytical. And in choosing the right strategy for the intervention in the classroom, the variety is not less perplexing. The teacher will have to decide whether she is willing to select a method that is based on a particular list of simple rules or a menu of specific techniques or if she prefers an approach that is grounded in a general expectation to be more open to any kind of hypothesis. And the large variety of options can be especially confusing in the third dimension. In this layer that involves feelings and a sense of commitment, one teacher can invest in creating a comfort level and a permissive climate in the classroom, another in finding an emotional hook with the topics that have to be taught, and a third teacher can put her efforts toward improving the sensitivity and concern for the thinking and insights of her students. This may be a natural expectation for a worker in the psychological clinic, but it is less common in classrooms, especially when many other tasks are sacrificed in the service of predetermined objectives and other external pressures.

WHERE IS A GOOD STARTING POINT?

There is a mixed feeling among scholars regarding the need to come up with a precise definition of what imagination and creativity really mean. We have shown elsewhere (Alexander & Shoshani, 2008) that even if a teacher has a pragmatic approach and does not want to be committed to a narrow definition of creative teaching and learning, it still makes sense to adopt a dialectic approach that moves between a series of possible extreme poles.

Many scholars are excited when they study the unique human ability of the creator to come up with an original and even fantastic idea and use it as a basis to see the world in a new way or even operate on the world and transform some elements in it.

Imagination, on the other hand, is usually perceived as contributing to the process but not so much as requiring a certain type of product. The power of the imagination can be in its ability to scaffold our thinking about the familiar in new ways. It can be, according to some theoreticians, a very romantic way, which is related to fantasy, and it can be restricted to a much narrower realm of our thinking that relates or is even subsumed under critical thinking and reasoning. In this latter option, the imagination still has a unique role in being the engine of new possibilities and alternative scenarios for an initial insight that has to be elaborated and implanted through the rigorous examination of the critical thinking.

If we maintain, like Egan and most of the scholars in the IERG group, that the imagination is our best source of hypothetical scenarios, then the emphasis in the classroom will be on the thinking process rather than using certain kinds of cognitive tools. Imaginative ideas can serve as raw materials to something that can be shared and is of value to others, but their significance does not depend on these latter achievements.

In looking for other characteristics of creativity, we can concur with Janet Hargreaves (2008), who warns us that "introducing creativity into an educational experience involves risk on a number of levels" (p. 5). She notes that the major barrier to creativity can be the fear "of the unknown, of ridicule, and of failure that engaging creativity may be a source of anxiety for students" (p. 5). The stimulation of the imagination can be less demanding and less risky in this respect. It is more tentative and plays with ideas or even partial explanation that one does not have to be fully committed to, and it does not culminate the deliberation with a definite kind of understanding or action.

What place can the imagination have in the conventional type of the classroom? The first and obvious one is that of a motivator that links the current interests of the student to topics and chunks of knowledge to which she does not feel connected. The trick is to find how and where and with what the student can identify. But the potential reliance on the imagination does not stop there. In Egan's (1997) educational scheme, each stage in the development of human understanding is engaging the imagination in a different manner. The imagination in the early phases of development has many somatic roots and many oral manifestations. And the more literally one moves the imagination to the background, the more it turns to be more dependent on a dialog and serves as foundation on which more sophisticated kinds of understanding like the philosophical and ironical can grow. Egan's conception of the imagination is transforming and changing as a result of the development and the cultural and educational experience that the student encounters. It has a collective aspect that is embedded in the language and in the cultural and historical formation of meanings (Alexander, 2006).

Some scholars see as a major attribute of the imagination the ability to generate images and mix these images with our perceptions and ability to verbalize and translate ideas into words (Thomas, 1997). Some others think that although the imagination facilitates our ability to think with images, this is not its main asset, and we should, rather, see "the ability to think about the possible as being so" (White cited in Egan, 1992) as the major contribution to a different kind of teaching and learning. It is interesting to note that one of the most successful efforts to integrate creative learning and teaching in England (NACCCE, 1999) started from a very similar standpoint.

To conclude this discussion on the ways in which a teacher can learn the meaning of the terms *imagination* and *creativity*, we can reasonably say that the imagination can be conceived as the source of images or the generator of new possibilities. In an educational context that is willing to combine the two terms, the imagination can be viewed as the powerful engine or locomotive that pulls the wagons packed with curious and committed learners. The use of the term *creativity*, in spite of its ambiguity, has several agreed-upon criteria. Most scholars concur that there is a need for a product or clear presentation of an idea. This product has to appear to be original and unexpected, at least in the eyes of the beholder or in those of the student who succeeded in challenging her existing knowledge with a new insight or hypothesis.

Epilogue: Accounts of Sporadic Solo Attempts by Courageous Teachers

In a course, "A Critical Outlook on the Educational System," I asked my students to find teachers who are considered creative by their colleagues and students. They were asked to interview the teacher and find out how creativity is related to the context of the work in her classroom, how she thinks that she manages to engage the imagination of her students, and what she would consider as creative thoughts or behaviors of her students. A detailed account of what came from these interviews that were, in part, accompanied by the examination of materials that students were asked to produce and an observation in the classroom is beyond the scope of the current chapter. It will suffice, though, to share with readers some of the accumulated impressions from the exercises that the students handed in that led me to the following conclusions:

- Many teachers are reluctant to commit themselves to a formal definition of creativity.
- There is a tendency to confuse creative teaching with creative learning.
- Creativity is often (wrongly) perceived as relating to the teaching of interdisciplinary topics or alternative methods for the teaching of traditional topics.
- The teachers reported that they experienced many unexpected reactions and contributions on the part of their students. This forced them to refresh their thinking about the selection of topics and assignments.
- There were disagreements about the need of the teacher to be creative as a precondition in enabling the students to use their own imagination and creativity.
- Creative abilities were perceived by some teachers as primarily depending on the innate talents of the students and by others as depending on the educational opportunities that one receives.
- Many of the teachers complained that they felt lonely in their efforts to introduce creative thinking and that they did what they did despite the lack of support and encouragement from their colleagues or superiors.

To end, I will discuss the implications of these insights and how they relate to the theory and acknowledged practices behind the possible place of creativity and imagination in school. In sum:

- The reluctance to be committed to a certain definition of creativity can be understood on several grounds.
- The term is ambiguous and defies most efforts to box it or confine it to a certain realm of meanings, or as Boden (1990) comments: "It is usually unhelpful to ask 'Is that idea creative: *yes* or *no?*' because creativity exists in many forms, and on many levels. Much of the illumination lies in the details" (p. 287).
- When the teacher does not explicitly subscribe to a certain conception of creativity, the odds for presenting many kinds of practices and even contradicting examples of creativity become greater.
- Many educators like Joseph Schwab (1969/1978) feel that the practical should have preference over the theoretical. It follows that an intuitive conception of the mission that is involved fits well with the practical knowledge that educators should rely on.
- This relates to the oxymoron that is mentioned in the title of this chapter. If creativity contains a possibility of surprise (as Margaret Boden [1990] and other scholars have noted), a precise definition could be limiting and could reduce the chance that such a surprise will occur.

INDIRECT WAYS TO ENCOURAGE STUDENTS TO USE THEIR IMAGINATIONS

We can ask, how are teachers able to plant the seeds of creativity without directing their efforts and setting the stage for such a move? The literature on teacher behavior and preferred methods of teaching tends to be silent on this issue. We know that one restaurant chef can cook in creative ways that are different from those of his colleagues, and this raises some questions about the ability to teach an organized corpus of skills dispositions and kinds of understandings.

We can look for ways to reduce unexpected results and lead to activities that are not common in most classrooms. As an appetizer, I will list here four different indirect ways to encourage such a move:

1. Learn from models, both live and historical figures, that are related to the knowledge in the curriculum.
2. Experience the process of discovery with its ups and downs and become aware of the dispositions that are needed in order to make it happen.

3. Create a transitional space in the classroom in which experimentation is encouraged.
4. Change the evaluation measures in a way that will deliver the message that there are many possibilities to excel, and they are not restricted to performance on standardized achievement tests.

Sizer's recommendation to replace standard testing with exhibitions is a move in this direction that does not require the sacrifice of some of the most cherished missions of the school.

Modeling is dependent on a complex mechanism, and there is a consensus that its indirect effects can have a much stronger impact than direct attempts to nurture something. Dreeben (1968) discovered in his *On What is Learned in School* that students are exposed to many types of examples during the school day—not all positive and not all norms that the schools would like to nurture. It is these norms and behaviors that are reinforced even when they represent the exact opposite of what the school believes in. Students learn how to cheat on tests, how to compete instead of to collaborate, and how to shout and adopt violent patterns of behavior in order to be able to survive and become popular in their social group.

Some Concluding Remarks

The attractiveness and popularity of the terms *imagination* and *creativity* can also cause them to become dangerous traps. When different and sometimes contradictory meanings are all attributed to the same objective, and the imagination is stripped of some of its critical qualities, the end result is chaos and a sense of uneasiness. Nevertheless, there is growing indication that schools are becoming more and more irrelevant, and the option of changing this course by introducing the idea of imaginative education and creative thinking seems tempting. Although there are many kinds of implications for teacher education that arise from the ideas I have presented in this chapter, I will leave them to other chapters in this yearbook and to other articles that need to be written. Having begun with provocative words from the book of Avot, I end also with a saying of another wise man from the same book (2:21): "It is not incumbent upon you to finish the task. Yet, you are not free to desist from it."

References

Alexander, G. (2006). Distributed imagination where the individual and the collective mind meet. *Imaginative Education Research Symposium*. IERG symposium conducted at Vancouver, Canada.

Alexander, G., Eaton, I., & Egan, K. (in press). Cracking the code of computer games: Some lessons for educators. *Teachers College Record.*

Alexander, G., & Goor, A. (1980). (in Hebrew). *Final report on the effectiveness of a two-year intervention promoting creative thinking in teaching and learning.* Jerusalem: The Center for Research on the Culturally Disadvantaged, Hebrew University.

Alexander, G., & Shoshani, Y. (2008). Dialectic explication of creativity. *3rd Annual Research Symposium.* IERG symposium conducted at Vancouver, Canada.

Bereiter, C., & Scardamalia, M. (2003). Learning to work creatively with knowledge. In E. D. Corte, L. Verschaffel, N. Entwistle, & J. V. Merriënboer (Eds.), *Powerful learning environments: Unravelling basic components and dimensions* (pp. 73–78). Oxford: Elsevier Science.

Boden, M. (1990). *The creative mind: Myths and mechanisms.* London: Abacus.

Bohm, D. (1998). *On creativity.* London: Routledge.

Boring, E. G. (1923). Intelligence as the tests test it. *New Republic, 36,* 35–37.

Caspi, M. (1985). (in Hebrew). *Introduction to creative education.* Jerusalem: The Faculty of Humanities, Hebrew University.

Coleridge, S. T. (1817, 1983). *Biographia literaria: The collected works of Samuel Taylor Coleridge.* Princeton, NJ: Princeton University Press.

Craft, A. (2005). *Creativity in schools: Tensions and dilemmas.* London: Routledge.

Craft, A., Jeffrey, B., & Leibling, M. (2001). *Creativity in education.* London: Continuum.

Cropley, A. J. (2001). *Creativity in education and learning: A guide for teachers and educators.* London: Kogan Page.

Cuban, L., & Tyack, D. B. (1997). *Tinkering toward utopia: A century of public school reform.* Boston, MA: Harvard University Press.

de Bono, E. (1968). *The mechanism of mind.* New York: Penguin.

de Bono, E. (1985). *Six thinking hats.* New York: Little, Brown & Co.

Dreeben, R. (1968). *On what is learned in school.* Reading, MA: Addison-Wesley.

Egan, K. (1992). *Imagination in teaching and learning: The middle school years.* London: Althouse Press.

Egan, K. (1997). *The educated mind: How cognitive tools shape our understanding.* Chicago: University of Chicago Press.

Egan, K. (2005). *An imaginative approach to teaching.* San Francisco: Jossey-Bass.

Egan, K., & Nadaner, D. (Eds.). (1988). *Imagination and education.* New York: Teacher College Press.

Esquivel, B. G. (1995). Teacher behaviours that foster creativity. *Educational Psychology Review. 7*(2), 185–201.

Finke, R. A., Ward, T. B., & Smith, S. M. (1992). *Creative cognition: Theory research and application.* Cambridge, MA: MIT Press.

Goodlad, J. I. (1979). *Curriculum inquiry.* New York: McGraw-Hill.

Goodlad, J. I., & Klein, F. M. (1974). *Looking behind the classroom door* (2nd ed.). Worthington, OH: Charles A. Jones.

Guilford, P. J. (1950). Creativity. *American Psychologist, 5,* 444–454.

Hargreaves, A. (2009). A decade of educational change. *Journal of Educational Change, 10*(2), 89–101.

Hargreaves, J. (2008). Risk: The ethics of a creative curriculum. *Innovations in education and teaching international, 45*(3), 227–234.

Joseph-Hassidim, D. (2007). *The appearance of educational champions in schools and their influence tactics.* Unpublished master's thesis, Ben-Gurion University, Israel.

Koestler, A. (1964, 1989). *The act of creation.* London: Arkana.

Lampert, M. (1985). How do teachers manage to teach? Perspectives on problems in practice. *Harvard Educational Review, 55*(2), 178–194.

NACCCE. (1999). *All our futures: Creativity culture and education.* London: Department for Education and Employment.

Nadler, G., Hibino, S., & Farrell, J. (1995, 1999). *Creative solution finding: The triumph of breakthrough thinking over conventional problem solving.* Los Angeles: Prima.

North, V., & Buzan, T. (2001). *Get ahead.* New York: Dorset Limited Edition.

Osborn, A. F. (1948). *Your creative power.* New York: Charles Scribner's Sons.

Perkins, D. (1981). *The mind's best work.* Cambridge, MA: Harvard University Press.

Perkins, D. (1992). *Smart schools: From training memories to educating minds.* New York: Free Press.

Schwab, J. J. (1969/1978). The practical: A language for curriculum. In I. Westbury & N. Wilkof (Eds.), *Science, curriculum, and liberal education: Selected essays* (pp. 287–321). Chicago: University of Chicago Press.

Sternberg, R. J., & Lubart, T. (1999). The concept of creativity: Prospects and paradigms. In R. J. Sternberg (Ed.), *Handbook of creativity* (pp. 3–15). Cambridge MA: Cambridge University Press.

Thomas, N. J. T. (1997). Imagery and the coherence of imagination: A critique of White. *Journal of Philosophical Research, 22*, 95–127.

Torrance, P. E. (1962, 1976). *Guiding creative talent.* Huntington, NY: Krieger.

Treffinger, D. J. (1995). Creative problem solving: Overview and educational implications. *Educational Psychology Review, 7*, 301–312.

Treffinger, D. J., Isaksen, S. G., & Dorval, B. K. (1992). *Creative problem solving: An introduction.* Sarasota, FL: Center for Creative Learning.

Weisberg, R. W. (1993). *Creativity beyond the myth of genius.* New York: Freeman.

Weisberg, R. W. (1999). Creativity and knowledge: A challenge to theories. In R. J. Sternberg (Ed.), *Handbook of Creativity* (pp. 226–250). Cambridge, MA: Cambridge University Press.

White, A. R. (1990). *The language of imagination.* Oxford, UK: Blackwell.

Williams, F. E. (1972). A *total creativity program for individualizing and humanizing the learning process.* Englewood Cliffs, NJ: Educational Technology Publication.

CHAPTER 3

Jumping to Conclusions or Jumping for Joy?

REFRAMING TEACHING AS THE ART OF TALENT DEVELOPMENT

F. Richard Olenchak
University of Houston

John P. Gaa
University of Houston

F. Richard "Rick" Olenchak, PhD, PC, is professor, psychologist, and co-director of the Urban Talent Research Institute at the University of Houston. Prior to his research career, he was a teacher, principal, and consulting psychologist. Having served in a number of ancillary professional roles, including service as president of the National Association for Gifted Children, he is interested in examining cognitive and affective interactions and exploring how educators and parents can enhance optimal development of young people.

John P. Gaa, PhD, is a professor of educational psychology and co-director of the Urban Talent Research Institute at the University of Houston. He has conducted research in a variety of areas, including applied motivational interventions, goal-setting, locus of control, gender identity and sex role development, and ego and moral development. Most recently, his research has focused on the affective and social-emotional development of gifted students, most specifically those students gifted in the arts.

ABSTRACT

Like many gifted students who do not present diagnosable disabilities but who nonetheless fail to accomplish at levels commensurate with their abilities, teachers who develop patterns of instructional underachievement develop behaviors and attitudes similar to those of gifted children who have multiple exceptionalities. The negative effects of underachievement eventually yield social and emotional underachievement as well, with individuals feeling as if they are less capable than they are and affectively living their lives in kind. More critically, otherwise highly capable teachers, due to inadequate support in the educational workplace, risk underachievement of a variety that can be much more damaging than simple failure in the classroom—underachievement, occasionally to the point of denial, *within* their domain of teaching talent potential that serves to erode healthy psychosocial, adult development. Case study data are used to examine the negative effects of underachievement in the affective domain on individual teachers. Included are explorations of several interventions for reversing social-emotional underachievement in a fashion likely to instill optimistic, hopeful, creative development in teachers.

"The art of teaching is the art of assisting discovery."

—Mark Van Doren, 1894–1972, Pulitzer
Prize-winning poet, educator, and critic

Teaching, like parenting, is perhaps one of the most difficult jobs there is. Imagine one adult in a typical classroom attempting to impart information, inspire a zeal for learning, and even entertain a group of as many as thirty-five young people who come to school with vastly differing needs, interests, ideas, and desires and whose individuality is shaped by a vast array of contrasting languages, cultures, expectations, values, and socioeconomics. Demands from society to prepare students for the ever-changing collection of knowledge and skills it has identified as requisite for successful citizenship, together with increasingly formulaic governmental attempts at accountability, have made teaching even more complex than the classroom image alone. Is it any wonder that many creative teachers determine quickly to find alternative career paths?

Educators hold approximately 3.8 million, or about 4 percent, of the available jobs in the United States, and during the 2004–05 school year, 621,000, or almost 17 percent, of teachers left their positions (American Association for Employment in Education, 2008). Slightly less than half of those teachers transferred to a different school. That represents a rate of almost 1,000 teachers per day who quit teaching and 1,000 teachers per day who transfer to a new school across the US. When schools with high levels of poverty are considered separately, the percentage jumps from 17 percent to 21 percent.

Research about attrition and mobility suggests that the shortage of good teachers is a skewed perception (Ingersoll, 2003; Ingersoll & Perda, 2008). These sources cite the high turnover of new teachers—nearly a third in their first three years of teaching and half by the fifth year. Labor statistics also show that nearly 18 percent of new hires are considered to be new teachers, or within their first three to five years of teaching. Ingersoll's empirical research has suggested that the ones who remain are dedicated to stay long term, thus skewing the data that appears to show a large number of retiring teachers when only around 2 percent of teachers leave for retirement. In a current study conducted for the Consortium for Policy Research in Education, a collective of researchers at the University of Pennsylvania, Columbia University, Harvard University, Stanford University, the University of Michigan, the University of Wisconsin–Madison, and Northwestern University, data indicate that there are sufficient numbers of qualified teachers in all disciplines, yet there are "not significant numbers of willing teachers" (Ingersoll & Perda, 2009, p. 37).

Why is it that there are so many teachers who are unwilling to teach? While a buffet of reasons is frequently conjectured, an extensive meta-analysis of empirical literature about teacher attrition answers the question from a data-driven perspective. Borman and Dowling (2008) concluded that:

- While some attrition is desirable (weeding out ineffective teachers from the profession), the reality is that the majority of teachers who elect to leave their jobs are in fact effective, conscientious educators.
- Although a variety of personal and professional factors influence teachers' decisions to leave the profession, these predominately cluster around weak or missing workplace support systems. Among the leading sources of dissatisfaction that precipitate attrition are inadequate time for preparation and planning, marginally attractive compensation that is not commensurate with increasingly high expectations, and lack of faculty influence and autonomy in terms of curriculum and instruction.
- The most significant aspects of teacher attrition are likely resolvable through policy adjustments at the state and local levels and through development of new initiatives specifically addressing the key sources of dissatisfaction mentioned in item two above: preparation time, compensation, and autonomy.

Based on this meta-analytic research, it is fair to extrapolate that when reasonably talented teachers choose not to exercise their skills in classrooms, they are in a sense behaving as underachievers—at least insofar as applying knowledge and skills that they hold with respect to educating children and youth. In fact, such calculated underachievement carries the same sort of traits and implications in adults as it does in school-aged students who selectively underachieve.

Comparing and Contrasting Underachievement in Teachers with That of Students

Interpretations of underachievement continue to be as diverse as people them-selves, though there is general agreement among researchers that underachieve-ment is a significant discrepancy between actual performance and some index of ability (Rimm, 1986). Typically, underachievement among school-aged youth is defined academically, but there is ample reason to believe that, in keeping with Rimm's widely accepted definition, persons—including teachers—underachieve whenever they fail to perform at a level commensurate with their ability *of any kind*. Particularly when students of fairly high ability underachieve and when teachers who have been rated as capable decide to forget teaching as a career, there is ample reason to believe that the reasons behind the underachievement are related to affective or social-emotional concerns stemming from cognitive issues.

For example, in the case of underachieving school-aged students who are otherwise capable, classroom attributes can precipitate and eventually insti-tutionalize underachievement, particularly in terms of students' talent areas. Features such as under-stimulating curriculum and instructional strategies that fail to allow for a range of individual learning and response styles, as well as classroom environments that inhibit nurturing of strengths, individually and collectively, serve to impede exercising one's abilities. The hyper-accentuation of weaknesses through remedial approaches or the unnecessary over-practice of basic skills gauged to relatively low-level summative assessments can often lead to and perpetuate underachievement (Kanevsky & Keighley, 2003).

Similarly, among educators who are capable of better-than-average teaching, it follows that an overemphasis on mundane tasks, tucked inside rigid school procedural structures that do not foster individual critical and creative thinking coupled with problem solving and decision making, can lead to teacher under-achievement. As with students, teachers who perform at a level less than that of which they are capable amidst unaccommodating settings, if prolonged and oppressive enough, can likely precipitate dropping out. School-aged students and teachers alike who drop out do so because of environments that do little to acknowledge and develop their individual talents (Ingersoll & Smith, 2003). Because talent development among both children and adults is rooted as much in cognitive as it is in affective aspects of the individual (Olenchak, 2009), it only makes sense that when the schoolhouse fails to address *both* cognitive and affec-tive needs of its students, there is probably the chance that it also fails to address the cognitive *and* affective needs of its teachers. Persons who do not feel affective support will not perform at their best, and persons who over time do not feel as if they can exercise their skills in a way that is personally meaningful are likely to drop out—students and teachers alike.

This chapter seeks to address issues related to the underachievement of talented students and teachers alike and to offer suggestions for the classroom that may strengthen both affective and academic achievement. In keeping with the yearbook's theme, we refer to the affective domain, which includes curiosity and creativity. Affective and academic underachievement are linked and must be considered together when examining issues of underachievement of talented students and the rate at which talented teachers stagnate and/or leave the profession. We seek to show that teachers, like students, suffer when their working environment provides no creative outlets.

Heretofore, largely restricted to academic performance among students, the construct of underachievement probably has been limited by the fact that even when school programming efforts do address strengths, they often focus on academic talents alone and seldom provide for developing affective abilities (Olenchak, Gaa, & Jackson, 2009). A persistent view exists in society, as well as among many educators, that spending time and money on noncognitive skills takes away from content learning and that affective education is unnecessary (Bluestein, 2001, p. 87). The federal No Child Left Behind legislation along with a number of legislative acts and policies in individual states have emphasized achievement test performance as the principle, if not sole, measure of success or failure in schools. This, in turn, has inhibited the design and implementation of curricula and instructional strategies targeting affective development. Additionally, while there is a paucity of evidence that such programming has currently been widely implemented, there is also strong indication that schools will continue to disregard explicit attention to the affective domain. As a result, students who may possess affective but not necessarily cognitive talent are out of synch with societal demands (VanTassel-Baska, Cross, & Olenchak, 2009), and the teachers who are equally in need of affective scaffolds in the increasingly high-stress classroom of the twenty-first century are literally left wanting.

Comparably, there is also evidence that specific attention to affective development and to affective talent is all but absent in preparatory programs for adults, including teacher education programs. An unpublished analysis of the courses and requirements of the fifty largest teacher education programs in the United States conducted by the Urban Talent Research Institute at the University of Houston in 2005 concluded that few intentional efforts were being undertaken to address affective development among individuals studying to become teachers. While practices such as reflection were identifiable as perhaps simple beginnings in this regard, the emphasis on cognitive activity was decidedly far greater than on affective activity. If modeling is the strong educator that it is believed to be, then it can be concluded that teachers who have been taught through models that reduce emphasis on affective development in favor of cognitive development will likely teach that way themselves. What remains unknown is how long it takes for such teachers to realize that something is missing in their own repertoire of psychosocial skills and to what degree that absence may cause them to leave education in search of it. It is also obviously problematic if teachers do not come to realize their own limitations and/or lack of support with respect to psychosocial development and skills. When this happens, it is, in turn, difficult to imagine that the teacher can adequately provide for the affective needs of his or her students.

Jumping to Conclusions

As societal demands for increased educational accountability and more rigorous, world-class standards seemingly prompted the increased federal and state attention to schools during the early part of this century, schools began to assume a new direction in which test outcomes became all but paramount. Indicators of the overemphasis placed on tests continue to abound. For example:

- Educators who felt increased pressure to raise test scores sometimes stooped to cheating (Axtman, 2005).
- Students, sensing the elevated emphasis on testing and emulating adults, also engaged in a variety of cheating scams on tests and assignments (Callahan, 2004).
- Incidents of school behavior issues increased in parallel with the test-based schoolhouse. While causal relationships have not been established, there is reason to believe that when students engage in negative behavior, they may very well be actualizing their frustrations with the school environment (Gottfredson, 2001).
- Flight to homeschooling or to private schools where testing is either not accentuated or is of low or no consequence has soared (Green & Hoover-Dempsey, 2007).

As society has apparently accepted the notion that single scores on tests accurately reflect both teaching and learning, it is interesting to note that an increasing number of families have opted out of the test-based school environment. For example, in 1999, the U.S. Department of Education National Center for Education Statistics (NCES) conducted a study through the National Household Education Surveys Program (NHES) that reported an estimated 850,000 secondary-aged students were homeschooled (NCES, 2008). The same study conducted eight years later estimated that 1,508,000 youths were being home-schooled in the spring of 2007 (NCES, 2008). Hence, between 1999 and 2007, the number of children being schooled in the home increased by 74 percent. According to Aurini and Davies (2005), many homeschool families worldwide opt out of public and private schools for many reasons, and the test-centered classroom is among the leading ones.

It is equally intriguing to note the increasing rate of teacher attrition both among educators new to the profession and among those who have substantial years of experience. In a study prepared for the Education Commission of the States that analyzed teacher attrition between 1980 and 2003, it was found that the highest attrition rates among teachers occurred in their first few years of teaching. However, it was also found that similarly high attrition rates took place after many years of teaching, when individual teachers were near retirement, thus producing a U-shaped pattern of attrition with respect to age or experience (Guarino, Santibanez, Daley, & Brewer, 2004). Furthermore, several studies link increasing teacher attrition to the increased use of high-stakes test results as the dominant steering mechanism for determining the nature of classroom instruction (Crocco & Costigan, 2006; Kersaint, Lewis, Potter, & Meisels, 2007; Kopkowski, 2008).

The notion that society continues to advocate more tests in public education, at the same time that both teachers and students are fleeing from public schools in larger numbers, is illustrative of a bigger problem than test scores themselves. Having jumped to the conclusion that at least some of schools', if not society's ills, can be "solved" by raising standards, testing for those standards, and then making decisions about students and teachers alike based on test results, those segments of society electing to find alternatives to public education may be indicative that many feel that this conclusion was not warranted. Perhaps test-based schools are not the answer; perhaps raising standards and expectations without simultaneously redefining what it means to learn and to teach is tantamount to cart-before-the-horse thinking. Simply preparing teachers cognitively without paying express attention to their affective growth and development in an era of pressure-cooker accountability is probably as myopic as attempting to teach school-aged youth without equal emphasis on both cognitive and affective attributes, of which curiosity and creativity are a part.

There is ample confirmation from neurological science that cognitive development is influenced to a great degree by affective development. In fact, it has been demonstrated that cognition is activated by emotional stimuli, and thinking, problem solving, and decision making are individually and collectively enhanced by positive emotions (Damasio, 1994, 1999; Isen, 2004; Zins, Weissberg, Wang, & Walberg, 2004). Indeed, there is increasing evidence that, even in an educational system that is devoted primarily to cognitive development, ignoring affective growth defeats the very purpose of the cognitive-based school. The overall ability of schools to succeed in attaining adequate yearly progress objectives in a test-driven, No Child Left Behind era in the US is actually imperiled by not addressing the social, emotional, and creative development of individual students. Hence, by essentially ignoring the scaffolding of the affectivity of teachers, it is plausible that teachers will be less able to provide the sort of psychosocial structures for students to perform well. Quite simply, the lack of explicit support for educators' psychosocial needs may well undermine their ability to provide in kind for their students, thereby yielding less-than-anticipated educational results from classrooms as well as failing to aid in the facilitation of the affective growth of students.

Recent research in neurobiology suggests that the aspects of cognitive ability to which schools are most oriented—learning, attention, memory, decision making, and social functioning—are all significantly influenced by the processes of emotion (Immordino-Yang & Damasio, 2007). More convincingly, it is now believed that each of these cognitive skills that schools, the general public, and political decision makers have elected to emphasize are actually subsumed within emotion—that the ability to transfer knowledge and skills from school to real life is highly dependent on an "emotional rudder" that governs judgment and action (Immordino-Yang & Damasio, 2007, p. 7). It is logical to conclude then that when schools and the larger society do not support educational efforts to develop critical social and emotional abilities, students and their teachers alike are likely to function less than fully.

Educational services that are out of alignment with individual students' needs contribute to underachievement (Baum & Olenchak, 2002; Baum, Olenchak, & Owen, 1998, 1995; Olenchak, 1994, 1995; Rimm, 1997). For example, otherwise talented students who have been diagnosed with learning disabilities, attention deficit hyperactivity disorder, social and emotional problems, and other attendant concerns that require federal educational accommodations (e.g., IDEA or Rehabilitation Act Section 504) are often served for their disabling condition first, rather than focusing on their talents. Interestingly (and ironically), this placement of disability first, while decidedly not in keeping with the talent development literature, may at least afford these students attention to social and emotional development, whereas their peers without disabilities may have access to few such services. In fact, accommodations for students with disabilities have long emphasized specific services for addressing social and emotional development (Morse, Ardizzone, MacDonald, & Pasick, 1980), and they continue to do so (Council for Exceptional Children, 2003). Unfortunately, there are no similar mandatory support systems and very few support systems of any kind to provide for the psychosocial aspects of teachers.

Underachievement Enigma

Considerations of underachievement are further confounded by the numerous methods through which professionals attempt to address the problems related to this incongruity between potential and actual performance. As with issues of definition, most paths toward reversing underachievement have been theorized and tested in cases of academic problems among children and particularly those otherwise judged to be capable of consistently superior academic performance (Seeley, 1993). Other than considerations of stress factors among artistically gifted young people (Kogan, 1995) and "blocks" inhibiting productivity among the creatively talented (Davis, 1992), little regard has been paid underachievement, aside from that which is scholastic. Underachievement among teachers is absent from research literature; instead, studies postulate about the increasing levels of teacher attrition. For otherwise capable teachers to leave the field is emblematic of underachievement.

The purpose of this chapter is to extend the construct of underachievement among students in the affective domain to teachers—showing that social and emotional underachievement is as insidious for teachers as it is for their students. Additionally, the chapter explores programs for reversing underachievement that concentrate on affective educational components for teachers. Excerpts from one of a series of case studies are included as illustration of intervention strategies useful for attacking social-emotional underachievement among teachers as well as for developing conclusions applicable to the breadth of underachievement issues among practicing teachers.

EXPLORING THE MEANING OF UNDERACHIEVEMENT THROUGH CHILDREN

With a full scale Wechsler Intelligence Scale for Children-Fourth Edition (WISC-IV) (Psychological Corporation, 2003) score of 157, Cho had been identified with enormous academic promise in first grade; equally superior creativity potential had been assessed using the Torrance Tests of Creative Thinking (both figural and verbal forms) (Torrance, 1966) as well as observational data collected during her preschool and kindergarten years. Those data included several instances in which Cho demonstrated remarkable creative talent. At age three, she directed and staged a "parade of dolls" play starring her stuffed animal collection. Later, she designed and constructed a bridge of common building blocks, rocks, and nails to ford a creek behind her house to allow her to get to a fellow kindergartner's home to avoid having to cross streets.

As a nine-year-old fifth-grader, Cho was enrolled in a magnet school for academically gifted students. Having performed extremely well scholastically, including a double promotion from second to fourth grade, Cho began fifth grade with an announcement to the school principal: "I have decided to take a sabbatical this year." When asked to explain, she told the principal that she had "worked hard enough and needed a vacation longer than the summer" had provided.

As the school year progressed, Cho proved she was a girl of her word; her grades were average at best, and she was not involved in the array of projects and activities that had previously been her choice. However, after returning from the winter break, she again approached the principal and told him her sabbatical had been long enough; her school and extracurricular performance quickly returned to the level known before Cho's original announcement.

In the interim, both Cho's parents and teachers were concerned that she had intentionally elected to become an underachiever, and all expressed fears that, for whatever reasons, Cho may have adopted a set of school behaviors likely to over-shadow her significant strengths. Though several professionals involved with the school also cautioned that this bright, young girl may well require special inter-vention aimed at curbing her underachievement, a few others felt the nature of her underachievement—self-described as a "sabbatical"—was not only transitory but, more importantly, was indicative of her need for social-emotional rejuvena-tion as a person who, despite her young age, obviously possessed a great deal of affective ability paralleling her cognitive potential. While it was the latter view that proved correct, this excerpt from Cho's schooling prompts a question critical to considering underachievement among gifted youth: is *real* underachievement ever knowingly self-selected? Without equivocation, the answer is affirmative. Ponder the case of Eduardo.

Eduardo was a thirteen-year-old eighth-grader in a typical public school. Although identified for participation in a specialized program for students with significant talent in the fine arts, he was no longer allowed to participate in the program because he had lagged seriously in all of his performance areas, includ-ing the music he had previously loved so dearly.

Through some intensive individualized counseling at school that took place after a referral for emotional/behavioral disabilities, it was discerned that Eduardo had *elected* to perform poorly in school. It was his way to gain attention from his parents, whom he felt had grown overly preoccupied with their careers, and it was also a means for him to feel a sense of emotional belonging among his neighbor-hood peers who were not involved in special school programs. Academically hav-ing fallen from customarily attaining grades of A in virtually all school subjects, placing first-chair trumpet in the school orchestra, and winning awards for his original musical compositions, Eduardo clearly looked like a *real* underachiever.

However, was he actually an underachiever socially and emotionally? Was his intentional decision not emblematic of a rather sophisticated level of affective self-awareness?

Perhaps the only difference between Eduardo and gifted youngsters who underachieve without any cognitive awareness of the reasons prompting their poor performance was Eduardo's degree of affective stamina and control. He knew he could again achieve at high levels, but like Cho, he knowingly chose not to do so. Still, the level of underachievement and its effects were no different from those experienced by underachieving gifted students who are unclear about themselves, their emotions, their roles, and their affective needs. The main distinction, of course, is that Cho and Eduardo could reverse their poor performance when *they* decided. Most other gifted students who experience underachievement, including those with formally diagnosed disabilities, do not have this luxury of control, nor have they achieved the level of social-emotional development that Cho and Eduardo had, their underachievement linked to unidentified sources seemingly *beyond* their direct command.

Regardless, underachievement, whether self-selected or adventitious, eventually produces the same outcomes for children and adults experiencing it. An emotional sense of pessimism eventually envelops all underachievers who otherwise possess superior potential, and feelings of frustration replace those of fulfillment (Olenchak, 1999). Note then that underachievement, while it is usually identified because of flagging performance results, is in reality sustained by *emotions* that are negative. Even those persons with histories of excellent performances and profiles of tremendous talent are placed at risk of a continuing cycle of failure due to the pervasive attitudes of negativism that develop as a consequence of their underachievement; truly, one might say that underachievement begets underachievement. Snyder (1994, p. 24), using statistical analyses to factor away the effects of previous accomplishment and high ability, describes the predictive ability of his construct of hope—the converse of pessimism—in a manner that clarifies the state of otherwise capable persons who underachieve: "high hope may assure people of some success in reaching goals; high intelligence or a record of achievement only gives them a chance."

SOCIAL-EMOTIONAL UNDERACHIEVEMENT

As described above, the notion of underachievement, whether among gifted or other students, has been consistently linked to academic performance. In the adult world, underachievement is also predominantly conceptualized as performance that is in some way less than that which would be anticipated, given an individual's ability profile. Whether or not later-life underachievement consistently has roots in childhood development is not conclusively known, but the way in which underachievement is defined is the same regardless of age and context—underachievers are seen as not actualizing their talents, abilities, and gifts at a level seen to be commensurate with their assessed or supposed potential (Borkowski & Thorpe, 1994). In any case and at any age, underachievement has over and over been attributed to the inability of the underachiever to integrate self-regulation and affect, the latter of which subsumes a variety of social-emotional traits and skills.

With the exception of studies in psychiatry targeting an array of serious mental health disorders such as schizophrenia (e.g., Ciompi, 1982, 1988, 1991, 1999), few theorists and researchers have examined underachievement in any way other than cognitively. To illustrate, Borkowski and Thorpe (1994) propose a meta-cognitive model for conceptualizing the interactions among executive functioning, attributional beliefs, and learning strategies: "We believe that it is the incomplete or inadequate integration of self-regulation, with strong motivational beliefs about the power and importance of self-efficacy, that is at the heart of underachievement" (p. 50).

It is of critical importance that the Borkowski and Thorpe view is the dominant one in psychology as well as in education, yet this perspective overtly lacks consideration for the affective aspects at play in each individual's functioning. It makes no sense that terms such as "self-regulation," "beliefs," and "self-efficacy" can be considered apart from the affective dimension of each person. How is it feasible that an underachieving person can be self-regulated, internally motivated, and self-efficacious in a manner that is emotionally free?

It seems not only unlikely but implausible, and when one contemplates the recent neurobiological research referenced above, it seems misguided ever to consider meta-cognition without also considering meta-affect. While it is not the purpose of this chapter to examine the notion of meta-affect or the theoretical and research underpinnings of this relatively new construct, it is useful to consider that meta-affect should be conceptualized as one of the foundations for human performance.

The Bull's Eye Model for Affective Development (Olenchak, 2009) and the attendant research from positive psychology (e.g., Seligman, 1990, 2004; Seligman & Csikszentmihalyi, 2000; Snyder, 1994) on which the Bull's Eye is constructed provide a clear means for grappling with the cognitive-affective interaction in terms of an individual's facility for scaffolding performance by more than just using his or her powers of thinking but by also using his or her powers of feeling. As a result, there is every reason to believe that underachievement is as much a social and emotional phenomenon as it is one that is cognitive, and there is every reason to believe that among teachers the importance of underachievement of the social-emotional type may be even more critical. This is crucial in understanding underachieving teachers and ultimately in assisting them in dealing with this phenomenon.

A Case Illustration of Social-Emotional Underachievement in a Teacher

Two case studies highlight the use of various affective-cognitive strategies to reverse patterns of underachievement among teachers in their personal lives. Each case study entailed a minimum of one academic year in a comprehensive in-school and out-of-school intervention program. Relying on methods delineated for qualitative research by Patton (1990), data were collected through triangulated sources of participant observations, interviews, and analyses of documents such as interview protocols and anecdotal notations. Following each case description is a discussion of the interventions utilized.

MARY'S SOCIAL-EMOTIONAL DILEMMA

After noteworthy experiences as a public school student that included award-winning performances in the classroom, on the basketball court, and on the theatrical stage, Mary went on to pursue studies in pre-medicine at a small liberal arts college in the Mid-Atlantic region. At the same time, Mary also secured her teaching license in biology and chemistry. Graduating with honors, she thought it might be wise to teach a few years as a means of bolstering her finances prior to pursuing medical school, despite the fact that she had gained admission to several top-ranked medical schools. After her first interview, she was offered a mathematics teaching position at a medium-sized middle school in an affluent suburban area not far from her undergraduate college. After three years in the job, she recalled:

> I fell in love with the kids. I guess a lot of them sort of remind me of myself. They were a group of exploring adolescents yearning to find meaning in life, and they would do virtually anything to gain acceptance from those they saw as important in terms of judgments, but definitely their peers came first and foremost. For me, I would do anything to have gained acceptance from teachers who were seen as experts—even if it meant tabling medicine even longer. I wanted to feel as though I was not only a competent teacher but an excellent one. The teenagers I teach all wanted to feel as if they were at least competent in terms of socialization and many would have liked be-

ing equated with the upper crust of the school's social pecking order. Academically, they were all over the map, some wanting to please self or parents or coaches or even teachers with elite academic success, but the majority really being interested in getting good enough grades that college admission would not be a problem but focused much more on their relationships with their peers. You would have thought that as an adult I would have been secure enough not to need approval from my fellow teachers, but retrospectively, all I wanted to do was be seen as successful. After all, I had always been smart and had always produced outstanding results; this teaching stuff was not about to be my undoing!

Mary, a creative individual who had been accustomed to achieving as a student and equally acclimatized to rave reviews for her accomplishments, was seeking the same degree of success and the same level of notoriety as a teacher. Fully aware that she held a strong grasp of her subject matter and having earned accolades in both content and teacher preparation courses, including her teaching internship experience as an undergraduate, she was not content with her three years of teaching, despite great diligence in preparations:

> I was unsure what to do. I spent many hours getting ready for my classes—to the point that I pretty much had eliminated anything else from my life. I was so concerned about the kids, and I wanted them to do well—to test well and to get into good colleges. But all the hours I spent preparing or the time I spent meeting with my students privately and going to support them at school events ended up meaning very little. Kids did not come ready for class half the time, and they did not seem to take it seriously—just wanting to get by well enough so that they were not in trouble with coaches or parents. Back then, I had asked a few of the better teachers for help and had even talked to the principal and a curriculum specialist at the district office, but they either just looked at me like I was crazy or shuffled me off with some collection of quick and dirty strategies—most of which proved useless, by the way. My department head spent a little time gathering materials to help me, but then she seemed upset that I wanted more. Honestly, I just wished we had had some time to discuss the students and the curriculum, but when we met those were the last topics we considered. In fact, near the end of the third year, I decided that I probably just ought to can teaching, but then something happened.

What transpired was that Mary had met and fallen in love and had decided that marriage was her next step and that medical school would have to wait. Her new husband was already locked into a stable career and was not mobile job-wise; as a result, Mary decided that she would teach a few more years and then would tackle medical school and having a family thereafter: "I just wanted to leave teaching as the success I knew I could be, and successful students would be the real report card if I had made it." She elaborated that the environment was lacking in the sort of support structures she felt equated with high-quality classrooms: "I felt as if I had to find the heart and soul—the humanity—in teaching so that I could be creative in how I taught. This is what drew me to it in the first place, but it had been diminished and maybe even hidden completely by demands to teach to the test."

Mary was unlike as many as 50 percent of new teachers who, in some socioeconomically challenged locations, elect to leave the field within the first few years (Ingersoll, 2004; Liu, Johnson, & Peske, 2004). Still, she was feeling the effects of a lack of professional support, including the ambiance conducive to creativity and innovation in teaching that has been identified in a number of national reports, including those developed by the National Education Association (NEA) (Johnson, 2006), by a number of researchers sponsored by state governments (Loeb, Darling-Hammond, & Luczak, 2005), and even by those concerned more than anything else with the ultimate economic impact of teacher attrition (Alliance for Excellent Education, 2005; Boyd, Lankford, Loeb, & Wyckoff, 2005).

Said Mary, "I began to search for things that would help me grow professionally—that would allow me to be innovative and still meet the demands from the state test, but I really didn't have a process." Mary explained that one day she saw a poster on a bulletin board at the school district's central office that advertised a competitive thinking skills program for students. She wondered if by getting at least some of her students involved she might be able to find a mechanism for developing her creativity in the classroom: "I wanted to see if there was anything that would let me act more like an artist than a test-slave with my students. I felt if I found it, they would do better on the tests and both the kids and I would feel less like we were in a straightjacket."

MARY'S INTERVENTION

Throughout the weeks that followed, Mary became increasingly involved in teaching herself about the Future Problem Solving Program (FPSP) (Torrance, 1976) (see figure 3.1), which fosters critical thinking and creative problem solving skills. While her initial objectives were built on integrating FPSP into her mathematics classroom to enhance student interest and learning with the hope that she could build a link for them to their real lives, she also was

Researching
Gathering cognitive and affective information about her teaching career

⇩

Describing the Dilemma
Developing a "fuzzy situation" about her teaching career, a scenario
reflecting the affective and cognitive impact of her concerns on the future

⇩

Conceptualizing Challenges
Creating a list of challenges or problems related to the fuzzy situation about
her career, using traditional rules for brainstorming, and then elaborating them

⇩

Identifying and Focusing on One Challenge
Focusing the list of challenges by categorizing them, selecting one specific category for
attack (affective), and articulating the challenge so that, in question form, it states what
needs to be accomplished, the purpose or "why" the task needs to be accomplished,
and the parameters of the future period in which the situation is being tackled

⇩

Generating Solutions
Using both feelings and thoughts; brainstorming a list of solutions that
responds directly to the focused question that has been developed

⇩

Criteria to Select the Best Solution
Assessing the solution options through a set of predominantly
affective criteria so that the best solution can be selected

⇩

Developing an Action Plan
Detailing the solution so
that it can be implemented

Figure 3.1   Mary's adapted version of the future problem solving process.

aware that she was seeking a solution to her own displeasure with teaching:
"I thought that maybe a structured logic program would help my kids, but
I also was hoping that I would find a way to bring some art back into what
was fast becoming nothing more than a mundane daily exercise. I was drilling
and killing my kids for test preparation, but I was also drilling and killing my
creativity and enthusiasm for teaching."

The plan Mary designed was facilitated by the FPSP director for her state
and included role playing as well as problem solving designed to stimulate Mary's

intelligent mind and those of her students. A number of realizations developed during her involvement with FPSP, including:

- Mary had no instructional support system for her professional development at school. As in so many schools and school districts, the sum total of professional development each year amounted to one or two of what Mary termed "command performances," where teachers were required to attend a day-long series of sessions often associated with topics and themes that had little direct relevance to their teaching. Worse, in direct conflict with research about stimulating the brains of children in schools by offering an array of interest- and style-based options (Coleman & Cross, 2001), such sessions for teachers seldom offered opportunities for self-selection based on interest; rather, they typically were decided by administration, at least some of whom had little if any knowledge of Mary, let alone recognition of her professional needs.

- Mary had no social support for her professional growth at school. Despite the fact that her school had developed a mentorship program in which seasoned educators were paired with novices like Mary, Mary described the program as "superficial . . . with little in the way of efforts to match new teachers with veterans." As a result, Mary was "matched" with a veteran teacher who seemed quite successful but with whom Mary had nothing in common, aside from being a teacher of mathematics: "It was as if she had her classroom and I had mine and the twain wasn't about to meet. She was busy with her own work, and the school did nothing to enable her or any of the mentors to work with us newbies." As a result, Mary described her first few years at the school as ones of "sheer isolation professionally—on my own to sink or swim." While her department chairperson extended as much assistance as he could, Mary again emphasized that the school had integrated no explicit system for facilitating mentoring: "The environment delivered a discrete yet decisive message that new teachers had best figure it all out and at the same time be happy and intact emotionally or we would be out fast. I felt abandoned."

- Although options certainly existed in her geographic area for Mary to enroll in graduate courses to strengthen her skills and to develop professional relationships with colleagues, she saw such study as an impossibility at the moment: "I had all to do with trying to prepare better than marginal lessons, to provide my kids my timely feedback, and to spend at least some time with my husband and to try to have a life outside of work." Mary saw the need for scaffolding her psychosocial and professional needs as falling primarily on the school itself, but "the absence of any meaningful collegial relationships and professional development programs pretty much left me and the other new teachers on our own." When asked about the feasibility of developing collegial relationships for the purposes of bolstering both social and emotional as well as professional growth, Mary responded, "It sounds good in theory. The fact was that we each were just trying to cope. I saw it as analogous to a group of captives or prisoners being expected to provide for each other psychologically. Yes, this has worked in some cases in some prisons or concentration camps, but mostly the ones imprisoned ended up with some pretty severe mental health issues." The very fact that Mary compared her situation to that of prisoners and concentration camp detainees illustrates the strong negative view that she held of her teaching situation. "Like a prisoner, I would either have to escape teaching completely or find some psychological and professional support to survive."

- Mary continued to love teaching, despite her struggle with the shortcomings of the school's support of new teachers. She was animated in describing her classroom: "I had fallen in love with the students and my work to teach them. Although I was never sure what would work and what wouldn't, each day became a sort of experiment for all of us. Would I motivate them to be interested and participative in math?" Still, she had expressed worry that because of the lack of what she called a "spirit fire" in her school for new teachers, she might have left the profession: "I was so disillusioned. I thought I could bring not only my math knowledge but also my inventive personality to the classroom, but mostly it was being squelched by the over-emphasis on test performance. My love for teaching was endangered even though I was trying to hold on to it, and I bet as my love for teaching was endangered so was the kids' love for learning. I was working nonstop just to survive, and my teaching was becoming hollow and without any pizzazz."

- Due to the challenges imposed by an unsupportive school professional program and the lack of a meaningful professional peer group, Mary was significantly underachieving not only in teaching but also in life in general: "My new marriage was even becoming turbulent because I was struggling to find my identity as a teacher." Her overall social-emotional ability to sustain herself in a way that would propel Mary to find her "personal niche" (Olenchak, 2009) was indeed imperiled. Personal niche is a place where one's emotions and thoughts complimentarily interact to undergird one's thinking and feeling performances through cognitive-affective integration in which one balances belonging with independence. Mary was experiencing serious intellectual as well as emotional dissonance due to her inability to find equilibrium between thoughts and feelings across both personal and professional aspects of her life.

- Due to the escalating psychosocial and professional demands of her teaching job, Mary was fearful that any special burden she placed on her home life would ultimately undermine what was in her words "the love of my life." Thus, she felt it better to abandon teaching because of the stress her career placed not only on her but also on her household, so she had secretly decided to submit her resignation during the spring of her third year of teaching. "I hated to leave—to quit something that I knew in my heart that I could flourish at, but I was losing myself and my life to administrative dictums that didn't care about me or the kids, to a test system that evaluated kids and teachers on marginal tests, and to a school program that was empty of empathy for people as people first and as performers second," Mary explained at one session, yet only a few weeks later she said that it would be "simpler to try another career." Mary, while capable of integrated cognitive social-emotional functioning based on previous history, was now at a crossroads where she was, in fact, underachieving affectively—confused and not sure how to juggle the seemingly incompatible demands of family, friends, school, talent, and sense of self.

As Mary continued to examine the circumstances, she mastered the problem identification and resolution strategy in Future Problem Solving (FPS) (Torrance, 1976) (see Figure 3.1) under the guidance of the therapist. By applying an adaptation of FPS over an extended period of six months, she engaged in gathering data and fully studying and weighing all options before attempting to arrive at a resolution. And while FPS is reliant on cognitive processing, it is laced with affective components in which one's emotions shape the decision-making process, a method that Torrance himself described as "affective as much as cognitive . . . People can only come to grips with the future if they account for their feelings about it" (personal communication, June 16, 1991). With the reassurance of her therapist, Mary eventually elected to teach in a small private school that was free of many of the mandatory features she felt were strangling what she frequently referred to as "the artisan's part of teaching." Meanwhile, Mary and her husband began saving to fund a future career direction for her: either a private school of her own or a consultative practice in which she would provide model and/or co-taught lessons. As a result, Mary had reason to believe that her frustration and sense of despair would be alleviated.

Underachievement's Emotional Tax

High-ability educators like Mary typify underachievement of a genre that continues to be disregarded: performing at a level less than one's capacity would allow one to govern oneself in the affective domain. The emotional concerns for such educators are both similar to and different from those of gifted children.

SIMILARITIES TO ACADEMIC GIFTEDNESS

Personality traits of gifted individuals tend to include high degrees of sensitivity, perfectionism, and intensity, each of which contributes to greater degrees of stress than in other individuals (Silverman, 1993). Paralleling these traits are tendencies for able children, whether gifted academically or otherwise, to become deeply concerned about moral issues at an earlier age than peers. Sophisticated awareness of world events, injustice, and ideals, when combined with feelings of impotence experienced by all children, is likely to have a serious impact on the emotional development of gifted children.

While previous studies of the emotional traits of gifted individuals have been primarily restricted to those with academic giftedness, the efforts of Dabrowski (1938, 1964) and later of Piechowski (1997) expand the conception of advanced emotional development. Dabrowski's "psychic overexcitabilities" have been described as heightened sensitivities in five contexts: psychomotor, sensual, intellectual, imaginational, and emotional. In and of themselves, each contextual overexcitability can be described as a "gift," but there has been conclusive evidence that individuals with academically oriented, IQ-delineated giftedness (that which is most frequently measured and served in schools) tend to have heightened overexcitabilities across all five contexts (Silverman, 1993).

However, there has also been significant investigation indicating that emotional development in *other* types of giftedness—including affective giftedness—parallels the amplified sensitivities found in the academically gifted (Lind & Olenchak, 1995). The following is an overview of psychic overexcitabilities (adapted from Dabrowski & Piechowski, 1977):

PSYCHOMOTOR

- Heightened excitability of the neuromuscular system
- Capacity for great activity and animation; love of movement for itself
- Organic surplus of energy demonstrated in various forms (rapid speech, marked enthusiasm, need for action)
- Psychomotor expression of emotional tension (compulsive talking, impulsive actions, acting out, nervous habits, drive, "workaholism," high degree of competitiveness)

SENSUAL

- Magnified sensual experiences (seeing, smelling, tasting, touching, hearing)
- Intense sexuality

- Sensual expression and outlets for emotional stress (overeating, buying sprees, wanting to be in the limelight)
- Appreciation of aesthetic pleasures (appreciation of beauty in objects, words, music, form, color)

INTELLECTUAL

- Amplified need to seek understanding and truth to gain knowledge
- Intense activity of the mind (curiosity, concentration, capacity for sustained intellectual effort, avid reading, keen observational skills, detailed planning and recall)
- Penchant for probing questions and problem solving (search for truth and understanding, tenacity in finding and resolving problems)
- Preoccupation with logic and theoretical thinking (love of theory and analysis, metacognition, introspection, morality, highly conceptual, independent)
- Tendency to want to develop new concepts

IMAGINATIONAL

- Enhanced use of imagination in terms of intensity and frequency
- Rich association of images and impressions, both real and imagined (frequent use of image and metaphor, inventive, detailed fantasy and visualization, poetic and dramatic perception)
- Spontaneous imagery as an expression of emotional tension (mixing truth and fiction, elaborate dreams, illusions)
- Potential for living in a fantasy world (predilection for fairy and magic tales, creation of private worlds, imaginary companions, escapism through imagination)

EMOTIONAL

- Extremely intense positive and negative feelings (extremes of emotion, complex emotions and feelings, highly empathetic, awareness of range and intensity of feelings, high ability to differentiate interpersonal feelings)
- Tendency toward somatic expressions (tense stomach, sinking heart, blushing, flushing)
- Powerful affective expressions (inhibitions, ecstasy, euphoria, pride, strong affective recall, fears and anxieties, feelings of guilt, concern with death)
- Capacity to develop deep relationships (strong emotional ties and attachments to people, places, pets, objects; compassion; responsive to others; sensitivity; difficulty adjusting to new environments; loneliness; intense desire to offer love to others)
- Well-differentiated feelings toward self (awareness of one's real self, inner dialog and self-judgment, meta-affect, sense of self-responsibility, awareness of one's growth and adjustments)

Previous research has determined that context-specific overexcitabilities must be integrated with all other overexcitabilities before there are influences on emotional development equating with characteristics of giftedness (Dabrowski & Piechowski, 1977; Piechowski, Silverman, & Falk, 1985). Using Dabrowski's theory, the emotional development associated with academically gifted persons has been confirmed in individuals whose talent domains are not particularly scholastic, in studies of artists (Piechowski & Cunningham, 1985), creative children (Gallagher, 1985; Schiever, 1985), and social reformers and leaders (Brennan & Piechowski, 1991; Grant, 1990; Piechowski, 1990). Hence, it appears that emotionality in gifted persons, whether academically or otherwise gifted, is parallel. While distinctions certainly exist in the emotional characteristics of gifted individuals, persons of high ability *of any type* tend to develop pronounced sensitivities and, therefore, require specialized affective curriculum and instruction (VanTassel-Baska, Buckingham, & Baska, 2009).

DIFFERENCES FROM ACADEMIC GIFTEDNESS

While the internal emotional traits of gifted persons appear to be similar regardless of talent domain, distinctions exist demarcating those who have great ability in fields aside from the academic; these appear to be external to the individual. A wide array of external variables—home, parents, peers, school, social values, among others—have significant influence on the emotional development of individuals, gifted or not. These are described as among the "world context" in the Bull's Eye Model for Affective Development (Olenchak, 2009). Due to the amplified sensitivities described above, these external variables likely have a heightened effect on gifted individuals' emotions, but a case can be made that they can have even greater significance on the emotions of those with non-scholastic gifts.

TALENT AND THE AFFECTIVE DOMAIN

Most persons with great potential must learn to live in a society that fails to celebrate their gifts and often rejects them due to their superior abilities. Certainly, terms like "nerd" and "egghead" symbolize society's apparent contempt for individuals who are academically gifted. For whatever reason, society generally has chosen to reject such individuals from its mainstream, and surely such rejection must prompt notable negative social-emotional reactions in the academically gifted population. However, the majority of gifted programs in schools today reflect identification procedures and programming efforts suitable only for the academically gifted. Other than athletic giftedness, perhaps the singular type of superior potential that society has elected to support avidly with special programs and opportunities, few other kinds of giftedness or intelligence are celebrated by educational institutions.

For example, as VanTassel-Baska, Buckingham, and Baska (2009) report, instructional efforts in the arts have been greatly reduced in just the past six years, and despite federal interest in increasing vocational and technical education, as expressed through the Perkins Act funding, "vocational education is caught up in the academic reform tide. Although these reforms may have helped raise academic content in many vocational courses, it often appears to be at the expense of vocational or technical skills and content" (Stasz & Bodilly, 2004, p. xxiii). Most assuredly, efforts on behalf of academically gifted persons are totally inadequate and pale in comparison to the often extravagant expenditures on athletic giftedness; nonetheless, the fact remains, there *are* programs available for persons of superior scholastic potential, and these often do not address social-emotional development, let alone affective talent.

While academically gifted students often quite sadly respond to social rejection by camouflaging their gifts, at least if specialized programs are available, students have some chance for adjusting their emotional development. Contrast this with students who possess remarkable talents in domains other than the athletic or academic for whom specialized school programs are seldom available. In the absence of suitable school programming, these children are frequently forced to hide their abilities, and worse, come to deny them (Kogan, 1995). Denial of one's abilities among gifted populations often leads to risk of underachievement, dropping out of school, delinquency, eating disorders, drug abuse, and other activities deemed not only unacceptable socially but also personally destructive.

A review of literature over the past decade indicated that previous investigations of this group have largely been limited to three categories: gifted students with concomitant disabilities; those from poverty, minority, and/or overlooked cultures or otherwise at educational disadvantage; and those who are underserved due to their gender and/or degree of giftedness. Although few studies were located that examined the emotional risks of students having significant talents aside from the academic, this group's strong similarities with those who have concomitant giftedness and disabilities place them equally in danger. One investigation that concentrated on extreme talent in dancers examined the negative outcomes, including serious health problems, that repeatedly occur as a result of inappropriate and/or inadequate training occurring in both schools and in specialized dance programs (Kogan, 1995). Apparently, where talents—regardless of their type—remain either underserved or unserved in schools, students are placed at risk of developing serious affective problems.

Academically gifted students, by virtue of the presence of at least some school programs, are less at risk of personal disaster than are those for whom programs seldom, if ever, are offered. Moreover, where social pressure to disregard certain talents in schools is personified by teachers and educational officials who do not, cannot, or will not understand gifted students' needs, there is every likelihood that emotional damage will be guaranteed. Such children have little reason to be optimistic, and persons who lack "optimistic willpower" are not likely to find or develop "optimistic waypower" (Snyder, 1994, p. 44). In all probability, they will suffer damaged motivation and an overall sense of despair more frequently than gifted students for whom programs are available. Due to the infrequency of programs for gifted students in domains other than the academic, gifted youth with non-scholastic talent, like gifted students with disabilities, are at more emotional risk than other gifted students.

Implications for Intervention with Teachers like Mary

Obviously, if professionals in education and psychology are aware that gifted youth with advanced abilities in areas other than the academic are more socially and emotionally fragile than other gifted students, it would seem that preventive measures would be appropriate. The first psychologist and counselor specializing in emotional needs of the gifted, Leta Hollingworth, suggested that gifted students be involved in "emotional education" (Hollingworth, 1939, p. 585) to assist them in handling the special problems they were likely to encounter in school. Hollingworth felt that such emotional programming would help prevent potential maladjustment and enhance full development of their talents.

What Hollingworth meant by emotional education was a comprehensive program integrating all aspects of emotional, social, cognitive, and physical development. Such a program would integrate sufficiently challenging curriculum and instruction appropriate to the individual interests and needs of each gifted student. Later investigations confirmed Hollingworth's suspicion that curriculum and teaching have an important link to lifelong emotionality—that messages transmitted to students indirectly can be as critical to emotional development as more direct, therapeutic approaches.

Terman and Oden (1947) found that gifted adults who did not find their work interesting were prone to higher mortality rates, while Ziv, Rimon, and Doni (1977) concluded that gifted students who underachieve academically are often successful outside of school because they find pursuits that are interesting and fulfilling in which to engage. Later, Whitmore (1988) determined that school negligence of any number of specific social, emotional, and intellectual needs—including interests—could trigger a spiral of underachievement in the gifted that would likely be irreversible without specific curricular interventions. Further, Emerick (1989) ascertained that consciously serving gifted students' interests could stimulate a reversal of academic underachievement. Olenchak (1991, 1994, 1995) concluded that underachievement in academic domains attributed to learning disabilities could be at least partially reversed when schools nurture significant, nonacademic performances of superior quality.

This recognition by schools that some students' strengths may not lie in traditional academic work legitimizes human pursuits of all kinds, thereby indirectly delivering a powerful message that talents of *all* types are important. And Baum and Olenchak (2002) have found that treating strengths and de-emphasizing weaknesses in gifted students who either have attention deficit hyperactivity disorder (ADHD) or are being confused with ADHD students, serves to reduce if not eliminate risks for underachievement and social/emotional concerns altogether.

Common to these studies as well as to Hollingworth's emotional education plan is a general willingness in schools to equip gifted students with information and techniques useful and rewarding for handling stress. Consequently, opportunities for gifted students to engage in purposeful reflection as a means for sifting through life's events, in addition to activities in which they learn to integrate various problem resolution strategies, are suitable for all gifted children. To prevent emotional maladjustment, personally rewarding curriculum and instruction, opportunities for interaction with others of similar ability and interests, and situations likely to teach how to relate to those with lesser abilities and differing interests are critical school components for all gifted youth (Hollingworth, 1942). However, no subgroup among the gifted is more at risk of emotional problems than those with abilities that are likely to be ignored or underserved by schools. This group includes not only gifted students with disabilities, gifted females, those from different cultures, and those representing low socioeconomic groups, but it also refers to young people with superior abilities that are not particularly valued by the educational system.

The primary intervention programs utilized with Mary illustrate some viable and relatively easy-to-employ options for frustrated teachers. The details of Future Problem Solving are described in terms of Mary's case.

FUTURE PROBLEM SOLVING'S IMPACT

The Future Problem Solving Program (FPSP) was originally designed by E. Paul Torrance (Torrance & Torrance, 1978) as a means for teaching the Creative

Problem Solving model and, concurrently, increasing awareness of and appreciation for the future. This futuristic orientation assists individuals in creating more accurate images of the future, their places in it, and their interaction with its development (Torrance, 1976; Torrance & Reynolds, 1978).

For socially-emotionally underachieving persons such as Mary, the importance of a healthy, futuristic outlook is linked very closely to the routes for reversal of their underachievement condition. It is virtually impossible, for example, to ameliorate underachievement if one perceives little opportunity in which to interact positively with the various aspects of personal life in the future. Moreover, by equipping underachieving persons with a heuristic that is effective both in problem resolution and in assessing the future, it is likely such people will begin to feel a sense of control over their own destinies. For underachievers, most of whom feel as if life "just happens" to them, a strategy for seizing control over at least some aspect of one's life has enormous value. More importantly, teaching a strategy that works amounts to handing those who feel both helpless and hopeless a tool that develops hopefulness. As Mary put it: "FPS has helped me realize that my career future is as unlimited as my career past is limited."

Numerous case studies of gifted underachieving students have been completed to date, each revealing that involvement in FPS, coupled occasionally with either individualized or family counseling, has instigated reversal of underachievement (Olenchak, 1990; Rimm & Olenchak, 1991). However, until now, case studies of using FPS with teachers have not existed. Mary's case represents one of a sample population of six educators who have noted that FPS has specifically marked the beginning of change from underachievement to achievement in at least one aspect of their lives.

Bright underachieving teachers can benefit from involvement in programs that emphasize learning and practicing a simple problem solving process, particularly when that process integrates cognitive with affective skill development. The opportunities to take risks, to identify and pursue a goal, and to adopt a proven strategy for effective problem resolution are rarely provided through any other component of life. The Future Problem Solving Program, in particular, addresses many of the major needs of high-ability underachievers that are so often mentioned: control, future perspective, and self-esteem.

FPS IN MARY'S CASE

After an individual has been involved in FPS for a period long enough to allow her time for practice with the process, there is a window of opportunity in which the teacher and/or therapist working with the teacher can intervene beyond FPS itself. This intervention can take the form of application of the FPS process to some aspect of real life in which the underachieving teacher finds herself, the teacher, demonstrating application to her *own* life. This latter stage is particularly useful as the teacher can begin to see how the heuristic taught to children is worthwhile in helping a reasonably successful adult to control aspects of her life.

In Mary's situation, she had not been involved in FPS as it was not available at her school. Nonetheless, her therapist felt that using this problem attack technique would be useful and easy for Mary to integrate both personally and professionally. As noted earlier in this chapter, Mary was able to use the process to arrive at a successful solution to her career dilemma, one that not only allowed her to find a school more suitable to her needs and interests but also one that would likely increase her sense of optimism—if not hope—as a teacher who had all but lost it insofar as balancing her interest in teaching with her intelligence, her need for professional independence, and her personal life.

Additional individualized counseling in Mary's case included discussions of other people—predominantly youth as models—and how they had applied FPS as a means for personal control in resolving situations. Such discussions, of course, retained the anonymity of others but also encouraged Mary to analyze how others had employed the process to their advantage. Emphasis was placed on the extensive applications of FPS in one's personal life. As Mary's needs occasionally dictated, other types of counseling were necessary to enhance the effects of FPS, but primarily, her circumstance of serious affective underachievement was fully reversed through FPS.

Pessimism Extinguishes Hope; Optimism Engenders Hope

Although underachievement academically is one issue that confronts all people of high potential—including teachers who have the capacity for tremendous classroom accomplishments, it appears more significant that educational and psychological scholars and practitioners begin to recognize the potential for underachievement in each individual's domain of talent with particular attention to its implications on social-emotional development. Though intellectual underachievement is of concern to the general population, there must be growing consciousness that cognitive success alone is unlikely to nurture in teachers the élan, commitment to task, ability, and creativity upon which gifted-like performances are founded and on which contentment and self-actualization can be constructed. If anything, an entrenched school system and social climate runs the risk of so alienating teachers of high potential that they may never fully realize their talents. Worse, their overall affective development could be stifled altogether.

The case study that served as the foundation for this chapter is but one among those these researchers have collected, and those, in turn, are simply a minor representation of the many cases depicting the social-emotional side of gifted teachers across the nation and around the globe. Regardless, they provide ample opportunity for professionals to reflect on the diversity prevalent among a population we too frequently refer to as if it were homogenous: good teachers. While there has been effort to alert the field to the needs of teachers because of rampant attrition, there has been little attention paid to teachers whose talents are significant yet are not in any way reflected in the support provided professionals within the teaching profession. In fact, underachievement and resultant affective dilemmas are the same for everyone; hence, gifted students and gifted teachers are all placed at enormous risk of failure.

If we are to embrace the reality that society needs teachers and particularly excellent teachers, such as Mary's case embodies, it is imperative that schools begin to design and implement effective proactive programs to provide support for teachers who are as cognitively-emotionally at risk of dropping out of school as are high ability students. The art of teaching must be nurtured, and where it is endangered, it must be redefined and scaffolded, lest we wish to perpetuate mediocrity in classrooms among students and teachers alike. As Mary best amplified the situation:

> My talent is teaching; I have finally come to recognize this fact. But if I did not find an environment in which I could *really* teach and not just go through the motions of test preparation with my students, I would have managed to kill my spirit for the profession and would have disposed of the paint and canvasses that I could use to design more than just a mundane test-driven classroom. My teaching is now my art, and my art is my teaching.

References

Alliance for Excellent Education. (2005). *Teacher attrition: A costly loss to the nation and to the states*. Retrieved May 24, 2009, from http://www.all4ed.org/files/archive/publications/TeacherAttrition.pdf

American Association for Employment in Education. (2008). *Educator Supply and Demand in the United States*. Columbus, OH: Author.

Aurini, J., & Davies, S. (2005). Choice without markets: Homeschooling in the context of private education. *British Journal of Sociology of Education, 26*(4), 461–474.

Axtman, K. (January 11, 2005). When tests' cheaters are the teachers. *Christian Science Monitor*, 1–3.

Baum, S. M., & Olenchak, F. R. (2002). The alphabet children: GT, ADHD, and more. *Exceptionality, 10*(2), 77–91.

Baum, S. M., Olenchak, F. R., & Owen, S. V. (1995). Gifted students with attention deficits: Alternate hypotheses, alternate solutions. *International Conference on Research and Practice in Attention Deficit Disorders*. Symposium conducted at the Hebrew University, Jerusalem, Israel.

Baum, S. M., Olenchak, F. R., & Owen, S. V. (1998). Gifted students with attention deficits: Fact and/or fiction? Or can we see the forest for the trees? *Gifted Child Quarterly, 42*(2), 96–104.

Bluestein, J. (2001). *Creating emotionally safe schools: A guide for educators and parents.* Deerfield Beach, FL: Health Communications.

Borkowski, J. G., & Thorpe, P. K. (1994). Self-regulation and motivation: A life-span perspective on underachievement. In D. H. Schunk & B. J. Zimmerman (Eds.), *Self-regulation of learning and performance: Issues and educational applications* (pp. 45–74). London: Taylor and Francis.

Borman, G. D., & Dowling, N. M. (2008). Teacher attrition and retention: A meta-analytic and narrative review of the research. *Review of Educational Research, 78*(3), 367–409.

Boyd, D., Lankford, H., Loeb, S., & Wyckoff, J. (2005). Explaining the short careers of high achieving teachers in schools with low achieving students. *American Economic Review, 95*, 166–171.

Brennan, T. P., & Piechowski, M. M. (1991). The developmental framework for self-actualization: Evidence from case studies. *Journal of Humanistic Psychology, 31*(3), 43–64.

Callahan, D. (2004). *The cheating culture: Why more Americans are doing wrong to get ahead.* Orlando, FL: Harcourt.

Ciompi, L. (1982). *Affektlogik [Affect Logic].* Stuttgart, Germany: Klett-Cotta.

Ciompi, L. (1988). *Psyche and schizophrenia: The bond between affect and logic.* Cambridge, MA: Harvard University Press.

Ciompi, L. (1991). Affects as central organising and integrating factors: A new psychosocial/biological model of the psyche. *British Journal of Psychiatry, 159*, 97–105.

Ciompi, L. (1999). *Die emotionalen grundlagen des denkens [The emotional bases of thinking].* Göttingen, Germany: Vandenhoeck & Ruprecht.

Coleman, L. J., & Cross, T. L. (2001). *Being gifted in school: An introduction to development, guidance, and teaching.* Waco, TX: Prufrock Press.

Council for Exceptional Children. (2003). *What every special educator must know* (5th ed.). Arlington, VA: Author.

Crocco, M. S., & Costigan, A. T. (2006). High-stakes teaching: What's at stake for teachers (and students) in the age of accountability. *The New Educator, 2*, 1–13.

Dabrowski, K. (1938). Typy wzmozonej pobudliwosci: psychicznej (Types of increased psychic excitability). *Biul. Inst. Hig. Psychicznej, 1*(3–4), 3–26.

Dabrowski, K. (1964). *Positive disintegration.* Boston: Little, Brown.

Dabrowski, K., & Piechowski, M. M. (1977). *Theory of levels of emotional development* (Vols. 1 & 2). Oceanside, NY: Dabor Science.

Damasio, A. R. (1994). *Descartes' error: Emotion, reason, and the human brain.* New York: Grosset/Putnam.

Damasio, A. R. (1999). *The feeling of what happens: Body and emotion in the making of consciousness.* New York: Harcourt Brace.

Davis, G. A. (1992). *Creativity is forever* (3rd ed.). Dubuque, IA: Kendall/Hunt.

Emerick, L. J. (1989). Student interests: A key to reversing the underachievement pattern. *Understanding Our Gifted, 2*(1), 1, 10–12.

Gallagher, S. A. (1985). A comparison of the concept of overexcitabilities with measures of creativity and school achievement in sixth-grade students. *Roeper Review, 8,* 115–119.

Gottfredson, D. C. (2001). *Schools and delinquency.* New York: Cambridge University Press.

Grant, B. (1990). Moral development: Theories and lives. *Advanced Development, 2,* 85–91.

Green, C. L., & Hoover-Dempsey, K. V. (2007). Why do parents homeschool? A systematic examination of parent involvement. *Education and Urban Society, 39,* 264–285.

Guarino, C., Santibanez, L., Daley, G., & Brewer, D. (2004). *A review of the research literature on teacher recruitment and retention.* Santa Monica, CA: RAND Corporation.

Hollingworth, L. S. (1939). What we know about the early selection and training of leaders. *Teachers College Record, 40,* 575–592.

Hollingworth, L. S. (1942). *Children above 180 IQ Stanford-Binet: Origin and development.* Yonkers-on-Hudson, NY: World Book.

Immordino-Yang, M. H., & Damasio, A. (2007). We feel, therefore we learn: The relevance of affective and social neuroscience to education. *Mind, Brain, and Education, 1,* 3–10.

Ingersoll, R. (2003). *Who controls teachers' work? Power and accountability in America's schools.* Cambridge, MA: Harvard University Press.

Ingersoll, R. (2004). *Why do high-poverty schools have difficulty staffing their classrooms with qualified teachers?* Washington, DC: Center for American Progress.

Ingersoll, R., & Perda, D. (2008). The status of teaching as a profession. In J. Ballantine & J. Spade (Eds.), *Schools and society: A sociological approach to education* (pp. 107–118). Los Angeles: Pine Forge Press.

Ingersoll, R., & Perda, D. (2009). *The mathematics and science teacher shortage: Fact and myth.* Philadelphia, PA: Consortium for Policy Research in Education.

Ingersoll, R., & Smith, T. (2003). The wrong solution to the teacher shortage. *Educational Leadership, 60* (8), 30–33.

Isen, A. M. (2004). Some perspectives on positive feelings and emotions: Positive affect facilitates thinking and problem solving. In A. S. R. Manstead, N. Frijda, & A. Fischer (Eds.), *Feelings and emotions: The Amsterdam Symposium* (pp. 263–281). Cambridge, UK: Cambridge University Press.

Johnson, S. M. (2006). *The workplace matters: Teacher quality, retention, and effectiveness.* Washington, DC: National Education Association.

Kanevsky, L., & Keighley, T. (2003). To produce or not to produce? Understanding boredom and the honor of underachievement. *Roeper Review, 26*(1), 20–29.

Kersaint, G., Lewis, J., Potter, R., & Meisels, G. G. (2007). Why teachers leave: Factors that influence retention or resignation. *Teaching and Teacher Education, 23*, 775–998.

Kogan, N. (1995). Motivational and personality patterns in performing artists. *Esther Katz Rosen Symposium on the Psychological Development of Gifted Children.* Symposium conducted at the University of Kansas, Lawrence, KS.

Kopkowski, C. (2008). Why they leave. *NEA Today, 26*(7), 21–25.

Lind, S., & Olenchak, F. R. (1995). ADD/ADHD and giftedness: What should educators do? *Eighth Annual Conference of the Association for the Education of Gifted Underachieving Students.* Symposium conducted at Birmingham, AL.

Liu, E., Johnson, S. M., & Peske, H. G. (2004). New teachers and the Massachusetts signing bonus: The limits of inducements. *Educational Evaluation and Policy Analysis 26*(3): 217–236.

Loeb, S., Darling-Hammond, L., & Luczak, J. (2005). How teaching conditions predict teacher turnover in California schools. *Peabody Journal of Education, 80*(33), 44–70.

Morse, W. C., Ardizzone, J., MacDonald, C., & Pasick, P. (1980). *Affective education for special education children and youth.* Reston, VA: Council for Exceptional Children.

National Center for Education Statistics, U.S. Department of Education. (2008). *1.5 Million Homeschooled Students in the United States in 2007.* Washington, DC: U.S. Government Printing Office.

Olenchak, F. R. (1990). Controlling underachievement through future problem solving. *National Association for Gifted Children Annual Convention.* Symposium conducted at Little Rock, AR.

Olenchak, F. R. (1991). Wearing their shoes: Role playing to reverse underachievement. *Understanding Our Gifted, 3*(4), 1, 8–11.

Olenchak, F. R. (1994). Talent development: Accommodating the social and emotional needs of secondary gifted/learning disabled students. *Journal of Secondary Gifted Education, 5*(3), 40–52.

Olenchak, F. R. (1995). Effects of enrichment on gifted/learning disabled students. *Journal for the Education of the Gifted, 18*(4), 385–399.

Olenchak, F. R. (1999). Affective development of gifted students with nontraditional talents. *Roeper Review, 21*(4), 293–297.

Olenchak, F. R. (2009). Creating a life: Orchestrating a symphony of self, a work always in progress. In J. L. VanTassel-Baska, T. L. Cross, & F. R. Olenchak (Eds.), *Social-emotional curriculum with gifted and talented students* (pp. 41–78). Waco, TX: Prufrock Press.

Olenchak, F. R., Gaa, J. P., & Jackson, S. (2009). Gifted education's latest challenge: Social-emotional underachievement, a new glimpse at an old problem. In B. MacFarlane & T. Stambaugh (Eds.), *Leading change in gifted education: The festschrift of Dr. Joyce VanTassel-Baska* (pp. 207–218). Waco, TX: Prufrock Press.

Patton, M. Q. (1990). *Qualitative evaluation and research methods* (2nd ed.). Newbury Park, CA: Sage.

Piechowski, M. M. (1990). Inner growth and transformation in the life of Eleanor Roosevelt. *Advanced Development, 2*, 35–53.

Piechowski, M. M. (1997). Emotional giftedness: The measure of intrapersonal intelligence. In N. Colangelo & G. Davis (Eds.), *Handbook of gifted education* (pp. 366–381). Boston: Allyn & Bacon.

Piechowski, M. M., & Cunningham, K. (1985). Patterns of overexcitability in a group of artists. *Journal of Creative Behavior, 19*(3), 153–174.

Piechowski, M. M., Silverman, L. K., & Falk, R. F. (1985). Comparison of intellectually and artistically gifted on five dimensions of mental functioning. *Perceptual and Motor Skills, 60,* 539–549.

Psychological Corporation. (2003). *Wechsler Intelligence Scale for Children-IV.* New York: Author.

Rimm, S. B. (1986). *Underachievement syndrome: Causes and cures.* Watertown, WI: Apple.

Rimm, S. B. (1997). An underachievement epidemic. *Educational Leadership, 54*(7), 18–22.

Rimm, S. B., & Olenchak, F. R. (1991). How future problem solving helps underachieving gifted students. *Gifted Child Today, 14*(2), 19–22.

Schiever, S. W. (1985). Creative personality characteristics and dimensions of mental functioning in gifted adolescents. *Roeper Review, 7,* 223–226.

Seeley, K. (1993). Gifted students at risk. In L. K. Silverman (Ed.), *Counseling the gifted and talented* (pp. 263–276). Denver: Love.

Seligman, M. E. P. (1990). *Learned optimism.* New York: Knopf.

Seligman, M. E. P. (2004). Can happiness be taught? *Daedalus, 133* (2), 80–87.

Seligman, M. E. P., & Csikszentmihalyi, M. (2000). Positive psychology: An introduction. *American Psychologist, 55,* 5–14.

Silverman, L. K. (1993). The gifted individual. In L. K. Silverman (Ed.), *Counseling the gifted and talented* (pp. 3–28). Denver: Love.

Snyder, C. R. (1994). *The psychology of hope: You can get there from here.* New York: Free Press.

Stasz, C., & Bodilly, S. (2004). *Efforts to improve the quality of vocational education in secondary schools: Impact of Federal and State policies.* Retrieved September 5, 2008, from http://www.rand.org/pubs/monograph_reports/2005/MR1655.sum.pdf

Terman, L. M., & Oden, M. H. (1947). *Genetic studies of genius: Vol. 4. The gifted child grows up.* Stanford, CA: Stanford University Press.

Torrance, E. P. (1966). *Torrance tests of creative thinking.* Bensenville, IL: Scholastic Testing Service.

Torrance, E. P. (1976). Career education of the gifted and talented: Images of the future. *Seventh Western Symposium on Learning.* Symposium conducted at Western Washington State College, Bellingham, WA.

Torrance, E. P., & Reynolds, C. R. (1978). Images of the future of gifted adolescents: Effects of alienation and specialized cerebral functioning. *Gifted Child Quarterly, 22,* 40–54.

Torrance, E. P., & Torrance, J. P. (1978). Developing creativity instruction materials according to the Osborn-Parnes creative problem solving model. *Creative Child and Adult Quarterly, 5,* 9–19.

VanTassel-Baska, J., Buckingham, B. L. E., & Baska, A. (2009). The role of the arts in the socioemotional development of the gifted. In J. L. VanTassel-Baska, T. L. Cross, & F. R. Olenchak (Eds.), *Social-emotional curriculum with gifted and talented students* (pp. 227–257). Waco, TX: Prufrock Press.

VanTassel-Baska, J. L., Cross, T. L., & Olenchak, F. R. (2009). *Social-emotional curriculum with gifted and talented students.* Waco, TX: Prufrock Press.

Whitmore, J. R. (1988). Gifted children at risk for learning difficulties. *Teaching exceptional children, 20*(4), 10–14.

Zins, J. E., Weissberg, R. P., Wang, M. C., & Walberg, H. J. (2004). *Building academic success on social and emotional learning: What does the research say?* New York: Teachers College Press.

Ziv, A., Rimon, J., & Doni, M. (1977). Parental perception and self-concept of gifted and average underachievers. *Perceptual and Motor Skills, 44,* 563–568.

CHAPTER 4

Aesthetic Themes as Conduits to Creativity

Christy M. Moroye
University of Iowa

P. Bruce Uhrmacher
University of Denver

Christy M. Moroye, PhD, is an assistant professor in curriculum and supervision in the Department of Teaching and Learning, University of Iowa. Her dissertation, "Greening Our Future: The Practices of Ecologically Minded Teachers," received the 2008 Outstanding Dissertation of the Year Award from the American Educational Research Association, Division B: Curriculum Studies. Her research interests include ecological and aesthetic approaches to education.

P. Bruce Uhrmacher, PhD, is a Professor at the Morgridge College of Education, University of Denver. He coedited *Intricate Palette: Working the Ideas of Elliot Eisner* and is the author of numerous articles on curriculum, teaching, and the role of aesthetics in education. Bruce is the faculty advisor to the Aesthetic Education Institute of Colorado.

ABSTRACT

The paper addresses two questions central to the theme of creativity: What practices and strategies spur the development of creative minds? And what does creative teaching look like? Responses explored here are derived from our ongoing research that examines the outcomes of aesthetically oriented activities used in aesthetic education institutes for teacher professional development and in K–12 classrooms. We suggest that certain ideas and processes exhibited by the teaching artists at the summer institutes aid in helping participants develop creativity. Likewise, these ideas and processes are useful for K–12 teachers in cultivating their own and their students' creativity. We refer to these ideas and processes as *aesthetic themes of education*.

Specifically, these themes include *imagination, sensory experience, risk taking, perceptivity, connections, and active engagement.*

Introduction and Background

Our approach to thinking about creative teaching stems from the arts. While creativity is certainly found in all of the academic disciplines, it is most readily apparent and inherent in the arts (dance, theatre, visual art, music, poetry, among others). It is true that scientists must be creative in thinking about experiments and in their interpretations of data, but it is also accurate to say that scientists generally want their experimental results to be replicated. In this sense, scientists seek nomothetic rather than idiosyncratic results. The arts, however, thrive on the idiosyncratic. Those of us who are grounded in the arts desire to see or hear the results of individual minds entangled with the world. We want to learn about life through the eyes of Toni Morrison or Philip Roth. The last thing we would want in the arts is a novel that could be replicated or a dance performance sanctioned by a committee. We embrace this focus on individuality and have sought to enrich educational endeavors through this perspective, as have many before us.

Understanding issues that relate teaching, curriculum, learning, and creativity from an artistic and aesthetic viewpoint has a strong tradition in the United States that dates to the 1960s. While writers in the West have touted the importance of the arts and the aesthetic for humanity at least since the time of Aristotle and have delved deeply into the importance of the arts in the Romantic era (e.g., Coleridge, 1983; Schiller, 1967), it was not until the 1960s that a full-blown curriculum came into being. The Central Midwestern Regional Educational Laboratory (CEMREL), for example, created an aesthetic education curriculum for grades K–6 and established eleven teacher professional development centers to support it. One goal of the curriculum was to teach students how "to perceive, judge, and value aesthetically what we come to know through our senses" (Madeja & Onuska, 1977, p. 3).

Today, a number of organizations aim to bring the arts and an aesthetic education into the schools. The Kennedy Center, the Lincoln Center, Young Audiences, and Think 360 Arts are a few of the institutions that aim to improve learning by having students engage in an aesthetic education. Our current research draws upon this tradition and is grounded in a particular teacher institute in Denver, Colorado—the Aesthetic Education Institute of Colorado (AEIC), which is jointly sponsored by the Morgridge College of Education at the University of Denver and Think 360 Arts.[1] In particular, we are interested in discerning important qualities of aesthetic educational experiences so that teachers may consciously employ these qualities in various lessons across the curriculum. Doing so, we argue, offers opportunities for both teacher and student creativity.

Aesthetic Themes

As organizers and teachers at the Aesthetic Education Institute of Colorado, as well as researchers of it, we have assisted in developing a new line of thinking that ties together aesthetics, art, and education. Briefly, we suggest that learning experiences can be ordinary or extraordinary. That is, people can learn in all sorts of situations and environments. The goal for schools, however, should be to provide exemplary situations and environments. This might be accomplished by providing aesthetic learning experiences, the upshot of which is creativity.

Let's examine these ideas more closely.[2] In his seminal text on aesthetics, *Art as Experience*, Dewey (1934) pointed out that an aesthetic experience can take place in the creation as well as in the appreciation of art works. Aesthetics, derived from the term *aesthetikos*, which means capable of sensory perception, generally referred to these kinds of person-art interactions. But Dewey unhinged aesthetics from art alone. He noted that aesthetic experiences can take place in all walks of life. In short, an aesthetic experience may be thought of as a time in which one feels a sense of awe or being "in the zone." Monroe Beardsley characterized one's feelings during an aesthetic experience as some blend of the following: a focus on a particular object or setting, a feeling of unity with that object or setting, a sense of timelessness, a feeling of self-expansion or edification, and a rush of sensory material (Csikszentmihalyi & Robinson, 1990, p. 7).

Thus, an aesthetic experience can happen while interacting with a work of art or with a particularly sensation-filled activity in life. It can happen the first time one sees the Mona Lisa, the hundredth time one sees a particular dance performance, while vacationing in the mountains or seaside, or even while simply walking down the street. Perhaps you noticed the rustle of the leaves on a grand oak tree, the slices of light that shone through to the sidewalk, and the smell of warm summer air stirring the nearby flowers. For a moment, perhaps you were engrossed in your immediate experience, unified with the setting around you. This is one example of an aesthetic experience.

Armed with Dewey's ideas about the aesthetic experience, we then examined activities taking place at AEIC. We noticed that the teaching artists tended to cultivate particular kinds of activities that led to enriched and enlivened teaching episodes. Next, by comparing these activities to Dewey's ideas on aesthetics, we eventually derived six themes that seemed to capture the teaching-artists activities. These include: connections, active engagement, risk-taking imagination, sensory experience, and perceptivity. Let's take a look at each.

Connections are the ways in which an individual interacts with an idea or object in the learning environment. These connections may be intellectual, emotional, sensorial, or communicative (Csikszentmihalyi & Robinson, 1990). Essentially, they describe the relationship one has with the object or idea of study. Not all individuals will connect in the same ways. Using *House on Mango Street*, a novella by Sandra Cisneros (1984), as an example, some students might be intellectually curious about the author's craft. Others may feel emotionally empathetic for the experiences of Esperanza. A communicative connection refers to the ways in which the object of study tells a story about the time in which it was made; some students may feel this connection to Esperanza's urban neighborhood. A sensorial connection could refer to the sounds of the words, the textures of the phrases, and the rhythm of the lines.

Our second theme, *active engagement*, requires that students be in the driver's seat; they are at the helm of their own learning. This could include physically being active, intellectually creating meaning, or making choices about how to represent their knowledge.

Third, *risk taking* refers to students' opportunities to try something new, to step out of their normal realm of experience. As with connections, risk taking is not the same for every student. For some, trying a new art form like dance or singing is risky; for others, simply working with a partner poses some risk. The goal, of course, is that the risk leads to a reward, to learning something new about oneself or an object of study. It is also important that the teacher provide safe conditions for the risks. As with Mike's drumming lessons (see below), the teacher is responsible for laying the ground rules, opening communication, and reaching out for participation from all members of the group.

We describe *imagination*, the fourth theme, as the internal manipulation of ideas, which may be characterized in several ways. Imagination may be intuitive, in which a person has a sudden rush of insight; fanciful, in which a person combines unexpected elements such as a talking clock; and interactive, in which a person works with materials to yield a product. We also discuss mimetic imagination in which the individual mirrors the creative expression of another, such as repeating the drum beats played by the teaching artist Mike. This type of imagination often leads into others, especially for those who are unsure of their imaginative and creative potential. We distinguish between imagination and creativity. Although some may use the terms interchangeably, we use imagination to refer to internal work, and consider creativity to be the external expression of this work. Hence, creativity cannot happen without imagination, but one might be imaginative without allowing their ideas to come to fruition. For example, an author is imaginative in designing his characters and plots and creative once those characters and plots have taken form on paper.

Fifth, an aesthetic experience depends on *sensory experience*: at least one person and a sensory interaction with an object. We use the term "object" metaphorically. It may of course refer to an actual object such as a vase or a painting, but also it can refer to a text, a soundscape, a landscape, an image, or simply something focused upon, such as birds flying over a barn. The key point here is that any kind of aesthetic experience depends upon the use of one's senses engaged in some aspect of the world. The object comes to life through the senses.

Finally, our sixth theme, *perceptivity*, is a deepened sensory experience. Perception is an achievement and as such can be developed. As an example, we could look at almost any object and notice its surface features, but when we really look and examine it, we begin to notice its subtle qualities. This deepened noticing is what we refer to as perceptivity.

Current Research

As part of our ongoing research, we asked two elementary school teachers who have been involved with AEIC as participants and as bridge builders—expert teachers who assist participants in creating bridges between the arts and their classrooms—to consciously incorporate the six themes into a curriculum unit of their choice. We interviewed the teachers formally both before and after teaching their units, and we observed them teaching several lessons over a period of two to three weeks. We used the qualitative method of educational connoisseurship and criticism (Eisner, 1997, 2002; Uhrmacher & Matthews, 2005) that calls for rich descriptions that are often presented in vignettes, such as those we include below.

Part of our research includes trying to understand the relationships among the themes and how they work together to create meaningful aesthetic educational experiences. While we are still pursuing this line of inquiry, our findings to date indicate that the themes appear to have significant import for teacher and student creativity.

In order to assist the reader in understanding our research and the connections between these aesthetic ideas and K–12 classrooms, we begin with a description and summary of AEIC activities. Since our current research focuses on classrooms rather than on institutes, we rely on Perlov's (1998) study that richly describes one aesthetic education institute. Next, we describe one teacher's implementation of the aesthetic themes. We do so to suggest how other teachers and teacher educators might infuse the ideas into more creative teaching practice. Finally, we provide interview data to reveal connections between the institute and classrooms and to indicate how the themes impact teacher and student creativity.

Teaching Creatively at the Institute: Artists as Teachers

The Aesthetic Education Institute of Colorado (AEIC) is held each summer at the end of June at the University of Denver. Cosponsored by Think 360 Arts, the institute is taught mostly by practicing artists in dance, theatre, visual art, music and poetry, and attendees are primarily pre-service and practicing K–12 educators. Artist selection is competitive and takes place in January. This selection process evaluates not only artistic ability but also aptitude for working with teachers and communicating about and through a particular art form. Oftentimes those selected are artists-in-residence who have extensive experience in K–12 schools. Once selected, the artists meet three times with institute directors to prepare for their teaching.

At their first meeting, artists think about and share their plans with each other for their art presentations, called focus pieces. At the beginning and at the end of the institute, each artist presents his or her focus piece, which acts as a point of reference. For example, the visual artist may show a slide show of his work; a dancer may perform a dance, either solo or with her troupe. The particular art works shown reveal qualities that the artists will help AEIC participants explore in their workshops. A dancer may exhibit a modern dance so that the participants can imagine the kind of movements they will experience. This is not to say that the participants are taught all of the skills to become modern dancers themselves, but they are taught a few skills, as simple as thinking about high, medium, and low space, so that they can engage in the creative process. As another example, a poet once shared her work about her farm in northern Colorado and all of her former pets that had been buried around the property over the years. She described their burials as forming a "necklace" of skeletons around their land. That summer her workshops focused on imagery and sense of place.

The focus pieces are then repeated at the end of the institute in order to allow participants to experience the artworks again, this time with a deeper understanding due to having experienced the art form for themselves. This is an example of *perceptivity*, or the ability to really see or understand the intricacies of an object (or experience) of focus. While a participant may not even think about paying attention to high, medium, and low space the first time he sees the dance performance, he is well aware of it the second time and can appreciate its usage. With their new perceptivity, participants are able to appreciate on a different level the creative process and product exhibited by the artist.

After presenting their focus pieces to the institute as a whole, the participants are divided into groups of about ten people. Each artist meets with each group three times. The goals of the workshops are to have participants engage in the creative process for the purposes of awakening their own artistic sensibilities and to begin thinking about education from artistic perspectives. That is, one aim is for participants to enjoy the workshops without worrying about issues of implementation. They are encouraged to relish their experiences for themselves. There is, however, time for participants to think about the application of their experiences for education in what is called bridge-building—additional blocks of time led by curriculum development specialists who are often practicing teachers.

In order to prepare for their workshops with the small groups, the other two meetings with institute directors focus on the process and elements of constructing a successful workshop. To prepare artists for their task, the following handout resembling a lesson plan template[3] is distributed and discussed:

AEIC WORKSHOP STRUCTURE

Set	*Time to talk about what you are going to do.*
Practice	*Model and time to do.*
Reflection	*Time to talk or write about what happened during the workshop.*

ELEMENTS
Create a Safe Environment

Respect	*Show respect for all individuals.*
Trust	*Develop a caring environment where everyone feels free to take chances.*
Community	*Create a sense of belonging for the entire group.*

Ownership

Choice	*Allow participants choices.*
Personal Relevance	*Allow participants to bring their own experience to activities.*
Challenge	*Be aware of each individual's skill level.*
Model	
Risk	*Encourage risk taking by sharing your work, your artistic process and experiences.*

Imagination	*Design activities that are out of the ordinary and that will spark the imagination.*
Response	*Respond to the efforts of each individual honestly and thoughtfully.*
Self-Correction	*Respond to participant concerns by engaging in conversation, clarifying ideas, and adjusting workshops. Take advantage of the teachable moment.*

The artists are asked to attend to three major categories: create a safe environment, provide participants with ownership over their own learning, and model the process or activity. By considering each of these categories, the artists build community, provide choices, and allow for risk taking and self-correction. These techniques have served the artists well in helping teachers explore their creativity at the institute, and these elements are also useful for practicing teachers as they strive to foster students' creativity.

To illustrate the workshops the artists create for teachers using the above template, we describe below the activities set out by Mike, who teaches African and Latin drumming. Notice that he includes each of the three categories but does so in a fluid manner that does not necessarily reflect a strict sequence. The elements are present but not prescriptive.

Mike's focus piece presented on the first day of the institute is a series of songs played by himself and a small ensemble of drummers:

> Mike is standing barefooted and slightly in front of a line of drummers. Mike begins the "call" as the curtain continues to open. *Bongto bongo fu my ae. Bongo ti bongo fu my ae.* The drummers respond. *Toe fay ah fu my ae. Toe fay ah fu my ae.* The call and response are repeated and then Mike begins the call again with *Hey bongo bongo fu my ae. Bongo ti bongo fu my ae,* infusing even more energy into it. The ensemble responds and then Mike starts clapping with his hands and arms raised about his head. He signals the audience to join in by clapping. There is a cacophony of rhythm, but Mike's drum can be heard clearly above the others. A sense of tremendous energy travels outward from the stage. The rhythms shift and change. (Perlov, 1998, p. 202)

After presenting this focus piece to the entire institute, he teaches his song to the smaller workshop group. In the first session, Mike begins with a warm-up, whereby participants ease into the planned activities. He teaches them the song from the focus piece. No one is singled out, and the group works together: "Mike tells them that the 'response is tricky' so they should not worry if they say 'tofu.' There is hearty laughter and the group really starts to warm up as he assures them that 'it takes a while to get used to the words'" (Perlov, 1998, p. 203). Mike takes the lead in the song, *modeling* the rhythms and responses, but over the next two workshops he has others take the lead when they feel ready.

Mike also had participants play the Nigerian "High Life" rhythm in the first workshop, encouraging them to play specific patterns on the shakere, the cowbell, the clave, and the drums. Subdivided into groups of four, the participants learn their patterns, often with Mike redirecting the beats as they get off course. In the first stage of this drumming workshop, Mike encourages his students to repeat his actions and to mimic what they hear and experience. We suggest that this is a type of mimetic imagination in which participants must experience someone else's creative expression and then repeat it with fidelity. This is not an end in itself in this context but a means to more individualistic imagination.

Mike's focus on this type of mimetic work has a purpose: it builds students' confidence and abilities, so they are more comfortable in taking risks in the next two workshop sessions. Near the end of the second workshop, Mike provides participants with the opportunity to explore the individualistic sense of imagination by informing participants that in small groups they will create their own rhythmic patterns. First, he asks students to listen to sounds and to write their reactions to them:

> "I'm gonna turn the lights down low, create a setting, so we can really listen and pick up on sounds that might move you in any way. If they don't move you, write about that, too. We'll incorporate it in a story in some kind of way. So there is a story to these sounds. . . . So we're listening to these sounds just to help you get an idea of how you might accent emotion, movement, the situation, anything to help create your stories. . . . After you hear these sounds you want to take them home, elaborate on them, and be prepared for Monday morning 'cause . . . everybody's gonna contribute to the story, and remember, everybody's gonna be a composer as far as adding music to it, or sounds." (Perlov, 1998, p. 212)

Mike encourages risk taking by building a safe community for his participants. One participant commented, "It is OK to fail or make a mistake" (p. 211). By including everyone's ideas in the "story" they will tell with music, Mike validates the imaginative contributions of all members of the group. He also explicitly acknowledges that not all participants might be "moved" by the same sounds, and he wants participants to connect with those that do move them.

Furthermore, Mike is sensitive to the fact that students, adults, and children alike learn in different ways, and he wants to model this idea for the teacher-participants. He focuses on students being actively engaged:

> "There are different ways to learn besides the linear way as far as the teacher teaching or lecturing to the students. I think more physical involvement would help a lot of students. . . . They need to be inter-active with whatever the program is, [to be] hands on and see how it's actually done as opposed to being told how it's done." (p. 211)

Making connections, encouraging active engagement, stirring imaginations, and creating a safe environment for risk taking characterize four of the ways Mike helps participants engage in creative activity. So what do these themes, present in the work of artists at the institute, have to offer K–12 teachers and students? We recognize that most K–12 teachers are not engaged in teaching drumming, so we asked two teachers to use the themes to teach their regular curriculum.

Teaching Creatively in the Classroom: Teachers as Artists

When we asked Maggie Baker, a fourth-grade teacher, to implement the aesthetic themes in her teaching, she responded with enthusiasm. Due to timing of the research as well as Maggie's interests, she decided to supplement a pre-planned curriculum unit from International Towne.[4] Students were engaged in an extensive exploration of globalization, and they were working to understand international cultures.

The following vignette shows how Maggie used the themes[5] inspired by her experiences with workshops at the institute to extend her students' understanding of culture and how it is expressed.

> After lunch, students stream into their sunny second-floor classroom. Maggie begins the afternoon by asking students to define culture. After a series of responses and negotiations, they describe it as the customs and traditions that make up a group of people or a commu-nity. She asks them to think about specific attributes or characteristics that could explain the way of life of an ethnic group. They come up with language, religion, food, clothing trends, treatment of animals, celebrations, currency, and the basic way of life and belief systems.

Maggie had told us before the lesson that she thinks her students have a difficult time with the concept of culture and that she wants to help them deepen their understanding of International Towne curriculum, which focuses on financial systems, by making international cultures more accessible. To this end, she designs the following lessons with the aesthetic themes in mind.

> First Maggie engages their imaginations and encourages connections through music and drawing. "I am going to play music from four countries," Maggie explains. "First close your eyes and listen to it. Second, draw what it makes you think of. Just your quick response. As you draw, think about what culture it is from." She places a basket of colored pencils on each table along with several sheets of colored paper. She begins the first selection. It has a strong bass line, reggae-like, and is upbeat. A couple of students rock to the beat, and a few have their heads on their desk with their eyes closed and pencils tapping. Maggie then prods them to begin their drawings. "It could just be colors or shapes, or you could draw a random design or a real image." She keeps the music playing while they draw. "Think of movement—how would the sound move?" One girl takes an orange marker and dots the paper to the beat. "What clues do you have about what country this is from? I see a lot of waves and scribbly upbeat drawings."

The music alone provides the opportunities for sensory and emotional connections. Some students clearly feel the beat. By asking students to find clues about what country the music is from, Maggie also engages students intellectually. Active engagement has also been elicited. From our observations, we note that every student is engaged and participating. Likewise, Maggie has sparked the students' imaginations. Each theme is drawn upon as the lesson continues.

> Maggie then puts on the next selection without discussing the first. "What do we do first?" Students close their eyes and listen to the new song. After a few moments she urges them to make connections. "Think about associations that come to your mind. What does this remind you of?" One student raises her arms over an imaginary piano and begins to play the air keyboard; another picks up the air guitar. The music has a Celtic flavor, and students bob to the beat and then begin their drawings. Many use different types of brushstrokes creating short lines or sweeping arcs of color.
>   The third selection of music begins with a low whistle—lonely, drawn out, breathy whisps of sound. Each note is separate, hushed but strong. Maggie again asks students to focus on connections. "Think about emotions. How does this make you feel?" A student whispers, "It is depressing." Maggie acknowledges her comment and then asks her to put it in her drawing, not into words. "What color

schemes go with the music?" Students select browns, blues, greens, and some yellow.

The final selection returns the room to an upbeat mood with bongos, piano, and a Latin beat. Students draw palm trees, rainbows, and ocean vistas. Two boys stand up and dance while they draw.

After playing each of the four selections, Maggie plays a short segment from the first.

Now that the class has warmed up to the music, she employs the theme of risk taking and asks students how they would move to the song.

"What does it make your body want to do?" Students move in different ways, some staying in the chair to sway back and forth or wave their hands, and others stand up and wiggle and shake. "What does this tell us about the culture?" Students respond that it is relaxed and happy. The music, they say, makes them want to move. Maggie continues this process for each of the songs; she asks them to move, to think about what it says about that culture, and to make some connections to countries with which they are already familiar. With each song, students move a little more freely about the room, and they share more specifically what they were thinking while listening and drawing. When she gets to the music selection of the low whistle, which was the sound of a didgeridoo, Maggie asks them to recall the emotions they felt or were reminded of. One student says, "It's all hazy, and there is a camel walking into the horizon. Then there's a guy with a flute." Another says, "It reminds me of a water buffalo." A third says, "I saw a hut with a horse coming out of the smoke."

Throughout the entire lesson, students are actively engaged, moving their bodies and their hands and creating individual responses to the music. For the final selection, students shimmied, wiggled, and rocked to the salsa beat. "This song is juicy!" one student hollered while circling around her table. "Now salsa your way to line up for PE." Maggie instructs, and students saunter out of the room.

DISCUSSION

Clearly, the descriptions of activities at the institute vary from those of actual classroom lessons. But the common themes are evident: connections, risk taking, imagination, sensory experience, and active engagement are woven throughout the classroom setting. Even perceptivity is brought in when Maggie replays the songs for the students. This recount is not unlike watching two focus pieces. In the second time through, students' awareness of the music is heightened by the fact that they had the opportunity to hear various interpretations.[6]

AESTHETIC THEMES AND TEACHER/STUDENT CREATIVITY

In addition to observing how the aesthetic themes might be brought to life in a K–12 setting, we were also interested in finding out if the teachers felt that the themes fostered their own and their students' creativity. Maggie said:

> "I believe that the themes enhance both teacher and student creativity. In the planning process, the themes pushed me to think of new ideas and different ways to teach material. I had to use my own creativity to think through alternative ideas. In doing so, a lot of the ideas I came up with were more creative for the students and encouraged them to use their creativity."

Claire Benson,[7] a third-grade teacher at an English Language Learners (ELL) magnet school, was the second participant in the study. She also perceived themes as influencing creativity. She said:

> "For me, there's a strong relationship between the themes and creativity, both for myself as a teacher and for the kids. The planning process really fulfills my need for creativity, both on a larger, long-term planning level, and also on a more spontaneous level when I'm trying to find ways to round out lessons by integrating the themes. For kids, I think my teaching, in a more creative way, generally makes the content more accessible and interesting . . . I have a large ELL population, coming from different cultures and learning styles, which adds to the variety of needs. Generally, the kids' creativity thrives when I use the themes. They tap into their imaginations much more, and they see things in new and different ways, from different perspectives. They also seem to approach their learning more creatively—they reach out to gather information in new ways, and they think about their own learning process a little more."

Conclusions

Our observations support the statements of the teachers in the study. We observed students producing externally their internal imaginative work. Therefore, while one might think that facilitating imagination in the classroom produces creativity as an outcome, our observations reveal that the situation is more complex. Before students exhibit creativity, they need to be connected to the lesson at hand. As we have shown, there are various ways to create such connections. That they need to be actively engaged is clear. Imagination and creativity cannot be forced on anyone. One must take initiative. In addition, it is our contention that imagination and creativity require sensory experiences. Whether dwelling in our own minds or manipulating actual qualities in the world outside our heads, we engage in something that is sensory. Finally, creativity almost by definition requires risk taking because one must take a leap into the unknown.

From a research standpoint, one might ask, just which themes exactly and with what proportion are needed to produce creativity? We, however, choose not to look at this issue in this way. To paraphrase Aristotle, seek precision only inasmuch as the subject matter will allow. It is not our goal to become too reductionist. In the same way that one might identify seven elements of design (line, shape, texture, color, etc.) but not be able to discuss how such elements need to be mixed and used to produce a great design, we believe that our six themes identify key elements in an aesthetic experience, but one cannot extract and correlate any given theme to any given outcome.

What we believe we can say, however, is the following: people go through life having various types of experiences. Some are ordinary, and some are extraordinary. Likewise, students are able to learn in a variety of situations. Some are mundane, and some are astonishing. When teachers provide the opportunity for students to have aesthetically oriented learning experiences, we move toward the astonishing end of the continuum. And when we move toward the stimulating end of the continuum, we increase the possibility for students to become creative.

Returning now to the two questions asked at the beginning of the essay— What practices and strategies spur the development of creative minds? And what does creative teaching look like?—we suggest one grand answer to each question. First, using the six themes as outlined in this paper offers the possibility of spurring creative minds. Second, creative teaching includes creating a safe environment, encouraging student ownership over learning, and modeling the creativity you seek.

Further Research

We have identified several aspects of our current work that could be extended for future studies. Someone interested in a particular content area, for example, could investigate the uses of the themes in teaching math or language arts. Additionally, the themes could be used more intentionally in certain combinations: what happens if perceptivity and imagination are used to explore a big topic such as photosynthesis? It would also be fruitful to more fully understand students' responses to lessons that contain the aesthetic themes. Furthermore, teachers who plan their curriculum together in teams may want to conduct an action research project in which they create lessons and share outcomes with each other. As we continue our own research on the aesthetic themes, we hope to understand them more fully so that they might provide conduits to greater creativity in teaching and in learning.

Notes

1. Visit http://www.think360arts.org for more information on this organization.

2. See Uhrmacher, "Toward a Theory of Aesthetic Learning Experiences," for further discussion on the theoretical grounding for these themes.

3. We are grateful to Barbara Barnhart, director of education for Think 360 Arts, for synthesizing the ideas for the workshop structure from a number of artists and thinkers that include Patty Ortiz, Jane Page, and Bruce Uhrmacher.

4. Visit http://www.yacenter.org/ for more information about International Towne and the Young Americans Center for Financial Education.

5. Although we discuss in the first section of the paper the three elements of creating a safe environment, providing participants with ownership over their own learning, and modeling the process or activity, we did not specifically ask the research participants to incorporate them. Therefore, we do not use them as points of analysis for their teaching but instead focus upon their use of the aesthetic themes.

6. Admittedly, we do not know whether students' perceptivity was truly expanded. We would need to conduct interviews with students to find this out. But what we do know is that the opportunity for perceptivity is there.

7. For a detailed description of Claire's work, see Moroye & Uhrmacher, "The Aesthetic Themes of Education."

References

Beardsley, M. (1966). *Aesthetics from classical Greece to the present*. Tuscaloosa, AL: University of Alabama Press.

Cisneros, S. (1984). *The house on mango street*. New York: Vintage.

Coleridge, S. (1983). Biographia literaria. In J. Engell & W. J. Bate (Eds.), *The collected works of Samuel Taylor Coleridge*. Princeton, NJ: Princeton University Press.

Csikszentmihalyi, M., & Robinson, R. (1990). *The art of seeing: An interpretation of the aesthetic encounter*. Malibu, CA: J. Paul Getty Center for Education in the Arts.

Dewey, J. (1934). *Art as experience*. New York: Perigee Books.

Eisner, E. (1997). *The enlightened eye: Qualitative inquiry and the enhancement of educational practice*. Columbus, OH: Prentice Hall.

Eisner, E. (2002). *The educational imagination: On the design and evaluation of school programs* (3rd ed.). New York: Macmillan College.

Madeja, S. S., & Onuska, S. (1977). *Through the arts to the aesthetic*. St. Louis, MO: CEMREL.

Moroye, C. M., & Uhrmacher, P. B. (2009). The aesthetic themes of education. *Curriculum and Teaching Dialogue, 55*(1&2).

Perlov, H. (1998). *Inspiring change in teacher practice: A qualitative study of an aesthetic education summer institute.* Unpublished doctoral dissertation. University of Denver.

Schiller, F. (1967). *On the aesthetic education of man, in a series of letters* (E. M. Wilkinson & L. A. Willoughby, Trans.). Oxford, UK: Oxford University Press.

Uhrmacher, P. B. (2009). Toward a theory of aesthetic learning experiences. *Curriculum Inquiry, 39*(5).

Uhrmacher, P. B., & Matthews, J. (2005). *Intricate palette: Working the ideas of Elliot Eisner.* Columbus, Ohio: Merrill Prentice Hall.

CHAPTER 5

Child Study/Lesson Study

A CATALYST FOR TEACHER CURIOSITY

Herbert P. Ginsburg
Columbia University

Joan V. Mast
Scotch Plains–Fanwood Public Schools

Merrie Snow
Scotch Plains–Fanwood Public Schools

Herbert P. Ginsburg, PhD, is a Jacob H. Schiff Foundation professor of psychology and education, Teachers College, Columbia University, New York. Dr. Ginsburg's research interests include the development of mathematical thinking (with particular attention to young children and disadvantaged populations) and the assessment of cognitive function. He has developed mathematics curricula for young children, tests of mathematical thinking, and video workshops to enhance teachers' understanding of student understanding of mathematics.

Joan V. Mast, EdD, is the district mathematics supervisor (K–12), Scotch Plains–Fanwood Public Schools, Scotch Plains, New Jersey. Dr. Mast holds a doctorate from Teachers College, Columbia University. Her research focus includes creating environments in schools where teachers' individual classrooms are laboratories for professional learning and the data source for continuous feedback, reflection, and improvement.

Merrie Snow, MA, is the elementary mathematics and science supervisor, Scotch Plains–Fanwood Public Schools, Scotch Plains, New Jersey. Ms. Snow collaborates with teachers to develop questioning strategies for clinical interviews. Ms. Snow's research focus is to improve student assessment to inform teachers' daily practice. She has created an extensive local professional development video library of clinical interviews addressing students' understanding of mathematics.

ABSTRACT

This chapter describes how teacher engagement in professional learning communities (PLCs) serves as a means of improving student learning as well as providing a tool for instructional improvement. Child study/lesson study, a new form of professional development, combines significant components of Japanese lesson study with clinical interviews to heighten teacher curiosity to understand student thinking. Student responses during these interviews often challenge teacher assumptions of how students make sense of a given lesson. Furthermore, teachers benefit from clinical interview outcomes in which the focus is on eliciting and analyzing student thinking. Vignettes from students (K–4) are discussed to illustrate how clinical interviews influence meaningful professional curiosity and discourse within PLCs. The vignettes were selected from approximately sixty interviews conducted and videotaped in an exploratory study in a suburban district in New Jersey.

The Need for a Change in Teachers' Practice

Teachers today are faced with an extraordinary set of challenges, including teaching all students content that was once reserved for an elite group of talented students. Additionally, teachers are strongly influenced by their own experience in school, having been immersed in the type of school system that the reform efforts are attempting to change, thus creating a cycle of teaching as they were taught. For example, the mathematics education that many teachers experienced in elementary and secondary school was typically procedural and fragmented, rather than conceptual and connected (RAND Mathematics Study Panel, Ball et al., 2003). Furthermore, teacher preparation has worked under the premise that elementary and middle school teachers learned all of the mathematics that they needed to teach during their own schooling (Conference Board of Mathematical Sciences, 2000). Yet many mathematics teachers today are being asked to teach for understanding rather than to simply teach mathematics as a set of procedures as they themselves were taught. The resulting challenge is to convince both teachers and other stakeholders such as parents that there is a need to change current practice in order to achieve more effective instruction. To accomplish these goals, teachers will need to experience transformative change, including a shift in deeply held beliefs and patterns of practice. A new paradigm in professional development is needed in order to achieve transformative change. The old norms of teaching have included autonomy, privacy, and noninterference. Now, opening the classroom for collaboration is a high priority, but it is also a process that includes many challenges (Little, 1990).

Professional Development and Curiosity

Sonnenberg and Goldberg (1992) stressed the need to foster curiosity in workplace learning situations because it encourages employees to investigate and learn. Similarly, Thompson and Zeuli (1999) maintain that professional development experiences must create a high level of cognitive dissonance for the teacher. This dissonance should be embedded in the teachers' own practice of teaching. To this end, teachers will have an increased openness to change. Child study/lesson study (CS/LS) situates teacher professional development directly in "live" lessons with "real" students. CS/LS provides two arenas where teachers can experience what Loewenstein (1994) describes as an information gap, where an individual becomes aware of a difference between "what one knows and what one wants to know" (p. 87). The first place where this information gap might occur is within the research lesson itself. In this case, what a teacher expects to happen with respect to student learning after implementing a lesson is different from the actual outcome. Secondly, as a result of the students' clinical interviews, teachers again often experience an information gap. In this case, the clinical interview results often challenge teachers' egocentric views on how students learn what they teach. Additionally, students often show different levels of competency in this setting from what a teacher anticipated.

In this job-embedded professional learning environment, teachers are motivated to explore the impact of their pedagogy on student learning. For example, we observed a fourth-grade teacher who taught her class the standard procedure for adding fractions. The students practiced the procedure in class, and they experienced success on an assessment. After a few weeks had elapsed, students were asked to add $1/2 + 1/3$. Some students got an answer of $2/5$. The teacher needed to make sense of why the learning did not endure for students who appeared to be successful when the rule was initially taught. The teacher was faced in a very direct way with the issue of determining when students really understand what has been taught.

CS/LS can provide opportunities for discussion and support that teachers need to think through dissonant experiences such as these and address the complexities of effective instruction. Furthermore, the incongruities and challenges that the teacher experiences can serve as a catalyst, raising curiosity for the CS/LS participants, perhaps prompting questions to find out what went awry in the development of student understanding. CS/LS provides a structure to support the systematic study of the complexities of classroom teaching, including the interdependence between pedagogy, content, and student learning outcomes.

Lesson Study

Lesson study is a specialized form of PLC that the Japanese have been implementing successfully for decades to transform Japanese education. In fact, lesson study has been credited for moving the dominant instructional model from "teaching as telling" to "teaching for understanding" (Lewis & Tsuchida, 1998). In the *Teaching Gap*, Stigler and Hiebert (1999) describe lesson study as a process where groups of teachers meet regularly to work on the design, implementation, and improvement of "research lessons." They recognize that the form can vary; however, they include the following steps that typify the process: defining the problem, planning the lesson, teaching the lesson, evaluating and reflecting on the lesson's effect, revising the lesson, teaching the revised lesson, evaluating and reflecting, and sharing the results. Lesson study, like PLCs, is built on the premise that the most effective place to improve teaching is in the context of a classroom lesson.

We propose that lesson study, particularly "evaluating and reflecting on the lesson's effect," can benefit greatly from intensive use of the clinical interview method. One-on-one clinical interviews with students can be used to help teachers understand how children think about mathematics (Ginsburg, Jacobs, & Lopez, 1998). Combining the "clinical interview" method for assessing children's mathematical knowledge while engaging in a lesson-study process across grade levels may provide the teachers with an invaluable opportunity to use insights into students' mathematical thinking and learning to improve instruction.

Implementing CS/LS

Meaningful implementation of CS/LS requires a combination of teachers who are open to reflect on all aspects of their current practice and how their practice influences student understanding. The nucleus of CS/LS is an intentional emphasis on "developing the mind" to investigate student thinking and understanding across grade levels and using this "formative assessment" to guide the analysis of lessons and improve instruction. The first significant component of CS/LS is the use of a vertical model. The research team is formed of one teacher from each grade level (e.g., K–4). The goal is to have teachers focus on the development of key mathematical concepts across a series of grades. For example, the teachers learn how first-grade addition builds on kindergarten enumeration skills and eventually helps students develop a sense of place value and the base ten system. Recognizing that U.S. teachers are typically generalists rather than content specialists, the vertical CS/LS model helps to address some of the limitations that U.S. teachers experience as a result of not teaching multiple grade levels (Ma, 1999). The vertical model provides opportunities for teachers to experience how the mathematical content, the teaching, and the children's understanding develop across the grade levels.

The second key component of CS/LS is that teachers create lessons using their district curriculum, supporting materials, and their own collective experience. CS/LS can be effective with any curriculum the teachers are required to use or choose to use, including reform curricula. Teachers participating in CS/LS identify a specific topic that is sequenced through grades K–4 (e.g., fractions). Then the teachers and a content specialist discuss the lessons, with emphasis on how the mathematical concept builds across the grade levels. As the lessons are taught, the CS/LS research team engages in a critical analysis based on events observed in the classroom or on insights gained through the clinical interviews with students at each grade level. Through this CS/LS approach, teachers' insights are gained from studying the lesson in action as well as observing students' understanding of the mathematical concepts through the clinical interviews.

The third component is that CS/LS is designed to include a series of "research lessons," one per grade level. This allows the teachers to gain a perspective on the curriculum's scope and sequence as well as on how the prototypical child develops through elementary school. Teachers gain cumulative experience as "researchers" when collecting student data and participating in multiple debriefing sessions.

The final and distinctive component of CS/LS is that clinical interviews are conducted with several students in each grade level after each "research lesson." In our case, an elementary supervisor with extensive elementary teaching experience conducted the interviews. Then each teacher reviewed and analyzed her students' interviews. The teacher shared her insights from the interviews during the debriefing session. Additionally, she selected video segments for viewing and discussion with the research team. The inclusion of the interviews reinforced the significance of students' thinking and learning. When we conducted lesson studies with interviews, teachers found it easier to focus and report on students' understanding. Prior to conducting CS/LS, some teacher discussions began with observations about bulletin boards or about how neat student desks appeared. The introduction of clinical interviews appeared to act as a stimulus for purposeful discourse about student thinking and learning.

Clinical Interview

The work of Freud, Piaget, and Vygotsky provides the theoretical foundation of the clinical interview (Ginsburg, 1997), which has been used widely in psychological and educational research. Piaget's monumental studies of cognitive development rest on the clinical interview method, and modern research in mathematical thinking (Ginsburg, Cannon, Eisenband, & Pappas, 2006) and science education (Clement, 2000) make extensive use of the method. The essential rationale for the method is that uncovering children's thinking requires a flexible, nonstandard approach that probes the individual child's responses in a more flexible way and in greater depth than is possible when using tests or observational methods (Piaget, 1976).

Conducting a series of interviews with students in the same grade and using the same questions provides PLCs with compelling student data to discuss and analyze. This segment demonstrates the interviewer testing a hypothesis and presenting a counterexample while collecting data on one student. The following excerpt provides a concrete example from a clinical interview with a fourth-grader named Sarah, who was identified by her teacher as an exemplary math student. The interviewer set out to investigate students' strategies for comparing the value of fractions. Throughout the interview, Sarah appeared to be adept at understanding the fraction concepts. In fact, because other fourth-grade students struggled with some questions, the interviewer was stretched to challenge Sarah's understanding.

I: Would you tell me what those fractions are?
S: This is one-half, this is one-fourth, and this is one-eighth.
I: Which is the largest of those fractions?
S: One-half.
I: And why is that?
S: Because it has the lowest denominator, and they all have the same numerator.

At this point, Sarah exceeded some of her peers who had been interviewed. Often, when students are developing understanding, they might neglect to consider the numerator when thinking about magnitude. The interviewer proceeded to challenge Sarah with a more complex task, testing the stability and depth of her understanding.

I: So if I show you this set of fractions (3/4 and 5/8), which would you say is the largest?
S: I would say three-fourths.

I: Why would you say three-fourths?

S: Even though it has the smallest numerator, it has a denominator that is really close to it.

I: Oh it is really close to it, so it has something to do with how you view those numbers together.

S: Yeah.

It can be seen from the above segment that this interviewer was testing the hypothesis that students will only consider the denominator when identifying the magnitude of fractions. Sarah demonstrated that she had an evolved understanding, and she could apply rules with flexibility. Of course, the interviewer must decide during the interview when enough evidence has been obtained to make definitive conclusions regarding Sarah's understanding.

The function of the clinical interview in our work is to investigate how students make sense of a particular topic their teacher has recently taught. Clinical interviews provide teachers with powerful feedback on student thinking. Often teachers discover that what they are trying to teach is not necessarily what students are trying to learn, and that teaching should take into account unsuspected strengths and weaknesses of student thinking.

In order to conduct a productive interview, some essential considerations must be addressed. Prior to the clinical interview, the interviewer must have a clear purpose and must develop a task(s) to engage the student in conversation. Additionally, materials must be available to provide students with a means to show their thinking in addition to providing verbal explanations. During the clinical interview, the adult must be mindful of all of the feedback the student provides, including gestures, responses, non-responses, inflections, and so forth. Based on the student's responses to the interview questions, the student and the interviewer together determine the direction of the conversation. At all times the adult is aware of the child's feelings and level of interest. In order to provide the greatest insight into student thinking, throughout the interview, the adult is "thinking on her feet," formulating hypotheses ready to modify or adjust the tasks instantaneously.

The clinical interview is a useful method for collecting data about each student's mathematical thinking and learning. The data collected can provide insight into student thinking as well as create curiosity regarding how students make sense of a given concept. In summary, the main features of the clinical interview include the following components: (1) the interviewer poses a specific (mathematical) task for the child; (2) the interviewer carefully observes the child's behavior and asks him/her to "think out loud" when solving the problem; (3) as the child's thinking unfolds, the interviewer uses implicit or explicit cognitive theory to generate hypotheses concerning underlying strategies and concepts that might explain the child's performance; and (4) the interviewer checks the hypotheses by giving new problems, asking some critical questions and making closer observations. Throughout the process, the interviewer treats the child with respect and crafts questions responsive to each individual case (Ginsburg, 1989).

Vignettes

In order to convey the significance of the clinical interviews to the CS/LS, vignettes of some students' interviews have been included. The students' names have been changed, but their work and the teachers' reactions to viewing their interviews are accurate. Teachers seldom have the opportunity to consider individual student thinking with the same level of intensity as they do through the analysis of clinical interviews in a PLC. As a result, it is a frequent occurrence in this environment for the teachers to discover something new about their students. This new learning shifts the focus of the research lesson from the "teacher-centric" perspective to a student-centered theme. The vivid visual images captured on video, combined with the teachers' personal knowledge of and connection with the students and their families, made this a very powerful component of the CS/LS.

CAN YOU SHOW ME HALF?

Much of our CS/LS work focused on students' understanding of fractions. As a result, the research team devised a series of questions that they wanted students to answer to help better understand students' thinking about fractions. The very first clinical interview began with what teachers thought would be an easy question, asking the student to show half. The question was presented to Lee, a five-year old girl who was looking at eight Unifix cubes scattered in a small group on the carpet. She said she could show half, and she proceeded to bring her hand down perpendicular to the floor dividing the cubes into two groups, with one group made up of two cubes and a second group of six cubes (see figure 5.1, figure 1).

Later as teachers watched the videotape of this clinical interview, the tape was paused after Lee's response to this question. The teachers were asked what they thought about Lee's understanding of half. Most of the teachers agreed that she did not understand half, and they indicated that they were somewhat surprised that she didn't understand this concept, based on what they had taught during the class lesson.

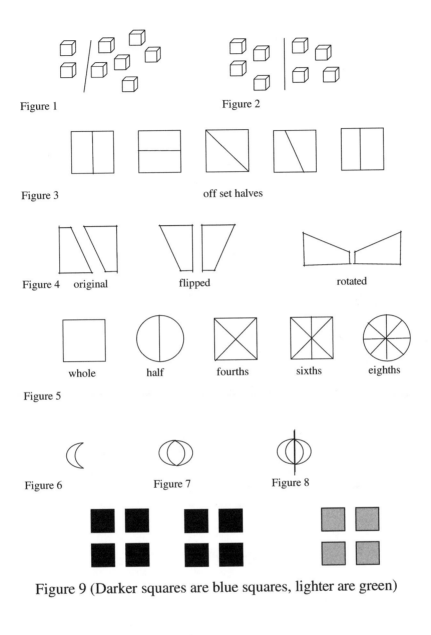

Figure 1

Figure 2

Figure 3

off set halves

Figure 4   original

flipped

rotated

whole

half

fourths

sixths

eighths

Figure 5

Figure 6

Figure 7

Figure 8

Figure 9 (Darker squares are blue squares, lighter are green)

Figure 10 (Darker squares are blue squares, lighter are green)

Figure 5.1   Children's answers to questions proposed.

After this discussion, the teachers continued to watch Lee's interview. The first question was followed with: "Is there another way you can show me half? You can move the cubes if you need to." In response, Lee picked up the cubes and made two separate groups with four cubes in each group (see figure 5.1, figure 2). Now she appeared to have a clear understanding of half. Teachers were curious about Lee's initial answer. After discussion and further investigation with other students, they came to understand that young children identify half based on their personal experiences, which often include cutting something in half. Additionally, teachers realized that they inadvertently contributed to the idea of "cutting in half" with both their visual and verbal representations of half as they talked about half in class discussions. This observation and discussion led teachers to expand and refine their classroom conversations about half.

WHICH OF THESE SHAPES SHOW HALF?

As part of another interview to investigate students' understanding of half using an area model, Joe, a five-year-old kindergarten student, was asked to identify shapes that were cut in half. In each "example of half," the original shape was a square. The bisecting lines for the squares were a vertical, horizontal, diagonal, or an offset diagonal line, with one additional square that was deliberately divided vertically with about a 45 percent to 55 percent division (see figure 5.1, figure 3).

Joe, who the classroom teacher had identified as an excellent mathematical thinker, correctly identified the vertical, horizontal, and diagonal halves. Additionally, he said that the square that was not divided equally was not half. He also said that the square that was divided with the offset diagonal line was not divided in half.

The videotape of the clinical interview was stopped at this point to permit teacher discussions. Teachers viewing this interview were not surprised when Joe said that the square that had the offset diagonal line was not half. During a brief discussion, they did speculate on why he said it wasn't half. Then viewing continued, and Joe was asked, "Why isn't that half?" He was very quiet for several minutes, and then he said, "The shape is wrong." He flipped and rotated one of the shapes until he could form a line of symmetry down the middle (see figure 5.1, figure 4), and then he said, "Now it's half." He returned it to the original position, and he said, "Now it isn't half." After moving the shape around again to several new positions, he found an additional way to arrange the two halves to show another line of symmetry, and he announced, "Now it's half."

Teachers were surprised and amazed by Joe's explanation and his careful reflection as he worked through several different arrangements of the "halves." The teachers wondered how many of their students might have a similar understanding of half. As they discussed Joe's explanation, they identified ways to include visual representations for half that would give students additional opportunities to see half in many different ways. The length of time that Joe took before he responded to the interviewer's question caused some discomfort for the teachers watching the interview. They initially wondered if Joe felt uncomfortable with the silence as the interviewer waited for his response. However, when the teachers saw the results of his thinking, they changed their minds. This interview provided an event in which teachers also discussed the benefit of providing time for students to manipulate the materials so that they could explore various configurations for half.

This same extended wait time phenomena was observed in different ways in CS/LS conducted in four elementary schools. While teachers make it a practice to include wait time before asking for whole class or group responses to their questions during lessons, they indicated that they were less comfortable with extended wait time when working with one student or even in a small group of students. The clinical interviews captured many students' thoughtful responses as the outcome of extended wait time. This result was noted with students of all skill levels.

Wayne, a second-grade student who usually answered most questions very quickly, was silent for a very long time after being asked if he knew another way to name one-half. This question was asked of Wayne following the use of paper cookies that were divided into fractional parts that represented halves, fourths, sixths, and eighths. After what seemed like five minutes but was really only one minute, Wayne got a huge smile on his face, and he said, "Two-fourths is the same as one-half." His enthusiasm and pride in figuring this out was very obvious. His interview prompted the research team teachers to discuss the need to allow students to have enough time to struggle or wrestle with problems as they work to find solutions. The teachers focused on the challenge of waiting long enough to allow students time for thoughtful responses without causing some students to become distressed.

Another discovery aroused teachers' curiosity as they viewed several kindergarten and first-grade interviews that included the question to determine half using area models. Some students did not appear to notice the difference in size between the two "halves" for the square with the 45 percent to 55 percent split. Interestingly, as girls examined the mismatched "halves," they usually picked up the shapes and placed one on top of the other to measure them. Most of the boys used only a visual comparison to make their determination. It must be noted that only seven students participated in this series of questions, so it was not a definitive survey. However, as a result of these observations, teachers were interested in gathering more information about representations of fractions and about gender differences as they worked with their students on future fraction lessons. The teachers recognized that some young students might not have developed the ability to make accurate visual discriminations to enable them to determine equal or unequal parts when the difference in size between two similar shapes is small. Again, the teachers realized the importance of having students manipulate materials to be able to prove their thinking.

IF I WERE A NEW STUDENT IN YOUR CLASS, HOW WOULD YOU HELP ME UNDERSTAND FRACTIONS?

This open-ended question became an important component of every clinical interview that focused on fractions. Kindergarten and first-grade students were asked to help a new student understand half. Older students were asked to help a new student understand fractions in general. The students' responses were very revealing and again prompted teachers to ask additional questions.

One of the most interesting results came from Holly, a second-grade student who appeared to have difficulty with most of the fraction work during the class lesson. She also found it difficult to answer most of the direct questions during the individual student interview. However, when Holly was asked to help the new student understand fractions, she chose to draw the following information on a white board using a dry erase marker (see figure 5.1, figure 5).

As she worked Holly said, "This is the whole. This is half. This is fourths. This is sixths, and this is eighths." While the representation for sixths was not accurate, her general understanding of partitioning the whole into fairly equal parts was clearly explained as she talked while she worked. She also chose to display the fractions from the largest to the smallest, deliberately beginning with the whole.

Holly received daily support for mathematics through special services. She did find it difficult to explain her thinking in whole class settings, and it was also challenging for her to answer the interviewer's direct questions. However, when she had the opportunity to share her understanding in a format of her own choosing, she was very successful at conveying her knowledge. Her attention to detail and her ability to organize and express her own understanding in this open-ended format were very revealing.

After viewing this interview, teachers reflected on the practice of providing more open-ended assessments to gain a clearer understanding of students' working skill levels. They wondered how many of their apparently struggling students would be able to provide the type of detailed, organized responses that Holly had provided with the final interview question. Clinical interviews helped teachers realize that some struggling students may possess greater understanding than they ordinarily display.

Careful examination of some primary students' responses to this question led to an intense review of additional student interviews. Neil, a first-grade student who always appeared to be a divergent thinker and one who was often considered to be "off topic" in class, gave the following explanation to the "new student." He began to tell about half by drawing a crescent moon on the white board as he talked about the sun and the moon. The interviewer almost decided to redirect Neil, thinking that he had misunderstood the question. His initial drawing looked like figure 6 in the set of figures (see figure 5.1, figure 6). He called it a moon and said that it wasn't half. However, he went on to explain his thinking as he added a second crescent moon in reverse to make figure 7 (see figure 5.1, figure 7). Neil called the joined parts a sun and said it showed half. When he was asked to explain half in figure 7, he drew a line down the middle of the "sun" making figure 8 (see figure 5.1, figure 8). Pointing to one side, he said, "This is half."

With extra questions for clarification, it appeared that he did have an understanding of half of a circle, but he chose to relate it to the sun and moon as a way of explaining it to the new student. Neil's unusual drawings and the accompanying narrative distracted the interviewer and the teachers watching the interview from his real understanding of half. The teachers on the research team agreed that in a whole class setting they would not have had time to pursue this unique explanation. They did see this as a pedagogical challenge to find ways to support students who are divergent thinkers.

During the teacher discussions that followed the viewing of these interview questions, teachers acknowledged that they very often think that their students are following along and actually understanding their peers' or teacher's explanations. For some skills and concepts this is an accurate statement. However, the research team teachers recognized that sometimes students make sense of the ideas or skills in unanticipated ways and can have misconceptions that go unnoticed by the teacher. In fact Lynn, a second-grade student, was able to mislead her teacher by enthusiastically saying, "Oh, I get it now." This was brought out when Lynn's evident confusion with fractions was captured during her clinical interview. Later, when Lynn's teacher reviewed the video of the interview, she was very surprised to discover Lynn's misconceptions. The teacher indicated that she knew Lynn was initially having some difficulty with fractions, so she reviewed several of the concepts individually with her after the lesson. At the end of the teacher's explanation, Lynn very cheerfully indicated that she understood. After viewing Lynn's confusion during the interview, her teacher thought Lynn might have a future as an actress, since she was so convincing in her affirmation that she "got it." Again, the teachers wondered how many of their students had managed to temporarily convince them that they understood a skill when they really didn't. This highlighted the need for the use of frequent informal assessments as well as formal ones. Teachers learn from interviewing that just as some students really understand when they seem not to, other students who seem to understand really do not.

PERSISTENCE AND RESILIENCE

The clinical interviews provided vivid images of the personal characteristics that students bring to their learning experiences. In particular, the videos of the clinical interviews aroused teachers' curiosity about how students learn to be persistent and resilient when they encounter challenging problems. Two third-grade students from the same class were interviewed with dramatically different results. George, who often had trouble completing class work in a timely manner, was very persistent during his interview, and he ultimately proved that he had a good grasp of fractional parts of a whole. His classmate Amelia, who usually finished most of her class work quickly and accurately, stopped answering questions during the interview when she encountered a challenging problem. Both of these students had the same teacher and the same classroom experiences, yet their reaction to difficult questions during the interviews were very different. During the discussion that followed the viewing of these interviews, teachers commented that they have found that students who occasionally have to struggle to find solutions seem to acquire the ability to persist at trying to solve problems. Conversely, they felt that students who usually arrive at correct answers easily may or may not have the same ability to be persistent. Teachers wondered why this happens, and they discussed how they might help students become more persistent. Some of their recommendations included praising and publicly valuing student efforts that exemplified persistence. Additionally, they indicated that they needed to provide wait time for students to engage in persistent thought processes. They acknowledged that when a student answers a teacher's questions or calls out an answer, most students stop thinking about the problem. This realization caused some teachers to change the way that they gathered solutions from students.

PROCEDURAL KNOWLEDGE VERSUS CONCEPTUAL KNOWLEDGE

Robert, an articulate third-grade student, was interviewed because his teacher noted that he loved to work on complex math problems. He attended a program after school that focused on extensive practice for procedural math problems using addition, subtraction, multiplication, and division. As a result, he was able to give equivalent fractions by multiplying the numerator and denominator of a fraction by the same number. It took very little time for Robert to solve this type of problem. During the interview, Robert was asked to use paper squares to show equivalent fractions for groups. When he was asked to use blue and green squares to show a group of twelve squares with three-fourths of the group using one color and one-fourth of the group using the other color, he displayed eight blue squares and four green squares (see figure 5.1, figure 9).

Robert was asked to explain his thinking, and he confidently pointed to the eight blue squares, indicating that the group was three-fourths and the other group with green squares was one-fourth. He maintained that this was the correct solution without being able to give more specific information to explain why. Finally, when he was asked to isolate the four-fourths, Robert counted the groups of four and recognized that he had only three groups. He thought about this and modified his solution by changing the squares to nine blue and three green (see figure 5.1, figure 10).

Robert's teacher said that this interview helped her resolve the differences that he exhibited in task performance in class. She indicated that sometimes his work was excellent, and sometimes he seemed confused by skills that he seemed to be able to perform on the preceding day. This discussion gave the members of the research team an opportunity to reflect on and discuss ways to support students' learning. They recognized that at various times students might appear to be confident of their skill levels based on their use of procedures to solve problems. However, when students forget the procedure or don't know which procedure to use, they may not have the conceptual knowledge to use problem-solving strategies to find a solution.

Summary

Over the years, we have conducted ten elementary mathematics lesson studies, with additional studies at the middle school and high school. Our first four lesson studies did not include clinical interviews. When we added clinical interviews to the research studies, the change in teacher discourse was immediately productive and positive. As a result, all of the successive lesson studies have included clinical interviews and eventually became known as child study/lesson study. Over time, we have managed to create CS/LS "envy" with teachers now requesting to be part of a research team. They willingly open their classrooms to present and reflect on public lessons. They look forward to discussing the lessons, curriculum, materials, and teaching practices with their colleagues in an effort to continue to improve student thinking and learning. The CS/LS continues to spark their curiosity, and it has become a part of the school culture.

NEXT STEPS

Those already doing lesson study might want to add some of the child study features, particularly interviews. Those not doing it should try it out. Exploratory research needs to document the practices of child study/lesson study in great detail and their effects on teacher thinking and classroom teaching. Eventually, large-scale rigorous research needs to be conducted on these issues—changes in (a) teacher understanding of kids' learning and thinking, (b) teacher understanding of math education and pedagogy, (c) actual teaching in the classroom, and (d) improvement in student math learning.

CONCLUSION

Our work with teachers suggests that child study/lesson study is a powerful method of professional development that promotes teacher curiosity. This model provides a well-defined structure to transform classrooms in all content areas into laboratories where educators closely examine teaching and learning.

References

Clement, J. (2000). Analysis of clinical interviews: Foundations and model viability. In A. E. Kelly & R. A. Lesh (Eds.), *Handbook of research design in mathematics and science education* (pp. 547–589). Mahwah, NJ: Lawrence Erlbaum Associates.

Conference Board of Mathematical Sciences. (2000). *The mathematical education of teachers. Issues in mathematics education* (Vol. 11). Providence, RI: The American Mathematical Society.

Ginsburg, H. P. (1989). *Children's arithmetic: How they learn it and how you teach it.* Austin, TX: Pro-Ed.

Ginsburg, H. P. (1997). *Entering the child's mind: The clinical interview in psychological research and practice.* Cambridge, UK: Cambridge University Press.

Ginsburg, H. P., Cannon, J., Eisenband, J. G., & Pappas, S. (2006). Mathematical thinking and learning. In K. McCartney & D. Phillips (Eds.), *Handbook of Early Child Development* (pp. 208–229). Oxford, UK: Blackwell.

Ginsburg, H. P., Jacobs, S. F., & Lopez, L. S. (1998). *The teacher's guide to flexible interviewing in the classroom: Learning what children know about math.* Boston, MA: Allyn and Bacon.

Lewis, C., & Tsuchida, I. (1998). A lesson is like a swiftly flowing river: How research lessons improve Japanese education. *American Educator, 22(*4), 14–17, 50–52.

Little, J. W. (1990). The Persistence of Privacy: Autonomy and initiative in teachers' professional relations. *Teachers College Record, 91*(4), 509–536.

Loewenstein, G. (1994). The psychology of curiosity: A review and reinterpretation. *Psychological Bulletin, 116*(1), 75–98.

Ma, L. (1999). *Knowing and teaching elementary mathematics: Teacher's understanding of fundamental mathematics in China and the United States.* Mahwah, NJ: Erlbaum.

Piaget, J. (1976). *The child's conception of the world* (J. Tomlinson & A. Tomlinson, Trans.). Totowa, NJ: Littlefield, Adams & Co.

RAND Mathematics Study Panel, & Ball, D. L. (2003). *Mathematical proficiency for all students: Toward a strategic research and development program in mathematics education.* Santa Monica, CA: RAND.

Sonnenberg, F., & Goldberg, B. (1992). Encouraging employee-led change through constructive learning processes. *Journal of Business Strategy, 13*(6), 53–57.

Stigler, J. W., & Hiebert, J. (1999). *The teaching gap: Best ideas from the world's teachers for improving education in the classroom.* New York: Free Press.

Thompson, C. L., & Zeuli, J. S. (1999). The frame and the tapestry: Standards-based reform and professional development. In L. Darling-Hammond & G. Sykes (Eds.), *Teaching as the learning profession: Handbook of policy and practice* (pp. 341–375). San Francisco, CA: Jossey-Bass.

CHAPTER 6

Nurturing a Creative Curiosity for K–2 Mathematics Teaching

LESSONS FROM THE DREAMKEEPERS

Patricia L. Marshall
North Carolina State University

Allison W. McCulloch
North Carolina State University

Jessica T. DeCuir-Gunby
North Carolina State University

Patricia L. Marshall, EdD, is a professor in the Department of Curriculum and Instruction. Her research focuses on the impact of culture and race in teacher development and the teaching-learning process. She has published work in *Action in Teacher Education*, *Journal of Teacher Education*, and *The Journal of Educational Research*.

Allison W. McCulloch, PhD, is an assistant professor of mathematics education in the Department of Mathematics, Science, and Technology Education. Her current research interests include perceptions of how the use of technology tools impact mathematical experiences and understanding and the complexities involved in teaching conceptually challenging mathematics in urban schools.

Jessica T. DeCuir-Gunby, PhD, is an associate professor of educational psychology in the Department of Curriculum and Instruction. Her research and theoretical interests include racial identity, mixed methods research, critical race theory, and emotions. Her work has been featured in *Educational Researcher*, *Educational Psychologist*, and the *Review of Educational Research*.

ABSTRACT

This chapter describes a multiyear research project designed to promote and study how kindergarten, first-, and second-grade teachers adopted a critical constructivist orientation to early mathematics teaching and learning. The primary goals of the study were to enhance teachers' mathematics content knowledge and to promote professional dispositions toward identifying and drawing upon children's outside-of-school experiences with mathematics in order to promote deep understanding of early number concepts. Critical reflection on the outcome of the project revealed that some participants developed what the authors characterize as a creative curiosity about their teaching. It is evidenced by the emergence of an instructional mindset and professional identity that is aligned with tenets of culturally relevant pedagogy and a mathematics teaching and learning orientation identified as conception-based perspective. The authors draw upon case studies from their research project to describe the nature of creative curiosity and implications for its promotion in teacher education.

To enter the classroom of the typical primary-level teacher is to enter a den of creativity. From imaginative student management techniques to ingenious uses of common household items, primary-level teachers can inspire admiration for their ability to create learning environments that excite young children about school. Yet accompanying this personal creativity can be evidence of a mundane pedagogy that falls short in its ability to promote deep understanding of elemental concepts endemic of primary level curricula. This is especially apparent in relation to mathematics. Therefore, as part of a multiyear professional development research project,[1] we sought to harness the creativity common among many primary-level teachers and to channel it toward professional introspection. Our goal was to foster "creative curiosity" about early mathematics teaching and learning.

In this chapter, we provide an overview of our research project, beginning with a definition of creative curiosity extrapolated from aspects of the theoretical framework. Next, we describe our research methods and intervention, followed by an analysis of case study data from our project that illustrates the implementation of creative curiosity in the primary grade context. Finally, we conclude with a discussion of the implications our findings present for teacher professional development vis-à-vis cultivation of the curious and creative mind in teaching early mathematics for deep understanding.

Nurturing Mathematics Dreamkeepers: A Professional Development Research Project

Teaching in today's schools is a complex intellectual activity perhaps surpassed only by the challenges involved in creating high-quality professional development to improve that teaching. The list of factors that contribute to the complexity of contemporary classroom teaching is long, and scholars agree that at its very top is the ever-increasing diversity among student populations (Hollins & Guzman, 2005).

Although diversity among students is increasing, there is a relative lack of diversity within the teacher population (Zumwalt & Craig, 2008). In light of this contrast, it is widely accepted that contemporary teachers need to acquire understanding of how the diverse cultural orientations, worldviews, and experiences children bring to school impact the teaching-learning process. A primary reason teachers need to learn about the impact of culture is that children draw upon what they already know to make sense of what they are taught in schools. Indeed, a number of scholars report that the teachers who are most successful with nonmainstream students are those who have developed facility in drawing upon students' outside-of-school experiences to promote understanding of school content (Boykin, Jagers, Ellison, & Albury, 1997; Deyhle, 1983; Ladson-Billings, 1994; Lipka, 1991; Thompson, 2004; Nasir, Hand, & Taylor, 2008). It was our own curiosity about culture, mathematics, and professional identity development that prompted us to begin work in September 2005 on Nurturing Mathematics Dreamkeepers (NMD), a study of the professional development of kindergarten, first-, and second-grade teachers.

The NMD project was an examination of how primary-level teachers understand and adopt standards-based teaching practices (National Council of Teachers of Mathematics, 2000) that promote children's conceptual understanding of the big ideas in early mathematics. Additionally, the project explored how teachers understand the impact of culture on the teaching-learning process and how they adapt tenets of culturally relevant pedagogy (grounded in knowledge of their own and their students' cultural ways of being, worldviews, and tendencies toward learning) in their mathematics instruction.

Our research plan was ambitious in that an aim of NMD was to facilitate an epistemological shift in the pedagogical orientations of K–2 teachers (Simon, Tzur, Heinz, & Kinzel, 2004) and, thereby, promote (provoke) changes in instructional behaviors and pedagogical worldviews. We theorized that the degree to which such a shift did occur would be attributable, in part, to the teachers' own enhanced understandings of mathematics. Based on their analysis of their own teaching and evaluation of their students' mathematical understandings, our goal was for the teachers themselves to perceive a need to alter (or change outright) their pedagogy. Such a change would involve replacing practices characterized by telling and demonstrating procedures with a pedagogy in which they would thoughtfully: (a) tease out and affirm children's out-of-school mathematics experiences, (b) recognize the form and function of children's emerging understandings of mathematics "domain" knowledge (Nasir, Hand, & Taylor, 2008), and (c) orchestrate learning moments (informed by the children's own learning goals) that promote deep mathematical understanding.

In order to promote children's conceptual understanding in mathematics, most primary-level teachers need to enhance their own content knowledge and skills and adopt different dispositions toward the teaching of mathematics (Ball, 2000; Borko, 2004; Ma, 1999). This means these teachers have to muster the professional (as well as the personal) courage to look squarely at their own experiences with the subject and revisit their own mathematics story. Similarly, teachers must acquire what we term a "creative curiosity" that prompts them to critically question and evaluate whether they are shaping the emerging mathematics stories of young learners in a manner that will facilitate future learning of more complex concepts and operations. For many primary-level teachers, reflection of this type can induce discomfort and anxiety, yet it can also constitute a symbolic professional emancipation.

PROMOTING CREATIVE CURIOSITY AMONG K–2 TEACHERS

The NMD project sought to provide a safe space for K–2 teachers to try on and possibly adopt a creative curiosity about their professional work. This meant that unlike previous professional development sessions in which many of the teachers had participated, NMD offered few "make and take" opportunities. Instead, NMD challenged the teachers to identify gaps in their own content knowledge and grapple with the consequences these gaps present for their students' future mathematics learning opportunities. Thus, teachers learned that to be part of NMD was to critically recognize that K–2 teaching has implications for the life chances of students, and, thereby, it constitutes sociopolitical activity (Haberman, 1995; hooks, 1994; Kincheloe, 2004).

Our definition of creative curiosity, therefore, relates to a professional view of self as well as a pedagogical orientation. When it comes to the teaching-learning process, creatively curious teachers are simultaneously confident in what they know and aware of what they do not know. Most importantly, they have the courage to question and grapple with both. To illustrate how creative curiosity was imbedded into the NMD project, we extrapolate from the two foci of the study, multicultural education and mathematics education.

MULTICULTURAL EDUCATION AS FOUNDATION FOR PROFESSIONAL IDENTITY AND HABIT OF MIND

An important feature of NMD was that the teachers were required to engage in ongoing professional reflection and introspection about the teaching-learning process. In preparation for this intellectual work, they participated in a series of conversations about the nature of teacher professionalism and professional identity. They explored what professionalism meant to them, how it manifests among classroom teachers, and how the professional differs from the nonprofessional or "semi-skilled technician" in a classroom setting. Ultimately, the teachers were invited to take a stand on their own status and professional identity.

These discussions about professional identity were situated in the context of the NMD research goal, which we informed the teachers was high-quality mathematics instruction for all students, with a particular focus on African American youngsters. Hence, our teachers became knowledgeable about the pervasiveness of innumeracy within the US (Paulos, 1988) and the international studies and national reports that provide chilling evidence that a high percentage of American students do not achieve a level of mathematical understanding needed to cope in today's increasingly technological society (National Center for Education Statistics, 1985, 1996; National Commission on Excellence in Education, 1983).

On an intuitive level, the teachers seemed to know that widespread underachievement in mathematics negatively impacts the larger society, and it thwarts many individuals' life chances by foreclosing access to higher education and to high-status professions (Gutstein, 2003; Moses & Cobb, 2001; National Council of Teachers of Mathematics, 2000; Paulos, 1988; Secada, 1992). Similarly, they were made aware that mathematics underachievement is particularly severe among African Americans. It was with this backdrop that we invited them to embrace the professional identity of culturally relevant pedagogue.

Culturally relevant pedagogy was one of the two organizing constructs in the theoretical framework for NMD; thus, cultural relevance is integral to our definition of creative curiosity. In the book *The Dreamkeepers: Successful Teachers of African American Children*, Ladson-Billings (1994) defined culturally relevant pedagogy (CRP) as a professional ideology in which teachers establish a success ethos in their classrooms that "allows African American students to choose academic excellence yet still identify with African and African American culture" (p. 17).

The professional ideology of CRP has three primary tenets: high academic achievement, cultural competency, and sociopolitical awareness. Teachers who effectively promote the achievement and overall academic success of their students use an array of resources and presentation styles (Foster, 1994, 1995) that align with their students' unique learning styles or tendencies. In short, teachers exhibit both curiosity (to learn multiple ways of presenting content and to learn about the extant knowledge their students bring to the teaching-learning context) and creativity (to incorporate multiple resources and presentation styles) in order to function as a critical pedagogue.

Since it is tailored to the needs and experiences of students, CRP-inspired instruction in one classroom may look different from that in another classroom. Nevertheless, all teachers whose pedagogy exhibits cultural relevance incorporate their students' cultural realities into instruction, and in so doing, they enhance students' interest in and success with academic learning. Gay (2002) reports that a critical characteristic of such teachers is that they do not allow students the "option to fail."

Cultural competency in CRP represents teachers' ability to "capitalize on the cultural practices and sensibilities of their students" (Nasir, Hand, & Taylor, 2008, p. 219), whereas, it also speaks to teachers' introspective capacities to recognize themselves as cultural beings. In other words, this second tenet of CRP requires an inquisitive (curious) mind on the part of the teacher that prompts reflection about one's own frame of reference and its impact on student learning. Teachers who embrace CRP recognize that without constant vigilance (in the form of self-reflection buoyed by professional curiosity about the impact of their teaching), they can either enhance or diminish the learning experience for different students through their (the teachers') own actions.

In order to create an affirming learning environment for all students, teachers must learn about and utilize the cultural frames of reference of their students in instruction. Therefore, as is evident in their pursuit of high academic achievement, culturally competent teachers are inherently curious about their own cultural ways as well as the ways of the students they teach.

Finally, CRP, as sociopolitical consciousness, relates to teachers' orientations toward status, resource, and power differentials among diverse groups in society. Put differently, CRP teachers openly acknowledge that demographic characteristics such as race, class, and gender, more commonly than not, do matter in gaining access to high quality schooling. Despite changes in society, the blight of bigotry in its various forms continues to taint many conventions of schooling; consequently, opportunities to learn for some children are thwarted in the very schools they attend (Darling-Hammond, 2004).

Teachers with a CRP identity find inventive ways to act individually and in collaboration with colleagues, parents/families, community members, and students to neutralize the impact of features of schooling that perpetuate inequality. In short, adoption of a CRP professional identity demands creativity because it requires teachers to think (and act) in imaginative and unconventional ways about doing school.

A CRITICAL PEDAGOGICAL ORIENTATION TO MATHEMATICS TEACHING AND LEARNING

In addition to reflecting upon their professional identities, the NMD project required teachers to reflect on the teaching-learning process, specifically the teaching and learning of mathematics. The teachers participated in activities that pushed them to analyze their own knowledge of mathematics, what it means to understand mathematics, and how students construct specific mathematical meaning. It was through their participation in these cognitively demanding experiences that the teachers were challenged to become critically aware of how they themselves engaged with mathematical tasks and to compare their experiences to what they thought K–2 students might experience on appropriately difficult tasks involving the same concept.

Most of the NMD teachers, like many K–2 teachers, were lacking a deep understanding of elementary mathematics concepts (e.g., the base ten system, equality, early algebra). As such, it was risky for the NMD teachers to analyze their own mathematical knowledge. On a daily basis in their professional environments, most of these teachers were teaching a subject with which they did not feel especially comfortable. To do so required creativity in the ways that they circumvented their own mathematical deficiencies while attempting to provide opportunities for their students to construct their own mathematical knowledge.

Simply by agreeing to take part in the NMD project, these teachers exhibited curiosity about mathematics itself: they were curious to learn more; although, initially they were not aware of the extent to which they would be guided through analyses of their own mathematical knowledge, skill, and thinking. In this regard, the project learning sessions provided the teachers with a safe space to think critically about their mathematical understanding as it developed over time while also linking their experiences to their students. Our goal was to promote a conception-based perspective of mathematics teaching and learning which served as the complementary organizing construct to culturally relevant pedagogy in the theoretical framework for the NMD project.

A conception-based perspective (CPB) characterizes teachers who operate from the assumption that a student's mathematical reality is not independent of that student's ways of knowing and acting, that what a student sees, understands, and learns is constrained and afforded by what that student already knows, and that mathematical learning is a process of transformation of one's knowing and ways of acting (Simon, Tzur, Heinz, Kinzel, & Smith, 2000, p. 584). In action, this means that the teacher recognizes that students must construct meanings for mathematical ideas on the basis of extant conceptions that may be quite different from those of the teacher (Tzur, 2002).

It is through CBP that teachers can think about knowledge development as well as the act of teaching. To hold a conception-based perspective of learning and teaching requires that one be both creative and curious. Simon et al. (2000) point out that this perspective represents a difficult shift in the ways one thinks about students' understanding. Teachers must let go of the notion that "we understand what we see" and recognize that "we see what we understand" (p. 585). For teachers to gain insight into the development of their students' current conceptions, they must be curious about what the students "see" (perceive) and creative in the ways (i.e., methods, strategies, and techniques) they employ to collect this information.

Thus, we view creative curiosity as a professional identity that requires teachers to be secure in *and* uncomfortable with the extent of what they know about teaching and learning. Because of this seemingly paradoxical reality, such teachers can experience (and they welcome) what might be termed "transgressive moments" (hooks, 1994) in which they may "act out." It is through actual or vicarious acting out that such teachers become inquisitive about possibilities in their pedagogy (curious), and they seek ways to work around or subvert business-as-usual teaching by becoming inventive (creative) in their own practice.

Creative curiosity in the NMD project represented a professional identity and a set of dispositions grounded in acceptance of teaching as intellectual activity informed by critical understanding of the multiple and sometimes conflicting contexts in which it occurs. Teachers with such sensibilities are necessarily curious because they must continually seek knowledge and understanding (in the case of NMD, through a conception-based pedagogical orientation) about context and meaning making as they relate to student learning.

The Dreamkeepers Project Methodology

The previous section described how creative curiosity was manifested through the two major theoretical frameworks that served as the basis for the NMD study. This section describes how the research methodology was designed to capture the development of the creative curiosity we sought to promote among the K–2 teachers who participated in the project. In this study, we employed a mixed methods approach, which is defined as "research in which the investigator collects and analyzes data, integrates the findings, and draws inferences using both qualitative and quantitative approaches or methods in a single study or program of inquiry" (Tashakkori & Creswell, 2007, p. 4). Ironically, a mixed methods approach would seem to exemplify creative curiosity in that it uses the best or most appropriate (and perhaps unconventional) research tools to address a research problem instead of strictly adhering to traditional methods that either a qualitative or quantitative research paradigm would dictate.

RESEARCH DESIGN AND PARTICIPANTS

The NMD project was a longitudinal, quasi-experimental study consisting of three treatment, or intervention, groups and one control, or standard practice, group. The intervention groups were organized into three levels called cohorts. Cohort I teachers participated in the project for three years while cohorts II and III participated for two years and one year respectively. Each cohort received the project intervention, while the standard practice or control group did not receive any intervention. The intervention involved approximately ninety hours of professional development delivered via four retreats[2] over the course of each project year. Retreats were structured for teachers to explore big ideas in K–2 mathematics along with tenets of culturally relevant pedagogy. In general, retreat activities were intended to strengthen teachers' mathematics content knowledge, understanding of the K–2 mathematics curriculum, children's thinking about mathematics, and the impact of cultural factors on the overall teaching-learning process.

Recruitment for NMD was school-based in that targeted schools, rather than individual teachers, were solicited for participation. Schools were chosen based upon several criteria, including a diverse student population consisting of at least 30 percent African American and 30 percent white American, a documented mathematics achievement gap between African American and white American students, and Title I designation. In addition, participating schools had to demonstrate a strong commitment to the improvement of mathematics achievement for all children. Although these were our school participation criteria, due to ongoing, district-wide efforts to maintain racial and ethnic balance throughout the school district, the student population demographics in all of our project schools changed to some degree throughout the course of NMD. By the end of the project, some of our project schools did not meet the original project requirements.

In the initial design of the study, our target was to recruit two teachers per grade in each of two or three consecutive target grade levels (i.e., K and 1st, 1st and 2nd, or K, 1st, and 2nd) to participate in cohort I. The goal was to identify a minimum of four or a maximum of six teachers per school. Then, for each subsequent year of the project, two additional teachers at each participating grade level were to be added. By the end of the project, there were to be a minimum of twelve teachers per school.

Same-grade pairs of teachers were required because the participants were to serve as "buddies" or same-grade professional peers within year I of the project. In the second year, the plan was to create cross-cohort, same-grade buddies with each cohort I teacher taking on a more complex role in year II by becoming "mentor" to a same-grade cohort II peer. Buddy teachers were to observe each other's teaching as well as participate in guided reflection sessions regarding their mathematics lessons. The reflection aspect was essential to the project because one of the goals was to help teachers understand their instructional decisions. But despite valiant attempts on our part, the project schools were not able to meet all our requirements. For example, because we could not implement our original plan for the number of cohort I schools, we re-configured the buddy structure so that in a few cases teachers worked as triads. Also, one project school had nine teachers in cohort I, no teachers in cohort II, and two teachers in cohort III. Consequently, after the first year, buddies were organized across cohorts, and in a few cases across grade levels within a school.

NMD participants (cohorts I–III) were provided a $1,000 stipend per year of participation, school district–based professional renewal credits, and support for National Board certification, if desired. Because of the reduced time commitment, control group teachers received $250 for their participation. Although the project involved sixty-five teachers from seven different schools by the 2007–08 school year, the data reported in this chapter focuses on two cohort I teachers, Rahquia and Johnetta.[3] A detailed description of cohort I, including the featured teachers and their respective schools, is provided later in this chapter.

DATA SOURCES AND DATA COLLECTION PROCEDURES

The project included multiple data sources, most of which were designed specifically for NMD. Some of these data sources (e.g., teacher dispositions questionnaire) were included at the start of our data collection, whereas others were refined or newly incorporated (e.g., one-on-one interviews) in subsequent years of the project. Although the project involved various sources, the data reported in this discussion focuses exclusively on the teacher dispositions questionnaire, videotaped mathematics lessons, and interviews. The following sections provide a brief explanation of each of these sources.

Teacher Dispositions Questionnaire

The NMD teacher dispositions questionnaire was designed specifically for the project, and its purpose was to capture teachers' dispositions (habits of mind) regarding the impact of culture on the teaching and learning of mathematics. This instrument consists of two sections: participant background information (twenty demographic items) and mathematics-culture teaching dispositions (twenty-four items on a five-point Likert scale). The subscales of the mathematics-culture teaching dispositions sections include parental role in schooling, student background, and affirming and valuing community. Teachers completed this questionnaire at the beginning and end of each school year they participated in the NMD project.

Videotaped Mathematics Lessons

For each teacher, two consecutive mathematics lessons were videotaped four times a year (twice each semester) by the project research assistants. Teachers were informed to teach a typical mathematics lesson with lessons averaging thirty to forty-five minutes. Also, teachers working as NMD buddies were required to observe each other teaching during the recorded lesson sessions. These teaching/observation sessions served as the focus of the post-teaching guided reflection sessions.

Interviews

Semi-structured interviews (Rubin & Rubin, 2005) were collected at the beginning and end of the school year. The interviews were used to help us gain a better understanding of individual teachers' dispositions regarding K–2 mathematics and the role or place of culture therein. The interviews were thirty minutes to one hour in length and were conducted at free periods before, during, or after school on each participant's school campus.

Data Analysis

In order to best illustrate the participants' development of creative curiosity, a case study approach was chosen. Utilizing case studies allowed us to "investigate real-life events in their natural settings" (Yin, 2004, p. xii). For the purposes of this study, we examined events and responses of two NMD teachers with similar project experiences yet different project outcomes. In creating the two cases, we analyzed the teacher dispositions questionnaire, videotaped mathematics lessons (through lesson mapping and rubric), and interviews.

Teacher Dispositions Questionnaire

For this discussion, we extracted teachers' responses from specific demographic items from the surveys administered during fall 2005 and spring 2008. We utilized these particular administrations in order to help illustrate the participants' thinking and experiences at the beginning and the end of the project.

Lesson Mapping

The act of "mapping" in the NMD project was the first step in the analysis process, and its purpose was to provide a detailed description of the structure of the particular mathematics lessons. Each lesson was mapped according to the categories of whole-class or small-group instruction, exploration, review, and sharing. A collection of lesson mappings for a given teacher is used to help describe the structure of the participant's teaching of mathematics over time.

Lesson Rubric

The second step of the lesson analysis was "coding" using a lesson rubric developed for NMD. Its purpose was to track the nature of the teacher's verbal communication (during mathematics lessons) that is consistent with CRP and CBP. The lesson rubric (used in conjunction with lesson maps) focuses on *teacher-initiated* verbal communication directed at an individual or group of students. More specifically, it focuses on whether and how a teacher: (1) introduces elements of cultural relevance to the lesson and (2) attempts to illuminate and utilize students' mathematical thinking to develop/direct the lesson.

The verbal communication codified using the rubric includes teachers' instructional directives, questions about the lesson, extraneous comments related to student attentiveness, behavior, and/or readiness for instruction. A tally (corresponding with the particular category) is recorded each time teacher communication aligns with rubric categories within two-minute segments of the lesson. The categories include learning connecting, illuminating thinking, affirming multiple representations, extensions of tasks, language matching, relevance making, cultural connecting, and communalizing.

Interviews

The interviews were analyzed using thematic content analysis (Coffey & Atkinson, 1996), which includes the processes of "classifying, comparing, weighing, and combining material from the interviews to extract the meaning and implications, to reveal patterns, or to stitch together descriptions of events into a coherent narrative" (Rubin & Rubin, 2005, p. 201). Significant themes were identified, organized, and interrelated into a broader analytical framework (Wolcott, 1994).

A Tale of Two Primary-Level Teachers

We have chosen to report findings from NMD cohort I, which was made up of eight[4] experienced primary level teachers (i.e., two kindergartens, four 1st grades, and two 2nd grades) from two schools in a large urban district. All members of cohort I were female, and the group was racially balanced between African Americans (50 percent) and white Americans (50 percent). This racial balance differed considerably from the demographic profile for teachers in the school district overall, where 89.4 percent are white American, 9.6 percent are African American, and 1 percent are classified as "other."

At the time they joined the project, the average teaching experience for cohort I teachers was approximately thirteen years, with the average tenure at their present schools being three years. The highest level of formal education completed by cohort I teachers when they joined NMD was a bachelor's degree; although, one member held a master's degree. All but one cohort I teacher was originally from the south; one was a northeastern transplant, having come south several years prior to NMD.

When describing their own mathematics histories, nearly all reported that their experience in learning mathematics changed for the worse in either middle (junior high) or high school. Similarly, all reported consciously taking the fewest mathematics courses necessary to complete degree requirements. This contrasts with their near-unanimous recollections of having enjoyed mathematics in elementary school. All but one of the cohort I dreamkeepers described herself as either liking or having been "good at math."

The two cases we chose for this discussion are Rahquia and Johnetta, who were selected because of their similarities and their differences. Rahquia was a kindergarten teacher at Farren Reese Elementary, a Title I school located in a small town on the outskirts of the school district county. The Farren Reese student population was very ethnically/racially diverse, with 35.1 percent white American students, 43 percent African American, and 14.7 percent Latino/Hispanic. In addition, just over 17 percent of students did not speak English as a first language, and 43 percent of the overall student population were eligible for free or reduced-price lunch.

During the 2007–08 school year, Farren Reese was named a "school of progress" by the district, as it had met all average yearly progress (AYP) goals. The principal of Farren Reese was very enthusiastic about the NMD project and in year I had enlisted the greatest number of participating teachers. Despite her enthusiasm, however, she was not as active in the project as was expected and at times did not seem to be supportive of her participating teachers.

Johnetta was a first grade teacher at Rhine River Elementary, a school that started NMD as a traditional nine-month calendar-schedule school but changed to year-round in year III of the project. During the 2007–08 academic year, the student population at Rhine River was 66.9 percent white American students, 15.8 percent African American, and 10.3 percent Latino/Hispanic. Also, approximately 8 percent of the students did not speak English as a first language, and 25 percent of the overall population were eligible for free or reduced-price lunch. Rhine River had previously been named an "honor school of excellence," and it is currently classified as a "school of progress," yet despite these distinctions, Rhine River did not meet AYP goals for the 2007–08 school year.

During the course of NMD, Rhine River had two principals, both of whom were supportive of the teachers from that school participating in the project. The original principal was actively involved in NMD until she was transferred by the district to serve as principal of a brand new school. This change abruptly ended her participation in NMD halfway through year I; however, her new school joined NMD as a control group in year III. The second (and current) principal of Rhine River was equally enthusiastic as the original principal about the teachers' participation and was very visible in NMD activities.

At the outset, we acknowledged that the similarities between Rahquia and Johnetta included their racial background (both are African American) and their general demeanor about NMD. As the project progressed, each seemed to assume a degree of informal leadership among the cohort I teachers from their respective schools. Other similarities we noted were in their previous participation in school district professional development workshops related to cultural awareness. The average reported from year I to year III was 4.5 workshops for Rahquia and 5 workshops for Johnetta. Also, each was a seasoned professional, having well over ten years experience.

On the other hand, there were a number of differences between them that extend beyond the manners in which they responded to the project intervention. For example, we observed striking dissimilarities in their teaching, professional environment, and general pedagogical identity at the conclusion of the research. Additionally, we noted distinct differences in the makeup of the children they had taught. Rahquia reported that approximately 20 percent of the students she had taught over the span of her teaching career were African American, whereas Johnetta reported only 1 percent. Correspondingly, another contrast was in the extent of personal, cross-racial interaction outside of work each teacher reported. Rahquia's self-report of cross-racial interaction was far greater than Johnetta's, with the former reporting an average of 6.5 friends of a different race with whom she socializes outside of work, whereas the latter reported one such acquaintance.

By drawing upon these two similar yet divergent cases, we illustrate the essence as well as the complexities of the creative curiosity we sought to promote in NMD. We were curious to examine the diverse manner in which two teachers in our project responded to our efforts to promote and study the development of creative curiosity in early mathematics teaching. Moreover, we believe our analysis of these particular cases adds to the extant scholarship on African American teachers in schools (Foster, 1994, 1995; Ladson-Billings, 1994).

RAHQUIA

A particularly uncomfortable school memory for Rahquia relates to her name and the fact that when she was a child, most of her teachers mispronounced it. Recalling the unhappiness she felt at this, Rahquia makes a concerted effort to learn the names of her students and pronounce them correctly. Enunciating clearly in a soft voice and an accent that belies southern roots, Rahquia pronounces her name for the group, "Ray-KEY-ah."

This is the first day of the first retreat, and Rahquia has arrived to the site with a cast on her foot that prevents her from moving about easily. Consequently, she cannot participate fully in *BaFá BaFá* (Shirts, 1977), the simulation activity introduced at the first retreat and used to set the stage for the discussion about culture (how we see ourselves, and how we see others). This will be an ongoing critical construct that will be revisited throughout the three years cohort I teachers will participate in the NMD project.

Throughout the first year of her participation in NMD, Rahquia did not volunteer to speak, but she offered thought-provoking insights if called upon to share. At times, she gave the impression that she would rather be elsewhere, though she never actually said so. Discussions about culture in year I tended to be met with polite non-engagement, and one suspects this may be because Rahquia is African American and, thereby, perceives such discussions as superfluous. An exception is the discussion about racial identity when, like the other teachers in her cohort, Rahquia seemed thoroughly intrigued by the notion that a teachers' own racial identity status can impact her receptivity to adopting a culturally relevant pedagogy.

At the conclusion of NMD year I, cohort I teachers were invited to return to the project, and Rahquia was among the first to express her intention to remain for year II. Moreover, she was among the first to invite colleagues to join as part of cohort II. It became apparent that Rahquia is an informal leader, and we learned later that this was due in part to her facility with technology. In the second year, Rahquia was more engaged in retreats, mainly because she was called upon during the sessions. By year III, she had become part of the leadership team at her school, and while this role was apparent in informal discussions with Rahquia and her colleagues, her leadership status was less apparent in the context of the NMD retreats. Overall, as the project drew to a close, it remained rather difficult to get a clear indication of how Rahquia has made sense of the culture-mathematics connection.

In fall 2005, the first semester of the NMD project, Rahquia's classroom looked like a typical kindergarten classroom. There were bright colors everywhere, student desks were arranged in groups of three to four, and up near the white board at the front of the room was a large rug with the alphabet on it. It was around this rug that Rahquia began her mathematics lessons. The students would be seated in an orderly way around the perimeter of the rug while she sat in a chair with them. When planning her lessons, Rahquia says that she focuses on "what I am supposed to do, and then I think about how I can make it fun and relevant for the children." All of Rahquia's lessons during her three years in the project, including those in fall 2005, began with a story (either one from her classroom or one she made up) and included some sort of "hands on" experience. She was dynamic and expressive and always seemed to be having fun.

That fall, her mathematics lessons were all whole class discussions, with little to no time for students to work independently or with their peers, and typically lasted about twenty minutes (about half the length of time of other kindergarten mathematics lessons at her school). The few questions that Rahquia asked her students were always focused on a correct answer, not an explanation or justification, and usually aimed at the group as a whole, with the tacit expectation of a unison response. There was little evidence of the classroom characteristics associated with teachers who embrace cultural relevance and beliefs about mathematics learning that were consistent with CBP.

As the NMD project progressed and Rahquia had increased opportunities (by way of NMD retreats) to engage in learning mathematics that she found to be very challenging and frustrating, she began to make a few adjustments in her mathematics lessons. The first change (which became evident in late spring 2006 and was consistent from that point forward) was a concerted effort to let her students know that it was okay not to know something. For example, in a lesson in which her students were comparing numbers represented on dominos, she pretended that she didn't know what a student meant when he suggested "counting them all." After the student showed her what he meant, she thanked him, and pointed out to the rest of the class how much better she felt since she had asked for help.

In discussing this strategy she said, "Sometimes I will tell them I need help. Because if I don't know something, I don't know it. And that's one thing I try to show them . . . I try to get them to understand that it's okay if they don't know. It's okay to ask for help."

Although she presented opportunities for students to feel comfortable in acknowledging not knowing a given concept, we found little evidence of Rahquia's "problematizing" those moments in a manner that would allow her to engage the students in discussion of what they *did* know. Neither did Rahquia seize opportunities to utilize these moments to build deeper understanding of concepts. Nevertheless, by spring 2008, Rahquia's interactions with her students during her mathematics lessons seemed much different on the surface. Her lessons were still structured very similarly to the way they were in fall 2005, but the interactions with her students were more personal. She asked far fewer questions of the whole class and instead targeted individual students.

Though Rahquia was interacting with the students on a more personal level, the questions she asked were still focused on answers and not explanations or justifications. Unfortunately, by the last semester of the project, there was still little evidence of the classroom characteristics related to CRP or CBP, leaving us to speculate about the degree to which Rahquia had gained a level of curiosity about early mathematics teaching and learning that could propel her to begin incorporating creative and innovative strategies grounded in the children's own outside-of-school experiences with mathematics.

JOHNETTA

In the fourth year of her association with NMD, as she engaged in preparation for a national conference at which she co-presented regarding the NMD project, Johnetta revealed, "I was suspicious of NMD in that first year." In year I, Johnetta enthusiastically participated in *BaFá BaFá*, but years later, she revealed that at least one point of the activity (i.e., impact of in-group prejudices on out-group members) was somewhat lost on her. She noted that she had long experienced being on the "outside" and, therefore, found the experience to be no big deal in the context of the simulation. This was surprising to learn, but not nearly as much as the fact that Johnetta had been particularly suspicious of members of the NMD research team.

In the first semester, after the conclusion of the project, Johnetta revealed that the nature of her suspicion of "Caucasian male teachers" grew out of her schooling experience that, unfortunately, had all but broken her spirit for learning and enjoying mathematics. Johnetta made it clear that she was participating in NMD because her principal encouraged her to do so. Her original principal was a "math person," but Johnetta's interest was more in the "culture piece" of NMD than the mathematics. She shared that her mathematics still was not where it should be but that she was ready for the challenge.

The exploration of place value, a standard concept taught in primary grades, was jolting for all the cohort I teachers when they were introduced to base four; however, Johnetta suspected the whole point of the base four exercise was to publicly embarrass those teachers whose skills were wanting. Moreover, she believed the African American teachers, in particular, were being targeted as those whose skills were the most lacking. In time, Johnetta became less suspicious, and her interest in the culture piece of the project became stronger and more pronounced. More than other teachers in the project, she broached difficult issues openly, even one time delving into possible reasons for interracial, male-female relationships.

Most striking in the first year, however, was Johnetta's interest in engaging in conversations about how race operates in schools—a conversation that was obviously more difficult for the other members of the first cohort. During a retreat break, she shared with a project co-principal investigator (PI) who was also African American that one of the white American teachers in the cohort used the term "colored" in reference to the African American children in her class. Incredulous, Johnetta noted that she informed the teacher that such terminology is inappropriate, noting that African Americans no longer use that term in reference to themselves. She wondered aloud in conversation with the co-PI whether use of this anachronistic terminology is indicative of how that teacher interacts with the African American children in her class.

Johnetta's classroom, much like Rahquia's, is a typical primary-level learning environment, albeit first grade. Colorful signs and posters are on the walls, student work is displayed, there is a rug near the white board where Johnetta regularly meets with her students, and the student desks are arranged in groups of four. Johnetta's mathematics lessons at the beginning of NMD usually began with her students seated on the rug at the front of the room. She would begin each lesson with a whole group activity and then have her students work in pairs or small groups. Even from the start, Johnetta seemed to have a sense of what it meant to be a culturally critical pedagogue. She regularly made connections between mathematics lessons and set high expectations for her students.

Johnetta's early lessons demonstrate that she understood the importance of interacting with her students individually, not just by posing questions to the class as a whole. Analysis of her questioning in the lessons from fall 2005 shows that she asked many questions and that they were fairly well balanced between those that were intended to elicit a correct response and those that were more intellectually engaging.

It became evident very early on that Johnetta was embracing much of what she was exposed to in the NMD retreats. By spring 2006, Johnetta had already made huge changes in her expectations for students during mathematics lessons. She no longer expected just correct answers from them, but consistently required her students to provide explanations and justifications for their work. Additionally, she was much more focused on methods and representations than on correct answers. When reflecting on the retreats, Johnetta pointed out that questioning was something she focuses on regularly. When asked to explain this, she said, "The questioning? Oh, it's more of 'Can you prove that to me?' 'How did you get that?' 'Can you come and explain that to me?' It's just deeper questioning." Johnetta recognizes that this change in questioning has had a big impact on her students' attitudes towards mathematics. She explains, "I think the children enjoy math better because they do have more ownership." It was through Johnetta's questioning that she raised the academic expectations for her students. In turn, her students have come to expect to be able to explain their work and justify their choice of methods, which she believes has resulted in their sense of ownership of their mathematical knowledge.

When reflecting on her three years with NMD, Johnetta explained that she had welcomed the critical thought around culture and mathematics: "I guess because I lived so much of that"—referring to school inequities grounded in cultural/racial differences between herself and her teachers. Although she had clearly embraced what she was learning about the relationship between culture and school, she specifically said that she didn't think anyone would be able to see her understanding of this relationship in her classroom actions, especially not in her mathematics lessons. Yet the analysis of her mathematics lessons over the three years revealed that, in fact, this growth was evident.

By the second year of NMD, not only had Johnetta's questioning changed, but she had consistently showed evidence of the classroom characteristics associated with CRP and CBP (as identified by our rubric coding) in her lessons. For example, in a two-lesson sequence on doubles in spring 2008, Johnetta asked her students to justify their responses and, in more than one case, prove that two representations were the same. In addition, she showed evidence of valuing their language through language matching (a rubric code) while also promoting a culture of learning for the good of all within the classroom (reflecting the rubric code "communalizing").

An illustration of this is when one student shared her representation for doubling the number of dots on the wing of a ladybug, Johnetta questioned and listened enough to recognize that not only was the student trying to represent the double, but also she was trying to show symmetry in her drawing by making the wings "right." As the student shared her work, she (the student) kept saying that she was "wrong but couldn't make it right."

Instead of simply letting the student know that her drawing was indeed "right" (it did represent the double that was expected), Johnetta listened (demonstrating her own curiosity) and questioned (exhibiting creative engagement) the student until she (Johnetta) understood what the student had been grappling with. Johnetta then pointed out how great it was that the student had made the connection between doubles and symmetry on the ladybug's wings. It is this type of interaction that exemplified Johnetta's curious and creative stance toward building a pedagogy that is consistent with CRP and CBP.

Professional Growth Grounded in Creative Curiosity

It is clear from our analyses of multiple mathematics teaching lessons of these two NMD cases that Johnetta and Rahquia did not interpret or respond to the goals of the NMD intervention in the same way. The goal of the retreats was to promote a creative curiosity about K–2 mathematics teaching and learning by nudging the teachers to think critically about themselves as learners and as teachers with respect to both CRP and CBP. When asked if she had struggled with figuring out how the ideas promoted in the retreat were related to her classroom, Rahquia said that she had not struggled. In fact, she explained, "I mean I was doing some things—I guess—I don't know if the fact that I have so many different cultures in my own family so you try to be [cognizant] of those things anyway. I don't know. I mean to me it just didn't seem to be an issue."

This response seems to reveal a pronounced disinclination to grapple with the possibility (let alone the reality) that the knowledge children bring to the teaching-learning process (which is in some ways informed by their cultural realities) has significant implications for their success (or lack thereof) in learning school mathematics (Nasir, Hand, & Taylor, 2008). Irvine (1990) referred to this disinclination as "cultural aversion" due to teachers' disinterest and discomfort with issues like culture, race, and racism and their likely impact on the teaching-learning process.

Culturally averse teachers fear that exploring such issues (which they perceive as controversial) will upset a precarious balance that exists between and among diverse groups in schools. Thus, they prefer to perceive the teaching-learning process as culturally neutral. We believe that due in part to a disinclination or inability to fully acknowledge and seriously grapple with differences between the children's mathematics understandings and her own, Rahquia enacted instructional moments that never substantially aligned with either aspect of the creative curiosity for mathematics teaching and learning that formed the core of the NMD project.

In contrast, Johnetta responded to the same question by stating that she had been struggling with thinking about how to promote conceptual understanding in her interactions with her students. "Now that was a challenge," she said, "conceptual versus procedural."

A striking difference between Rahquia and Johnetta on this point was the former's disinclination and even reluctance to grapple with the issue of the impact of culture on the teaching-learning process, whereas Johnetta readily explored the issues and did so in a way that clearly reflected interest in further exploring how this factor may well have been affecting her ability to promote deep understanding of the mathematics concepts for her students. In the case of Rahquia, we observed a definite leaning toward color blindness and a disinclination to question the possible connections between children's outside-of-school, culture-based mathematical knowledge and its impact on their acquisition of deep understanding of school-based mathematics. Johnetta's reaction to diversity was quite different. Rather than claiming (either directly or indirectly) not to see color, she readily acknowledged cultural difference and seemed to be questioning possible impacts on the teaching-learning process.

During the retreats and in their interactions with students, the teachers were expected to think critically about what it means to understand a procedure and a concept. As mentioned above, Rahquia said that she had not struggled with making connections between what she learned about these ideas in the retreats and implementation into her classroom because she was "already doing some things." A closer look at Rahquia's interpretation of procedural and conceptual understanding, however, helps to elucidate her stance.

When asked to describe procedural understanding, Rahquia explained, "Well with procedural understanding . . . I mean it's just a process; this is how we do it, etc. You're not necessarily thinking about culture." Furthermore, she described conceptual understanding as, "It's basically knowing really what you're supposed to teach and why you're supposed to teach it." Given her interpretation of procedural and conceptual understanding, it is reasonable that Rahquia did not "struggle" with how to best draw upon students' extant, culture-influenced mathematical knowledge to promote understanding in her lessons because she perceived that the pedagogy she espoused was already consistent with what was being promoted in the retreats.

Conversely, Johnetta openly acknowledged the emergence of tension in her thinking and teaching practice that was introduced by the NMD experience. As such, Johnetta's interpretation of procedural and conceptual understanding was quite different from Rahquia's. She explained,

> So my whole mathematical thinking shifted with knowing the difference. Because in the past it's been procedures . . . I'll teach you the steps, and if you don't do the steps the way I do the steps, then you didn't get it. So it was not looking at 'Well how would you do this?' 'What do you already know about doubling or word problems or any mathematical concepts?' I taught procedures. And so there's been a

> big shift with that. And having taught procedures so long, you have to gradually turn it loose to where you start trusting children to have some conceptual knowledge because that's not the way it's been for so long. So now I can put a word problem up and talk about the word problem and make sure they understand what I need. 'And then show me how you would answer that.' 'Why did you do it that way?'

The length of Johnnetta's response alone exhibits a more thoughtful and more critical reflection than Rahquia's response to the same question. Furthermore, when asked to explain why she struggled with this issue in her teaching, Johnetta reflected,

> Because I knew the ways to do it. I knew my way would get you the results that I was looking for. So turning that loose means I'm giving my power and ownership away not realizing it wasn't about me anyway. I already knew how to do it. But just because I knew how to do it didn't mean there weren't other avenues.

Here, we see evidence of comfort with the internal tension (between what the teacher knows and what she doesn't know) as well as the desire to free or emancipate herself from old ways that she (Johnetta) now recognizes have been devoid of connection to her students' own ways of meaning making. The ability to engage in this level of self-critique demands courage on the part of the teacher, whereas to implement more effective ways of teaching that draw upon students' extant knowledge requires inquisitiveness and inventiveness (creative curiosity). We believe that Johnetta exemplified a basic principle of the NMD research. That is, it is reasonable to expect a teacher who is herself truly grappling with comprehending different types of mathematical ideas (that she is attempting to promote among her students) will likely change her pedagogy as a result.

While there were clear differences between the classroom outcomes of Rahquia and Johnetta, it should also be noted that the larger contexts in which they worked (the schools) were different as well. Earlier in this discussion, it was noted that Johnetta's original principal was transferred to another school and, therefore, (for a time) was not involved in the project. This principal's replacement, however, was equally enthusiastic about the project, and, to learn about it, the new principal spent an entire day with her teachers in the fifth retreat that first year. This contrasted sharply with the principal at Rahquia's school, who, although she expressed support for her teachers to the project principal investigators, apparently gave a different impression about teacher participation at the school site. In the latter years of the project, Rahquia and other cohort I teachers from her school expressed exasperation with what appeared to be mixed messages they received from their principal about being part of the NMD project. One reported that, on the one hand, their principal enjoyed being able to say that her school was part of a research project, but on the other, she fell short in offering the support and scheduling flexibility the teachers needed at times to participate fully.

These two contrasting cases point out the possibility that administrators' expectations for and encouragement of teachers to act in a creatively curious manner might impact teacher engagement in these activities. In the case of Johnetta, her principal encouraged all teachers at the school who have participated in the NMD project (all three cohorts) to begin discussions about culture in the teaching-learning process with the rest of the teachers (across all grade levels) who were not participants in the project.

Lessons from the Dreamkeepers

In this chapter, we described major features of a multiyear research project, which included an extensive professional development intervention that focused on promoting teaching for deep understanding of early mathematics concepts by drawing upon tenets of culturally relevant pedagogy. Participants in the research were primary-level teachers who became known to their colleagues in their respective schools as dreamkeepers.

We detailed the cases of two of these teachers, Rahquia and Johnetta, each of whom had participated in the research for three consecutive academic years. Our analysis revealed that both teachers began the project quite similarly, yet over time, they exhibited marked differences in their responses to the goals of the project as discovered through careful examination of their instructional practices and one-on-one interviews. Initially, the teachers showed caution and perhaps even skepticism about our research precepts; however, both eventually embraced the dreamkeeper professional identity, albeit to varying degrees.

In this regard, Johnetta's classroom practices as well as her articulated understandings of critical NMD concepts demonstrated far more consistency with the research precepts and intervention ideology than did Rahquia's. We, therefore, conclude that the NMD experience resulted in a substantively different professional development trajectory toward what we have termed "creative curiosity" for Johnetta than it did for Rahquia. Further, we conclude that as a result of their participation in NMD, these two teachers have amassed substantively different pedagogical capital to facilitate primary-level students' development of deep understanding of early mathematics concepts, skills, and operations.

Undoubtedly, there are many explanations for the dissimilarity in the outcome for these two teachers, and foremost among these may be each teacher's perception that through her principal she consistently had the firm support and encouragement to critically question her pedagogy and make changes to facilitate student growth. As noted, Johnetta characterized her original principal at Rhine River as a "math person," and she (along with her dreamkeeper colleagues) received considerable support from their second principal. The year after the conclusion of the project, the Rhine River principal allowed the dreamkeepers at that school to make two different professional development presentations (covering concepts the teachers had learned from their participation in NMD) to the rest of the school faculty.

The level of principal support at Rhine River contrasts sharply with the situation faced by Rahquia and the other dreamkeepers at Farren Reese. Indeed, during the last year of the project, Rahquia and the other Farren Reese dreamkeepers openly wondered whether their principal truly supported their continued participation. Other explanations that likely influenced the outcomes for Johnetta and Rahquia may include each teacher's own inclination and security to question the effectiveness of her pedagogy and the genuine "buy-in" each teacher had for our research precept linking mathematics knowledge and cultural knowledge. Although an investigation of each of these explanations is beyond the scope of this discussion, they are currently in progress.

Conclusion

We offer that our present discussion effectively illustrates the nature and complexity of creative curiosity as implemented in early mathematics teaching. Therefore, in conclusion, we present the following insights or lessons drawn from our project that speak to implications that may be presented for cultivating or "nurturing" the creative and curious mind for teaching in general and for the teaching-learning process in early mathematics in particular.

Cultivation of the creative mind and the curious mind for teaching should occur in tandem.

The foci of the NMD project, as well as the experiences described in the two cases reported in this chapter, suggest that as related to early mathematics teaching for deep understanding, the notions of the creative mind for teaching and the curious mind for teaching have limited pedagogical power as separate entities. This is to say, individually, neither represents a difference-making factor when added to a pedagogy that fails to draw upon the mathematical experiences children bring to the learning environment. Recognizing this, we coined the phrase "creative curiosity" to describe what we believe to be the symbiotic relationship that needs to exist between the two in order for either to positively impact a teacher's professional identity, pedagogy, and, ultimately, students' academic success. A habit of mind and professional inclination that results in inventiveness in teaching is a prerequisite to the creation of learning moments that promote deep mathematical understanding. Our experience in NMD informs us that such inventiveness exists within, and is necessarily nurtured by, a professional identity accompanied by an inquisitive spirit.

Provocation may be the most fertile action for the cultivation of creative curiosity.

Prescribing an ideology is ineffective in affecting change, and as such, in a professional development project like NMD, which was designed to promote particular ideologies (e.g. CRP, CBP), it becomes necessary to *provoke* the need to think critically about components of one's pedagogy that are central to the ideology. In the context of teaching mathematics, these components include but are not limited to the nature of classroom interactions, student understanding, and mathematical content.

Interpretation of key constructs related to these components will inevitably impact a teacher's beliefs about teaching and learning. For example, two key constructs for CBP related to students' mathematical knowledge include procedural and conceptual understanding. We saw that Rahquia and Johnetta interpreted these two key constructs quite differently. Furthermore, we hypothesized that the differences in their interpretations might have affected the ways in which they attempted to integrate them into practice.

The notion of provocation as a key component of the cultivation of creative curiosity prompts us to pose questions that in hindsight might have changed the nature of the NMD experience for at least some of the dreamkeepers. In this regard, if Rahquia had experienced a provocation, for example, in the form of a discrepant event in her teaching that sufficiently challenged her to develop a conception of procedural and conceptual understanding that was consistent with CBP, might she have acted in a more creatively curious fashion toward integrating these ideas into her pedagogy? Likewise, in relation to CRP, might we have observed more instances of communalizing, a key construct in CRP, if the teachers had been clear that communalizing is more complex than just working in groups?

Thus, the second lesson learned from the dreamkeepers is that professional development (where teachers are invited to critique and challenge their own pedagogy) cannot be designed to simply prescribe an ideology towards teaching and learning. Before teachers can critically consider a change in their pedagogical stance, it is necessary that they understand and buy into the components involved. Had we helped Rahquia resolve the issue of her misconceptions regarding procedural and conceptual understanding, she might have on her own become curious about the effectiveness of the ways she had been attempting to promote mathematical understanding in her classroom and creative in her efforts to align her pedagogy more closely to the children's own mathematical knowledge.

Finally, arguably, all professional development for teachers represents an ambitious undertaking when considering the potential outcomes. In this regard, Guskey (1986) suggested that participation in professional development can result in change in teachers' classroom practices, a change in student learning outcomes, and, eventually, a change in teachers' beliefs and attitudes. The NMD project was an ambitious undertaking because we sought simultaneously to challenge and support groups of primary-level teachers to be curious about their pedagogy and to adapt a creative discipline to revise their instructional practice where necessary in order to promote deep mathematical understanding for all children. Our work in NMD revealed that adopting a creatively curious mind for early mathematics teaching may be afforded and constrained by the professional identity and overall courage of the individual teacher.

Notes

1. The research reported in this chapter was supported by a grant from the National Science Foundation (Award #0353412). Any opinions, findings, and conclusions or recommendations reported herein are those of the authors and do not necessarily reflect the views of the National Science Foundation.

2. Originally, teachers were required to attend six two-day professional development retreats; however, because of school recruitment difficulties and teacher feedback, the number of retreats was reduced to four two-day retreats by the second year of the project. Each cohort attended a separate collection of retreats with the content covered in the first year for cohort II and cohort III being similar to what had been covered in the first year for cohort I. In year III, cohort II retreats were similar to those that had occurred for cohort I in its second year, whereas cohort I was required to help plan and deliver retreat contents (in conjunction with the project co-PIs) to either cohort II or cohort III teachers. To facilitate cross-cohort interactions, we added a cross-cohort, 3-hour "intersession" where teachers from both retreats (in year III, all three retreats) came together to work and have dinner at the project site.

3. All teacher and school names are pseudonyms.

4. Cohort I began as twenty-one teachers from three area schools; however, as the project progressed, teachers had to withdraw for a variety of reasons, including new school leadership, teacher reassignment to different (non-NMD) schools in the district, teacher relocation to a different district in the state, teacher relocation to a school outside the state, and pregnancy. Only one teacher opted not to return to the project in year II for "personal reasons."

References

Ball, D. L. (2000). Bridging practices: Interweaving content and pedagogy in teaching and learning to teach. *Journal of Teacher Education, 51*(3), 241–247.

Borko, H. (2004). Professional development and teacher learning: Mapping the terrain. *Educational Researcher, 33*(8), 3–15.

Boykin, A. W., Jagers, R. J., Ellison, C. M., & Albury, A. (1997). Communalism: Conceptualization and measurement of an afrocultural social orientation. *Journal of Black Studies, 27*(3), 409–418.

Coffey, A., & Atkinson, P. (1996). *Making sense of qualitative data: Complementary research designs.* Thousand Oaks, CA: Sage.

Darling-Hammond, L. (2004). What happens to a dream deferred?: The continuing quest for equal educational opportunity. In J. A. Banks & C. A. M. Banks (Eds.), *Handbook of research on multicultural education* (2nd ed., pp. 607–630). San Francisco: Jossey-Bass.

Deyhle, D. (1983). Measure success and failure in the classroom: Teacher communication about tests and the understandings of young Navajo students. *Peabody Journal of Education, 61*(1), 67–85.

Foster, M. (1994). Educating for competence in community and culture: Exploring the views of exemplary African-American teachers. In M. J. Shufaa (Ed.), *Too much schooling, too little education: A paradox of black life in white societies* (pp. 221–244). Trenton, NJ: African World Press.

Foster, M. (1995). African American teachers and culturally relevant pedagogy. In J. A. Banks and C. A. McGee-Banks (Eds.), *Handbook of research on multicultural education* (pp. 570–581). New York: McMillan.

Gay, G. (Speaker). (2002). *Culturally responsive teaching* [DVD]. Washington, DC: National Association for Multicultural Education.

Guskey, T. R. (1986). Staff development and the process of teacher change. *Educational Researcher, 15*(5), 5–12.

Gutstein, E. (2003). Teaching and learning mathematics for social justice in an urban, Latino school. *Journal for Research in Mathematics Education, 34*(1), 37–73.

Haberman, M. (1995). *Star teachers of children in poverty.* West Lafayette, IN: Kappa Delta Pi.

Hollins, E. R., & Guzman, M. T. (2005). Research on preparing teachers for diverse populations. In M. Cochran-Smith & K. M. Zeichner (Eds.), *Studying teacher education: The report of the AERA panel on research and teacher education* (pp. 477–548). Mahwah, NJ: Lawrence Erlbaum Associates.

hooks, b. (1994). *Teaching to transgress: Education as the practice of freedom.* New York: Routledge.

Irvine, J. J. (1990). *Black students and school failure.* New York: Praeger.

Kincheloe, J. (2004). *Critical pedagogy primer.* New York: Peter Lang.

Ladson-Billings, G. (1994). *The Dreamkeepers: Successful teachers of African American children.* San Francisco: Jossey-Bass.

Lipka, J. (1991). Toward a culturally based pedagogy: A case study of one Yup'ik Eskimo teacher. *Anthropology & Education Quarterly, 22*, 203–223.

Ma, L. (1999). *Knowing and teaching elementary mathematics: Teachers' understanding of fundamental mathematics in China and the United States.* Mahwah, New Jersey: Lawrence Erlbaum Associates.

Moses, R., & Cobb, C. E. J. (2001). *Radical equations: Mathematics literacy and civil rights.* Boston: Beacon.

Nasir, N. S., Hand, V., & Taylor, E. V. (2008). Culture and mathematics in school: Boundaries between "cultural" and "domain" knowledge in the mathematics classroom and beyond. In J. Green, G. J. Kelly, & A. Luke (Eds.), *Review of research in education* (Vol. 32, no. 1, pp. 187–240). Washington, DC: American Educational Research Association.

National Center for Education Statistics. (1985). Second international mathematics study: Summary report for the United States. Washington, DC: Author.

National Center for Education Statistics. (1996). Third International Mathematics and Science Study. Washington, DC: U.S. Department of Education.

National Commission on Excellence in Education. (1983). *A nation at risk: The imperative for educational reform* [Chairman's Revised Draft]. Washington, DC: U.S. Government Printing Office.

National Council of Teachers of Mathematics. (2000). *Principles and standards for school mathematics.* Reston, VA: NCTM.

Paulos, J. A. (1988). *Innumeracy: Mathematics illiteracy and its consequences.* New York: Hill and Wang.

Rubin, H. J., & Rubin, I. S. (2005). *Qualitative interviewing: The art of hearing data* (2nd ed). Thousand Oaks, CA: Sage.

Secada, W. G. (1992). Race, ethnicity, social class, language, and achievement in mathematics. In D. A. Grouws (Ed.), *Handbook of research on mathematics teaching and learning* (pp. 623–660). New York: Macmillan.

Shirts, R. G. (1977). *BaFá BaFá: A cross culture simulation* [Simulation activity]. Del Mar, CA: Simulation Training Systems.

Simon, M. A., Tzur, R., Heinz, K., & Kinzel, M. (2004). Explicating a mechanism for conceptual learning: Elaborating the construct of reflective abstraction. *Journal for Research in Mathematics Education, 35*(5), 305–329.

Simon, M. A., Tzur, R., Heinz, K., Kinzel, M., and Smith, M. S. (2000). Characterizing a perspective underlying the practice of mathematics teachers in transition. *Journal for Research in Mathematics Education, 31*(5), 579–601.

Tashakkori, A., & Creswell, J. W. (2007). The new era of mixed methods. *Journal of Mixed Methods Research, 1*, 3–7.

Thompson, G. L. (2004). *Through ebony eyes: What teachers need to know but are afraid to ask about African-American students.* San Francisco: Jossey-Bass.

Tzur, R. (2002). From theory to practice: Explaining successful and unsuccessful teaching activities (case of fractions). In A. D. Cockburn and E. Nardi (Eds.), *Proceedings of the 26th Annual Meeting of the International Group for the Psychology of Mathematics Education* (Vol. 3, pp. 297–304). Norwich, UK: University of East Anglia.

Wolcott, H. F. (1994). *Transforming qualitative data: Description, analysis, and interpretation*. Thousand Oaks, CA: Sage.

Yin, R. K. (2004). *The case study anthology*. Thousand Oaks, CA: Sage.

Zumwalt, K., & Craig, E. (2008). Who is teaching?: Does it matter? In M. Cochran-Smith, S. Feiman-Nemser, D. J. McIntyre, & K. E. Demers (Eds.), *Handbook of research on teacher education: Enduring questions in changing contexts* (3rd ed, pp. 134–156). New York: Routledge/Taylor & Francis Group & Association of Teacher Educators.

CHAPTER 7

The Impact of Creativity within the Inquiry Process in Science Education

Terri R. Hebert
University of Central Arkansas

Dr. Terri Hebert, EdD, assistant professor, Teaching, Learning, and Technology Department, College of Education, University of Central Arkansas, is interested in the impact of standardized testing on teachers' ability to effectively teach. She teaches in both the Advanced Studies in Teaching and Learning Program, which is aligned with the National Board of Professional Teaching Standards (NBPTS), and the Master's of Art in Teaching Program (MAT).

ABSTRACT

Humans are naturally inquisitive. One only need reflect upon the questions of a child to see how those questions become a driving force in learning. The innate desires of human beings to question and create remain, even though we find less and less time to allow for such deep learning experiences. Even as our allotment of time and resources is being streamlined, teachers and administrators are becoming more aware of the lack of innovation and creativity within classrooms. The push toward rigorous teaching and higher stakes because of testing leave many asking where the joy in teaching and learning has gone. What role might inquiry-based strategies play in helping to bring back the creativity and passion found lacking, specifically within the realm of science? Can teachers, positively impacted by high quality professional development, be the change agents so desperately needed in today's classrooms? This chapter seeks to address these queries and other questions related to the impact of creativity within the inquiry process in science education.

> When education is viewed as inquiry, important things
> happen. The focus of education becomes learning and
> the task of teaching becomes one of supporting the inquiry
> process.
>
> —Harste (1994, p. 1232)

The copy machine hummed as its engine warmed. The teacher, Mrs. Bell, waited patiently after what seemed an extremely long day. If only she could hurry up the task of copying the next day's science ditto sheets, then Mrs. Bell could go home. In an effort to multitask, she decided to check her mail while the machine collated the work. She noticed an envelope in her mailbox addressed to her from a neighboring university.

As she began to read the letter, it became apparent that this was an invitation to attend a three-week summer professional development opportunity focused on experiential methods and inquiry-based learning within the science content area. Mrs. Bell's interest was piqued. She knew that her passion for science teaching had faded some time ago, and her students were now paying the price of her less-than-enthusiastic attempt to engage them. The university may have provided the perfect solution to Mrs. Bell's inner struggle.

The Background

The local university's education department boasted an innovative program aimed to improve mathematics and science teaching, including faculty members in both the education department and the mathematics and science department as well as mathematics and science teachers in surrounding school districts. An assistant professor, Dr. Ben Carrillo, within the College of Natural Sciences, became intrigued with the methods being promoted—specifically, the inquiry method in science education. The predominant method being used within his college was direct instruction aided by PowerPoint slides. However, Dr. Carrillo had dabbled in the use of inquiry and cooperative grouping. He had personally noticed the level of student engagement would increase when these methods were used in place of the more traditional ones.

Dr. Carrillo sought the advice of those involved with the education department's innovative program. Dr. Mary Rein, also serving as director of the program, immediately connected with Dr. Carrillo. She brought in a third member of the group, a teacher-in-residence named Ashley Kelso. Ashley had been hired to serve as liaison between the university and the area schools and was aware of current resources available to both university and public school mathematics and science teachers. As the three colleagues visited about options for extending Dr. Carrillo's biology students' learning experiences, the discussion turned to include an established professional development opportunity offered on-site at the Exploratorium: The Museum of Science, Art and Human Perception. Ashley suggested that the three apply to participate in the next scheduled Institute for Inquiry. The idea soon became a reality, and within a semester, Dr. Carrillo, Dr. Rein, and Ashley boarded a plane for California.

The week moved at a rapid rate, each day filled with thought-provoking activities designed to move participants systematically through a sequence of learning experiences. Time was also allocated at the end of each day for each team to connect and share personal "aha" moments. It was during one of these sessions and near the end of the week that Dr. Carrillo, Dr. Rein, and Ashley began to discuss the three types of inquiry they had personally experienced—specifically, the structured, the guided, and open types (see figure 7.1)—and how this might fit within a classroom setting. A visual representation of the continuum of inquiry, ranging from structured to open, provided a basis to assess where one currently stood, in an effort to shift one's positioning on the scale. According to the developers of the Institute for Inquiry, good science education requires both learning scientific concepts and developing scientific thinking skills. Inquiry is an approach to learning that involves a process of exploring the natural or material world, and that leads to asking questions, making discoveries, and testing those discoveries in the search for new understanding (Exploratorium, n.d.).

Another way of viewing "good" science education was provided to institute participants in the form of a table entitled, "Essential Features of Classroom Inquiry and Their Variations" (see table 7.1). Embedded within the variations of student engagement and teacher instruction are found the three types of inquiry, as indicated on the continuum and implied in the "Essential Features" table: structured, guided, and open inquiry.

A more traditional type of inquiry—the structured method—allows the teacher to provide students with step-by-step instructions, while opening the door for them to add their own touch to the activity, such as in the form of a unique data table. Learners must decide what observations are important to record and then must wrestle with the meaning of the collected data in determining the end result. The value in this type of inquiry is found in the students' ability to learn the basics of investigating as well as the techniques required in using equipment and following procedures. This foundational type of learning can easily transfer in later, more complicated research (Beacon Learning Center, 2000–2005). This is also a good starting point for teachers to "test" the inquiry

Structured   Guided   Open

Figure 7.1   Types of inquiry

Table 7.1   Essential Features of Classroom Inquiry and Their Variations

Essential Features	Variations	
Learner engages in scientifically oriented questions.	Learner engages in a question provided by the teacher.	Learner poses a question.
Learner gives priority to evidence in responding to questions.	Learner is given data and told how to analyze.	Learner determines what constitutes evidence and collects it.
Learner formulates explanations from evidence.	Learner is provided with evidence.	Learner formulates explanations after summarizing evidence.
Learner connects explanations to scientific knowledge.		Learner independently examines other resources and forms the links to explanations.
Learner communicates and justifies explanations.	Learner is given steps and procedures for communication.	Learner forms reasonable and logical argument to communicate explanation.

Less ⟵ *Amount of Learner Self-Direction* ⟶ More

Less ⟵ *Amt. of Teacher Direction or Materials* ⟶ More

Adapted from: National Research Council. (2002). *Inquiry and the national science education standards: A guide for teaching and learning.* Washington, D.C.: National Academy Press.

method and see how it works within their classroom setting. Conventional activity sheets can be used with minimum alterations.

As one shifts toward the right on the teaching methods' continuum, guided inquiry is found nested in the middle of the line. Teachers provide the problem for investigation as well as all required materials. Students not only select what data to record and interpret but also the procedural process that will ultimately address the preselected investigable questions befitting of their science inquiry.

Open inquiry is found on the far right of the continuum and seeks to radically extend the students' learning experience in science education. It is truly student driven in that all decisions related to the investigation are made by the student, much like a true scientist would encounter, including the establishment of an investigable question, the decision of how to carry out the investigation, the method of what and how to collect data, and the presentation of valid interpretations of data (Colburn, 2004; Banchi & Bell, 2008). Together, the three types of inquiry provide the teacher and the learner varying degrees of participation while shifting ownership of the learning away from the teacher and toward the student.

As the week at the Exploratorium ended, the team was even more convinced that inquiry was a valid and reliable method of teaching and learning in science education. The discussion shifted from the changes that had occurred within their own personal mindsets to how they might share this experience with others, specifically local school teachers. Their first challenge presented itself to the team: how to convince both teachers and administrators that scientific inquiry was a necessary and proven vehicle for teaching and learning. This would prove to be a daunting task because deeply embedded in the minds of educators is the fact that schools operate within a standardized framework.

How could teachers be expected to shift their teaching methods—methods that are clearly and systematically aligned with the standardized tests? Textbook publishers and test preparation developers had created learning tools that boasted of their alignment with state and national standards and which were also used to formulate items found on high stakes tests. For a teacher to leave behind the safety of a "sure thing" and to step into a world where students' questions would become the guiding force in a lesson or unit may be too much to ask. A second group—the administrators—would prove to be challenging as well. With the retention of their jobs resting on student test results, they, too, may find the inquiry focus in science—a more recently tested content area in most locales—as a too risky endeavor.

Another question surfaced among Dr. Carrillo, Dr. Rein, and Ashley: how might the act of creativity found within scientific learning experiences stir a teacher's passion, even if it had grown cold over time? The team had witnessed this resurrected passion among the institute participants, and they believed that it could happen among others. Options, including grant funding, surfaced as to how the team might reach teachers in order to share the knowledge and skills. It was not long before a completed grant proposal was submitted to the state's education department, requesting funding to provide its own summer institute of inquiry.

RESEARCH BEHIND THE PROPOSAL

John Dewey, regarded by many as the greatest educational thinker of the twentieth century, believed experiential education to be the answer to students' disconnectedness with the curriculum. He argued that a one-way delivery style of transmissive schooling simply does not provide a good learning experience.

Instead, Dewey held high those educational experiences that allow students to connect what they are learning to their lives outside of school. An example of such an experience uses problem-solving methods mirroring scientific inquiry.

In *My Pedagogic Creed* (as cited in Hickman & Alexander, 1998), Dewey clarifies his concept of experiential learning: "This [educational] process begins unconsciously almost at birth, and is continually shaping the individual's powers, saturating his consciousness, forming his habits, training his ideas, and arousing his feelings and emotions" (p. 229). Dewey also believed that learning should be grounded in the natural curiosity of our world and in how it works.

INQUIRY-BASED LEARNING

Humans are naturally inquisitive, as evidenced by the number of questions a young child will ask of an adult standing nearby. Acknowledgement by key science leaders of the innate desire to both question and create, which remains as a critical component of authentic learning, prompted the establishment of the National Research Council's (1996) *National Science Education Standards*. These standards serve as the culmination of an extensive and collaborative writing project that began in 1991. Its goal was to better define inquiry and how it might look within science classrooms in school settings.

The National Research Council's (1996) findings indicated distinct connections between students' natural curiosities and how they inquire about their world and scientists' more formalized approaches to problem solving (National Institutes of Health, 2005). As learning occurs in both children and adults, similar stages of discovery are experienced: explore, explain, extend, and evaluate.

To understand the shift from a traditional teaching method to one that includes inquiry-based strategies, one must first understand the definition of inquiry. According to the National Research Council (1996),

> Inquiry is a multifaceted activity that involves making observations; posing questions; examining books and other sources of information to see what is already known; planning investigations; reviewing what is already known in light of experimental evidence; using tools to gather, analyze, and interpret data; proposing answers, explanations, and predictions; and communicating the results. Inquiry requires identification of assumptions, use of critical and logical thinking, and consideration of alternative explanations. (p. 23)

Berghoff, Egawa, Harste, and Hoonan (2000) compared inquiry to a prism, which embodies and reflects a multifaceted perspective. As the prism's position alters the image, so it is with the learning experience as it continues to be driven by the learner's questions. "What does this mean?" becomes a profound question that must be revisited in an effort to reach clarity. Of course, all questions proceed from what is already known. However, if the learning is not first surrounded by the experience, then it becomes virtually impossible to ensure that all students will learn. If no experiences exist or serve as a foundation for future learning, then the depth of the student's ability to question will be shallow.

Ronsberg (2006, p. 25) summarized this shallowness in a poem entitled, "There's More to Teaching Science," which is relevant to this discussion:

> There's more to teaching science than stuffing kids with facts—
> Cause unconnected data flows like rain right off their backs.
> Help kids discover nature, stars and waves, and tracks,
> Dinosaurs, and temperature, and killer bee attacks.
> They have to learn to question, to observe, and to explore—
> To seek the basic causes: to measure, count, and more.
> So shelve that fault-line lecture; it'll bore them to the core.
> Active learner engagement is the key to learning's door.

Bransford, Brown, and Cocking (1999) surmised, "An alternative to simply processing through a series of exercises that derive from a scope and sequence chart is to expose students to the major features of a subject domain as they arise naturally in problem situations" (p. 127). Originally, science educators sought to prepare all students in their quest of academic excellence while maintaining their sense of wonder about the world around them. Sadly, pacing guides and curriculum chunking have become the focus in this era of increased accountability.

For at least ten years, professional learning experiences specifically designed for educators have been scrutinized due to society's outcry for educational reform (Corcoran, 1995; Houghton & Goren, 1995; National Commission on Teaching & America's Future, 1996; National Foundation for the Improvement of Education, 1996). As a result, it was realized that for there to be transferability of knowledge and skills from the workshop into the classroom, there must be (1) an integration of support at the state, district, and local levels; and (2) a mental, physical, emotional, and intellectual connection established between the teacher, the content, and the school (Scribner, 1999). If there is a breakdown in either of these, then the chances of sustained improvement will be slim to none. Against the backdrop of accountability, with its huge cost in terms of time and money, an investigation into the support of quality professional development regarding inquiry beckoned us.

TEACHERS AND INQUIRY

Teachers search for and share ideas that, according to the original source, are deemed "best practices." Many have personally experienced the notion of "here today and gone tomorrow" kinds of reform. Even though the topic of change has been addressed by educators, school boards, legislative bodies, and even presidential candidates, little consensus has been reached as to the most productive reform path to take. However, one commonly agreed upon theme for change within the science classroom remains that of active involvement with the learner—in other words, inquiry-based learning (Hammrich, 1997).

Numerous professional organizations (e.g., National Research Council, American Association for the Advancement of Science, National Science Teachers Association) have settled upon the importance of advancing students' knowledge and skills with specific regard to science literacy. Because the educational system was found to be desperately in need of reform, as based upon reports such as *A Nation at Risk* (U.S. Department of Education, 1983), the call went forth to improve curriculum and instruction methods. Vast sums of federal money were pumped into local schools with the intent of providing curricular materials and additional after school programs. Governmental agencies sought accountability of the schools to prove to taxpayers the outcome of the funding. Thus, accountability standards were developed as a means of evaluating the progression of learning. Additional financial incentives were promised to those school districts showing marked improvement as well as to those districts experiencing distress.

Several years have passed since the institution of No Child Left Behind (2001), and we still do not have any substantial indicators of change occurring in the overall knowledge and skills of our students. In fact, as the accountability bar continues to be ratcheted up, it becomes increasingly difficult for all student groups to attain success. Large numbers of English language learners (ELL), special education students, minorities, and low socioeconomic sub-population groups find the standards to be out of their reach. Many simply fail or drop out. Those that remain are labeled "successful" because their test scores have indicated it.

Thinking skills cannot be developed in a contrived and controlled setting where students and teachers leave their personal experiences at the classroom door. Their personal experiences must be called upon as relevant issues are naturally connected with subject content. Resnick (1987) reinforces this thought:

> Cognitive research has established the very important role of knowledge in reasoning and thinking. One cannot reason in the abstract; one must reason about something. Each school discipline provides extensive reasoning and problem-solving material by incorporating problem-solving or critical thinking training into the disciplines. (pp. 35–36)

Bredderman (1982) examined the experiences of 13,000 students in 1,000 classrooms to determine significant benefits of using the inquiry-based method of teaching and learning. He reported that students had a substantially improved performance in science, specifically in the areas of process and creativity. He also reported significant improvement in perception, logic, language development, science content, and math, although a somewhat lessened improvement in attitudes toward learning. Bartels (1999) furthermore reported:

> Today, with the increasing demands on schools and the growing importance of science and technology, the nature of science education—what children should know and how they should learn it—may be the most important discussion of all. It is not a new question or a settled one, but it is the obvious starting point for rethinking the science education enterprise. (p. 15)

Teachers must be challenged to think outside the box and to reflect upon how they might incorporate such authentic experiences into the classroom, providing students with opportunities to explore and to question. Even though many administrators are suggesting budgets be mainstreamed and such encounters curtailed, and textbook publishers and test makers are seeking to add to the ever-growing list of what is "best" for our students, educators must remain focused on what they know as truth and continue to be steadfast in the mission to reach and educate all.

The fundamental beliefs about scientific inquiry are grounded in the following principles: (a) learning to think independently and scientifically is a worthy instructional goal; (b) learning to think independently actually requires the students to do just that—think independently. Critical thinking is a complex skill requiring instructional guidance, practice, and ongoing feedback; (c) thinking is not a context-free activity but one in which students must grapple with the content; and (d) students must be ready—developmentally and logically—to understand and comprehend the scientific idea embedded within the content (Colburn, 2004).

In order to assist students in the acquisition of such habits of mind, researchers have suggested that teachers move along a continuum of teacher-explicit to student-exploratory instruction. This approach begins with the teacher modeling the steps of inquiry to his or her own students then, gradually, transferring the leadership role to the student, taking into account his or her own social and educational needs (Lee & Avalos, 2003).

Explicit instruction moves beyond a traditional, closed-ended activity that centers on teacher lectures and/or worksheets into an atmosphere of guidance as all students become involved in the phases of inquiry. This transition requires the teacher to be familiar with and actively practice instructional scaffolding, in which students are moved from a non-questioning, just-tell-me-the-answer approach, to inquiry-based habits of mind (Lee & Avalos, 2003; Bencze & Hodson, 1999), which is a very important development.

One method of determining the level of decision making within a classroom setting is found in a simple activity containing three questions: (a) who decides the question to investigate? (b) who decides the procedures to follow in addressing the question? and (c) who decides the data to collect and analyze? (Colburn, 2004). If the answers lie within the teacher's decision making, then there will be little student involvement other than simply following through on the instructions provided. However, if it is the student who decides on the questions, the procedural issues, and the method of data collection and analysis, then one likely will observe stark differences in the engagement of the learner and in the amount of information actually learned. One teacher in Lee's (2003) scholarship struggled with this challenge:

> I had to make my students understand that I didn't know everything. It was a shock. Sometimes I find myself wanting to tell them the answers because I know that's what they expect. It has taken me longer to get into inquiry where they start to ask questions and find out their own answers because it feels so unnatural.

This "unnatural" feeling, as described by the teacher, is awkward, in a sense, simply because our educational system has downplayed the fact that learning is wrapped up in one's ability to question and reflect with the intention of solving one's own problems. Textbook publishers and test-preparation writers design the chapters and units of study to fit nicely within a given period of time. Such materials are devoid of any open-ended, thoughtful questions, leaving the students with nothing to ponder. Students simply move from one classroom to another, as if they are skimming the surface of a thin layer of ice. At what point, though, will the ice crack and send the learners into a state of frozenness unable to think or act in a given situation requiring creativity? And if they do fall, then what impact might this have upon our society as we continue to increase our reliance on foreign understanding of science and technology?

Limitations of Today's Test-Driven Classrooms

Assessing science through paper-and-pencil tests is akin to assessing a basketball player's skills in a similar fashion. We may find out what someone knows about basketball—the knowledge behind the skill—but we will not know how well that person can play the game until we give him or her a ball (Hein &

Price, 1994). Similarly, paper-and-pencil tests will not prepare scientists to break new ground in laboratories, producing new innovations, medications, and the like.

Traditional tests in the form of multiple-choice, short-answer items given at the end of a grading period or at the end of a chapter or unit simply cannot thoroughly assess the multiple levels of learning acquired in an inquiry-based experience. Yet we see more and more states requiring additional tests written in this format and given to students as a means of predicting possible outcomes on the end-of-year tests. Because of this pernicious trend, we have before us a heightened level of expectancy with regard to student performance, resulting in an increased time allotment dedicated to test preparation and administration—and all for tests that inaccurately measure the student's scientific knowledge and skills. In essence, we have a reading and comprehension test being given to serve as an indicator of science content knowledge. One teacher, for example, expressed her frustration in this way:

> This is my struggle every year. I know my children remember what they do much longer than what they are merely told or read, but as the testing time approaches I feel the panic rising in my throat. I don't know for sure if they will be able to transfer what they know to paper. So I freak out and give in to the test-prep material provided by the district. Instead of doing what I know is best, I give in to the demands of the test. (Hebert, 2006)

There is no time left in the day for children to *do* science—to examine, observe, design, collect, discuss, or interpret anything. Students are no longer pushed to create independent thoughts or to wrestle with a problem to create a solution. Textbooks have replaced higher-order thinking and student-led debates concerning relevant issues. Many simply do not understand the terms mentioned in a science classroom, words such as hypothesize, infer, or analyze, simply because there is no substantive connection to the words, no prior experience giving the terms meaning in science education.

Experience was significant for children living in earlier times. Farming families understood firsthand issues such as birth and death; seasonal changes; tools, such as levers, pulleys, and blades; and how plants developed from seeds. Natural connections to the words they read, letters they wrote, and historical perspectives about changing times occurred within the schoolhouse setting (Morrison & Morrison, 1989). Relevancy and connectedness remain key factors in a child's understanding of science concepts and trends; however, we have greatly limited the experience—both inside and outside of the classroom—due to the enormous hours dedicated to streamlined curricular offerings. Because of this growing limitation, the overall educational opportunities have diminished as well.

Members of the local community are often overlooked by many in the educational system, but when asked to partner with schools, have proven quite capable of providing diverse and rich learning experiences to all students. In fact, in many instances, informal science educators have often succeeded where formal structures have failed. Sussman (1993) states that these partnerships work because they draw from rich, scientific resources actually used in the field, increasing the odds connections will be made and deep learning will occur.

During the last two decades, we have witnessed a profound shift in the perception of community involvement within a typical school day. As school districts continue to struggle with financial barriers and lower test scores, committees are seeking creative solutions to these and other problems. What may seem innovative is simply resurgence in extending, once again, an invitation to the community at large to come and join in the education of its young people.

Zoos, science museums, water treatment plants, and hospitals, for example, offer authentic experiences relevant to today's science classrooms. Agencies such as these can assist in establishing a materials support center, providing technology expertise, offering human resources, and even organizing professional development, including summer institutes. Field trips to community agencies can open the eyes of many students to possible career choices, while at the same time enrich their vocabulary and increase their experiential learning. Even when field trips are not possible, teachers can travel to these sites with a video camera in hand and capture a virtual field trip on tape, then return to their classrooms, ready to share the experience with their students.

Until educators begin to think outside the box and become creative themselves, it will remain nearly impossible to understand the importance of reconnecting their own students with the power found in creativity. The task of educating students will suffer because the desire to learn will be weakened.

The Scientific Literacy Institute

With this background in place, Dr. Carrillo, Dr. Rein, and Ashley were certain that with the awarding of grant money from the state department, the scientific literacy institute could bridge the gap that had developed between creativity and science learning. Area teachers were contacted and over a period of four weeks, the twenty-five participants were selected with their teaching assignments ranging in grades fourth through tenth. The purposeful mixture of science teachers—representing a wide array of student ages and racial and cultural makeup—provided a rich background of experiences and an even richer dialogue.

The summer institute would occur within a three-week time frame, with ten follow-up Saturday sessions during the forthcoming school year. The purpose of the institute would be to model the Exploratorium's Institute for Inquiry. The Saturday sessions would then focus on strengthening the science content knowledge of each participant, while providing unique learning experiences situated within the community.

Participants were expected to write journal entries on a daily basis, exposing their thoughts and struggles as they shifted their teaching styles to include inquiry-based learning experiences in their science teaching. Team leaders were permitted to read the comments, questions, and feelings represented in either written words or drawings. They would then respond to whatever was included in an attempt to provide feedback and encouragement throughout the process. The following comments reflect some of what the entire group was dealing with as they mentally worked their way through this change.

Sam, a teacher of rural fourth grade Hispanic children, found the institute to be just the answer to the issues with which he had been struggling. The demands of inquiry-based science, it seems, ran contrary to the cultural norms of Hispanics:

> Hispanic students who have not been exposed to inquiry science may not feel comfortable when asked to develop probing questions. They tend to look at the teacher as an authority figure who must give them guidance on how to proceed. My students are accustomed to being told and shown how to conduct scientific investigations, and I have found this to be true in all of my years of teaching Hispanic students.

Yet when Sam came to understand the processes found within the three levels of inquiry and gained confidence in content knowledge, he learned to creatively solve some of those very issues related to the cultural norms of some of the students peopling his classroom. Sam was able to more effectively communicate with parents of his students about what he was attempting to do in the science classroom and to even invite them to join the classroom's learning community.

A married couple—Marilyn, the wife, teaching seventh graders in a rural district, and Bishop, the husband, teaching tenth graders in a separate rural district—wrote of their strong desire to acquire new strategies appropriate to their science subject matter yet unique to their students. Marilyn captured her own desire to learn:

> As a science teacher I think that one of the most important things I can offer my students is my enthusiasm for learning. I am curious about the natural world and because of this curiosity I have an inward drive to learn more about it. When I learn new things, I can't wait to share them with others, in particular, my students. My understanding

of my own excitement over learning helps me to feel a little of what my students may feel. And if I feel this strongly, then I definitely see the value in helping my students experience new things for themselves, so that they may feel just as passionate about their own learning. Inquiry is the perfect strategy to ensure that this happens.

Another participant, Michelle, shared her thoughts on the importance of a child's creativity within the classroom setting:

> Today has made it clear to me the need for creativity to flourish within my classroom. I am seeing how and why it is important to raise the level of student investigations. Often, I am the questioner, the creator, and I have realized how important it is for them to be the questioners, the creators, of their own learning experiences. I cannot do it for them, but I can help them get there.

Towards the end of the institute, Mrs. Bell—the teacher featured in the introduction—summed up what actually had been the team's desired effects of hosting such an institute all along: "The stuff you work on, create, and find out is the stuff that you will remember—long after the tests have been handed in and the grades have been posted."

What had begun as merely a dialogue between colleagues discussing teaching practices had flourished into the actualization of a vision. And the vision—a call for a return to authentic learning experiences relying on the creativity of children—would continue beyond the boundaries of this university.

Conclusion

Nationwide, school districts have been steeped in the No Child Left Behind (2001) policy. Curricular choices and teaching methods have continued their alignment to state and national standards as teachers and students prepare for accountability tests. What began as a public affirmation of high stakes testing (Phi Delta Kappa, 2001: 44 percent believe there to be an appropriate amount of testing), now has shifted (Phi Delta Kappa, 2008: 80 percent prefer schools to be judged by growth in student achievement instead of increased test scores) (Haury, 2001; Hull, 2008).

Furthermore, teachers and administrators are becoming more and more alarmed at the lack of innovation and creativity within classrooms. Many are simply leaving the profession, either because of increasing levels of stress or boredom (Blair & Archer, 2001). Still others leave wondering where the joy in teaching and learning has gone.

Within the science classroom, research studies have indicated that "high-stakes testing has led teachers away from strategies consistent with a constructivist view of science teaching. Such testing has narrowed the range of instructional practices . . . narrowing the purposes of education itself" (Wideen, O'Shea, Pye, & Ivany, 1997, p. 9). As Dr. Carrillo, Dr. Rein, and Ashley discovered, it is possible—no, it is imperative—for creativity to impact the inquiry process in science teaching and learning. Years after the university's scientific literacy institute, the ripple effects are still apparent. One participant went on to become a science consultant with a nearby education cooperative, another transferred to a larger school district that was opening up a science magnet school, and a third—our Mrs. Bell—continued to work closely with her peers, ultimately transforming science teaching within her school district.

The concept of inquiry-based learning remains a strong contender for reaching diverse students of all ages (Dyasi, 1999). Teachers who learn to use this method experience a win-win situation: their students' social and intellectual development expand, while the teacher's own passion for education becomes reignited and burns once again. It will no longer only be about how many standards have passing marks at the end of a grading period but about the depth of questioning and investigation that has occurred. Hopefully, creativity and passion will return to the hallways of our schools as students, teachers, and communities engage the mind as well as the soul in the experience of learning through inquiry in science education.

References

Banchi, H., & Bell, R. (2008). The many levels of inquiry. *Science & Children, 46*(2), 26–29.

Bartels, D. M. (1999). An introduction to the National Science Education Standards. In *Foundations: A monograph for professionals in science, mathematics, and technology education* (Vol. 2: *Inquiry: Thoughts, views, and strategies for the K–5 classroom*, pp. 15–21). Arlington, VA: Directorate of Education and Human Resources, National Science Foundation.

Beacon Learning Center. (2000–2005). What is inquiry? *Just Science Now!* Retrieved April 9, 2009, from http://www.justsciencenow.com/inquiry/index.htm

Bencze, L., & Hodson, D. (1999). Changing practice by changing practice: Towards more authentic science and science curriculum development. *Journal of Research in Science Teaching, 36*(5), 521–539.

Berghoff, B., Egawa, K. A., Harste, J. C., & Hoonan, B. T. (2000). *Beyond reading and writing: Inquiry, curriculum, and multiple ways of knowing.* Urbana, IL: National Council of Teachers of English.

Blair, J., & Archer, J. (2001). NEA members denounce high-stakes testing. *Education Week*. Retrieved October 24, 2008, from http://www.edweek.org

Bransford, J. D., Brown, A. L., & Cocking, R. R. (Eds.). (1999). *How people learn*. Washington, DC: National Research Council.

Bredderman, T. (1982). Activity science: The evidence shows it matters. *Science & Children, 20*, 39–41.

Colburn, A. (2004). Inquiring scientists want to know. *Educational Leadership, 62*(1), 63–66.

Corcoran, T. C. (1995). *Transforming professional development for teachers: A guide for state policymakers*. Washington, DC: National Governors Association.

Dyasi, H. (1999). What children gain by learning through inquiry. In *Foundations: A monograph for professionals in science, mathematics, and technology education* (Vol. 2: *Inquiry: Thoughts, views, and strategies for the K–5 classroom*, pp. 9–13). Arlington, VA: Directorate of Education and Human Resources, National Science Foundation.

Exploratorium. (n.d.). *What is inquiry?* Retrieved April 7, 2009, from http://www.exploratorium.edu/ifi/about/philosophy.html

Hammrich, P. L. (1997). Teaching for excellence in K–8 science education: Using Project 2061 benchmarks for more effective science instruction. *Journal of Teacher Education, 48*(3), 222–232.

Harste, J. C. (1994). Literacy as curricular conversations about knowledge, inquiry, and morality. In R. B. Ruddell, M. R. Ruddell, & H. Singer (Eds.), *Theoretical models and processes of reading* (4th ed., pp. 1220–1242). Newark, DE: International Reading Association.

Haury, D. L. (2001). *The state of proficiency testing in science*. (ERIC Document Reproduction Service no. ED 465544 2001-12-00). Retrieved October 24, 2008, from http://eric.ed.gov/ERICDocs/data/ericdocs2sql/content_storage_01/0000019b/80/1a/1d/67.pdf

Hebert, T. R. (2006). *The impact of state-mandated, high-stakes testing on fifth-grade science teachers' instructional practices*. Ann Arbor, MI: UMI Company.

Hein, G. E., & Price, S. (1994). *Active assessment for active science: A guide for elementary school teachers*. Portsmouth, NH: Heinemann Educational Books.

Hickman, L. A., & Alexander, T. M. (Eds.). (1998). *The essential Dewey* (Vol. 1: Pragmatism, education, democracy, pp. 229–230). Bloomington, IN: Indiana University Press.

Houghton, M., & Goren, P. (1995). *Professional development for educators: New state priorities and models*. Washington, DC: National Governors Association.

Hull, J. (2008). *Phi Delta Kappa poll: Public gives mixed messages on national standards*. National School Boards Association. Retrieved October 24, 2008, from http://www.nsba.org

Lee, O. (2003). Teacher change in beliefs and practices in science and literacy instruction with English language learners. *Journal of Research in Science Teaching, 41*(1), 65–93.

Lee, O., & Avalos, M. (2003). Integrating science with English language development. *SEDL Letter XV*(1), 21–27.

Morrison, P., & Morrison, P. (1989). *Keynote address*. Speech given at the summer 1989 National Science Resources Center Elementary Science Leadership Institute, Washington, D.C.

National Commission on Teaching & America's Future. (1996). *What matters most: Teaching for America's future.* New York: Author.

National Foundation for the Improvement of Education. (1996). *Teachers take charge of their learning: Transforming professional development for student success.* Washington, DC: Author.

National Institutes of Health. (2005). *Doing science: The process of scientific inquiry.* Colorado Springs, CO: Biological Sciences Curriculum Study. Retrieved April 9, 2009, from http://science.education.nih.gov/supplements/nih6/Inquiry/guide/info_process-b.htm

National Research Council. (1996). *National science education standards.* Washington, DC: National Academy Press.

Resnick, L. B. (1987). *Education and learning to think.* Washington, DC: National Academy Press.

Ronsberg, D. (2006). There's more to teaching science. *Science & Children, 44*(1), 24–25.

Scribner, J. P. (1999). Professional development: Untangling the influence of work context on teacher learning. *Educational Administration Quarterly, 35*(2), 238–266.

Sussman, A. (Ed.). (1993). *Science education partnerships: Manual for scientists and K–12 teachers.* San Francisco, CA: University of California.

U.S. Department of Education. (1983). *A nation at risk: The imperative for educational reform* (Archived information). Retrieved April 9, 2009, from http://www.ed.gov/pubs/NatAtRisk/index.html

U.S. Department of Education. (2001). *The No Child Left Behind Act of 2001* (Public Law print no. PL 107-110). Retrieved April 9, 2009, from http://www.ed.gov/policy/elsec/leg/esea02/index.html

Wideen, M. F., O'Shea, T., Pye, I., & Ivany, G. (1997). High-stakes testing and the teaching of science. *Canadian Journal of Education, 22*(4), 428–444.

CHAPTER 8

Capturing Teacher Learning, Curiosity, and Creativity through Science Notebooks

Carole G. Basile
University of Colorado Denver

Sharon Johnson
University of Colorado Denver

Carole G. Basile, EdD, is an associate professor at the University of Colorado Denver. She is also co-principal investigator/director for the Rocky Mountain Middle School Math and Science Partnership. Over her academic career, her research efforts have included teacher education and teacher leadership, professional development schools, environmental education, and interdisciplinary learning.

Sharon Johnson, PhD, is an adjunct professor at the University of Colorado Denver. Currently retired from K–12 education, she has a long career record as a science educator and administrator.

ABSTRACT

In teacher education, dispositions are often difficult to discern and understand. Curiosity, in particular, is a disposition of utmost importance if we want teachers to engage students as lifelong learners. How teachers view curiosity is essential to how they will respond to the manifestation of this characteristic in children (Chak, 2007). The work presented in this chapter illustrates how science notebooks were used to capture teacher curiosity in both content and pedagogical learning.

In science, curiosity is the critical element to discovery and learning. In young children, we see curiosity at every turn—in their questions, their reactions, and their movements. As we get older, curiosity becomes harder to define and harder to measure. As teacher educators, we want teachers who are inquisitive and curious because we believe that makes them better teachers and better at engaging students as thoughtful learners. How teachers view curiosity is essential to how they will respond to the manifestation of this characteristic in children (Chak, 2007).

The beginning of contemporary efforts to explore teachers' professional knowledge is typically attributed to Lee Shulman and his presidential address at the 1985 annual meeting of the American Educational Research Association, entitled, "Those Who Understand: Knowledge Growth in Teaching." In the published version of that address, Shulman (1986) suggested that "we distinguish among three categories of knowledge: (a) subject-matter content knowledge, (b) pedagogical content knowledge, and (c) curricular knowledge" (p. 9). Educational scholars have built upon and extended Shulman's seminal work on teachers' professional knowledge, particularly within the domains of subject-matter and pedagogical content knowledge (Ball, Thames, & Phelps, 2005).

However, as professional development opportunities grow for teachers in these areas, researchers should not dismiss attitudes and dispositions of teachers as critical learning components as well. The teacher's attitudes and dispositions can impact teaching methodologies and the amount of time spent in teaching the content (Paulson, n.d.). Specifically, more exploration is needed about how to capture whether we have piqued a teacher's curiosity through our teaching and how this curiosity impacts classroom practice and change.

In this chapter, science education forms the context for our work. Within this discipline, we examine the use of science notebooks with teachers and how these notebooks illustrate teacher curiosity and learning. Initially, the study was designed to analyze notebooks for content, content pedagogy, and general pedagogical or curricular knowledge. As a matter of fact, we did find tremendous insight into how and what teachers were learning, but we also found that the notebooks revealed teacher dispositions as well—the key disposition being curiosity.

Context and the Use of Science Notebooks

The context for this study is a Math and Science Partnership (MSP) project funded by the National Science Foundation. The primary purpose of this project is to enhance middle school student achievement in math and science, predominantly through the provision of math and science content courses to middle level teachers. Since the project's inception in 2004, seventeen content-based math and science courses have been developed, primarily as two- or three-week summer institutes with a four-session follow-up during the academic year. Summer sessions primarily focus on content while the academic year follow-up sessions focus primarily on pedagogy. Courses are co-taught by a team of instructors, including math and science faculty, university math and science education faculty, and K–12 math and science education administrators. Courses may be lab-based or field-based, depending on the content being taught. All courses have been developed using an inquiry-based instructional approach.

In the beginning of the project, the instructional teams struggled with how to assess what teachers were learning in the courses. Because science notebooks are currently a popular instructional and assessment tool (Ruiz-Primo & Li, 2004), the science instructors decided to use notebooks in addition to teacher content inventories as a possible way to discover just how much teachers were internalizing content. Ruiz-Primo and Li (2004) have described science notebooks as a "compilation of entries that provide a record, at least partially, of the instructional experiences a student had in her or his classroom for a certain period of time"(p. 62). Science notebooks allow students to illustrate the skills and processes related to scientific inquiry, promote application and integration of new information, provide a venue for expressing personal meaning and ownership of the learning, and provide a good source of information about student conceptions and understanding of the content.

At the beginning of the summer institutes, each teacher was provided with a lab notebook. Lab notebooks with carbonless paper were used so that instructors could have teachers turn in the carbon copy at the end of the day, and the teachers could keep their notebooks for continued writing and homework in the evening. Guidelines for the notebooks were developed by the instructional teams and were given to each teacher participant. At the end of the summer, instructors turned in their notebook copies for analysis by the research team, and instructors were interviewed to determine fidelity of implementation. The guidelines are as follows:

Science Notebooks provide instructors with:

- A window into teachers' thinking and learning and a reflection of the instructional tasks carried out in the science class
- An explicit way to model good content pedagogy
- A tool for formative assessment

Science Notebooks allow teachers to:

- Illustrate the skills and processes related to scientific inquiry
- Promote application and integration of new information

- Provide a venue for expressing personal meaning and ownership of the learning

Entries should include (these are the types of entries and prompts found to be of greatest value to find out if teachers/students gained new conceptual and pedagogical understandings):

- Defining concepts in own words
- Prewriting activity/assessment about prior knowledge (e.g., "quick write")
- Predicting/hypothesizing
- Designing experiments or field observations
- Procedures of experiments or field observations designed by teachers or the class
- Reporting claims and evidence
- Interpreting results/concluding/reasoning
- Providing new and/or multiple examples illustrating concepts
- Reporting new content understandings
- Application to content pedagogical knowledge and pedagogy
- Reflections related to lab experience, discussions, readings, and so forth
- Reflections related to readings related especially to world view

Formative assessment: Specific feedback from *all* instructors to teachers is critical to the process. At different points throughout the class, the instructors should collect notebook pages with specified entries and provide written feedback about the content and/or pedagogy. Instructors can sample notebooks every night and/or review notebooks during the course while someone else is teaching. Feedback should include comments that:

- Correct misconceptions
- Expand teacher knowledge
- Ask new questions that allow teachers to respond in depth

Final prompt and collection of notebooks for review: At the end of each course, please provide your teachers with the quick write prompt provided below. We will use the information gathered to assess the teacher's perception of the value of their notebooks.

Final notebook quick write prompt: Reflect upon the Rocky Mountain Middle School Project's use of science notebooks by responding to the following questions:

1. How did you use your science notebook during the class?
2. How did your instructor use the science notebooks during the class?

> 3 What types of entries and/or parts of your notebook do you value the most? Please refer to specific examples by page number or a marked page.
> 4. Will you use, or continue to use, notebooks with your students? Why or why not?
> 5. What are your new learnings, if any, about the use of science notebooks?
> 6. Are there any additional comments you would like to add?

Of the 196 notebooks turned in to the research team, seventy (ten from each of seven science courses offered) were randomly chosen for analysis. A constant comparative analysis (Lincoln & Guba, 1985) was used to determine which types of teacher knowledge were present across courses and science notebooks, gain insight into how teachers used the notebooks, and determine other uses of the notebooks besides those explicitly suggested in the guidelines. The average notebook was approximately eighty pages; some were more than one hundred; none were less than fifty.

Implementation of the Science Notebooks

After implementation in the 2007 summer institutes, the research team interviewed instructors from each instructional team to assess the actual implementation of the science notebooks. Four of the instructors interviewed taught more than one course, two were university science faculty members, one was a university education faculty member, and two were representatives from K–12. Interview questions fell into the following broad categories: prior experience with notebooks, perceived purpose of the notebooks, presentation or introduction of the notebooks to teachers, how the science notebooks were used as an instructional tool, how the science notebooks were used as a formative assessment tool, and how the science notebooks were used as a self-reflective tool to inform their own teaching. These interviews also gave us initial insight that science notebooks would reveal more than content and/or pedagogy.

Prior Experience with Notebooks

All representatives had some experience with science notebooks but not as a learning tool with teachers. Science, Technology, Engineering, and Mathematics (STEM) faculty had either used science notebooks in their own research or had used them with undergraduate or graduate students in traditional college classrooms. Education faculty had used science notebooks with middle and high school students. None had used them as part of teacher professional learning, which became part of our puzzle.

Purpose of the Notebooks

Faculty representatives had similar viewpoints about the purpose of the science notebooks within teacher professional learning. Initially, they all stated that the purpose of the notebooks was generally to provide teachers with a place to keep their lab notes, their reflections, new understandings, and self-reflections on their own learning. As the courses progressed and notebooks were used, faculty stated that the notebooks fulfilled multiple purposes beyond what they originally imagined. One faculty member noted that teachers constructed their own purposes—there was much more reflection of attitudes and dispositions than he thought would be present. Instructors were fairly open to including the type of entries established by the guidelines as well as to any other type of content relevant to their courses.

SCIENCE NOTEBOOKS AS AN INSTRUCTIONAL TOOL

As we asked faculty questions about science notebooks as an instructional tool, we urged them to point out specific examples from a random sample of notebooks to illustrate some of the ways they encouraged teachers to use the notebooks. Instructors were not consistent in the manner in which they used the science notebooks. Sometimes the notebook was used in a more directive fashion, sometimes less directive and more open and reflective. They felt the balance of the two provided greater purpose and allowed for more insight into attitude and disposition about what they were learning. However, instructors did encourage teachers to use "proper" field note techniques (i.e., incorporating drawings, showing calculations, not erasing, use of proper symbols).

SCIENCE NOTEBOOKS AS AN ASSESSMENT TOOL

At this point, there was no programmatic expectation that the science notebooks be used as an assessment tool. Only two of the instructors collected the pages on a regular basis, but they all talked about constant monitoring while teachers were working in small groups or out in the field. A few were surprised at how much they learned, not only about the teachers' content knowledge but also about general organization and problem solving skills. All instructors talked about how the notebooks helped their instruction from a content point of view: what content to re-teach or provide in more depth. Some instructors pointed out that it helped them to see how teachers were thinking, especially where teachers had common misconceptions.

For example, the following two entries show how two different teachers approached writing an explanation of the candle experiment. The first entry shows proficiency and uses scientific vocabulary to correctly explain observed events. The second entry also shows understanding but reveals a common misconception the teacher has about the meaning of the term "vacuum."

Teacher One's Entry: "When the candle is burning, air temperature increases in cylinder, molecules spread out and escape out of the bottom of the cylinder. When the candle goes out, air temperature in cylinder drops, air molecules slow down and move together, enter the cylinder again, increasing the height of water in the cylinder."

Teacher Two's Entry: "Candle heats air. More collisions. Air escapes. Candle goes out. Temp decreases so less KE and less collisions and less pressure. Vacuum. Water pushed in. Evidence is more candles, more temperature, more molecules escape, more vacuum, more water rises."

Here again, instructors pointed out that the notebooks also helped them to see the big "ahas," what teachers were curious about, what they really wanted to know more about, and what questions they still had.

SCIENCE NOTEBOOKS AS A SELF-REFLECTIVE TOOL

As instructors were asked to reflect on their use of the notebooks, what they learned about their own teaching and about the content knowledge gains of their teacher participants, there were consistent themes. Instructors had a lot of "next times," and every one of the teams would definitely use the notebooks again. They were amazed at how much they learned about their teachers' content knowledge and/or misconceptions. They found themselves re-teaching more than they had before and found the tool informative for both formative and summative assessment. All agreed they would definitely use the science notebooks again and felt that they learned a tremendous amount about their own instruction, the depth and breadth of teacher content knowledge, skills, as well as dispositions about various, sometimes controversial, science topics.

Teacher Learning, Curiosity, and Creativity

After the instructor interviews, the science notebooks were analyzed for common characteristics or categories across the courses. The categories included those that we expected to see: science subject matter knowledge, pedagogical content reflections, general pedagogical knowledge, and world view. However, a deeper analysis showed that curiosity, or the desire for teachers to want to know more, was the most prevalent disposition exhibited across all categories. Across the categories, curiosity looks a bit different. For example, in science subject matter knowledge, teachers are curious about new content they have learned, but in the other categories, we saw teachers who were curious to see if certain instructional techniques or tools used in the content courses would help students in the classroom. For organizational purposes, we will show how curiosity often appeared within each of the categories and discuss the nature of curiosity within each.

TEACHER LEARNING

Since all of the courses spent a considerable amount of instructional time engaged in inquiry-based laboratory experiences, the majority of the notebook entries were connected to teacher lab experiences. These experiences took various forms: explorations, investigations, observational verifications, experiments, and field studies.

The notebooks were full of content-focused questions elicited by the teachers' lab experiences. Most of their questions centered on their need to simply learn more. For example, in the chemistry class, every teacher had at least one unsolicited question in his or her notebook about solutions as he or she worked through a series of solubility labs. A few of these queries are noted below.

Are the only things that are not soluble in water things that are non-polar?
What are the liquids that don't dissolve in water?
Why do oil and water not mix?
The question I have would be, "How does the gas dissolve into the water?"
Are there other substances that have a solid phase less dense than their liquid phase like water?

Although many of the questions in the science notebooks were basic questions about content, some teacher questions reflected higher levels of thinking and a deeper interest in the subject. In many cases, the teacher would begin his or her question by saying, "I know this might be too far off the subject but . . ." or "For my own knowledge I would like to know . . ." or "Even though I wouldn't teach this to my students, what about . . ."

There were also comments that show how teachers were integrating ideas that had not been previously connected. This type of comment shows an intrinsic desire to inquire beyond the intended curriculum. A few samples of these entries are:

Why do I believe that DNA is a hereditary material?
What really drives these [chemical] reactions?
I would just really like to go over the "Big Ideas" more and connect the math to the purpose because I feel lost in the purpose behind the calculations.
I need a better understanding of bonding as well as more accurate ways of measurement.

It is important to note that as the content of each lab experience was debriefed, many of the teachers referred back to their lab notebooks to pose questions for discussion. In many instances, they would begin their question with "I have students who ask about . . ." "How would you answer their question?" But, it is also critical to point out that a number of the teachers never posed their notebook questions for class discussion. Whether or not the teachers' curiosity led them to seek the answers on their own is unknown; however, it does indicate that when science notebooks are used to record inquiry-based laboratory experiences, teachers with a disposition for subject matter curiosity will demonstrate that disposition through their notebook entries.

However, it is not just content-based questions and comments that show the degree to which teachers expressed their inquisitiveness. In the next entry, the teacher first provides an explanation for the actions of the "Dippy Bird," a toy bird that seems to dip up and down endlessly into a glass of water. The explanation shows that the teacher has a proficient understanding of the basic chemistry concepts involved in Dippy's actions: evaporation, condensation and the effect of temperature on gases and air pressure. Yet, a review of the reflection entry that follows the explanation provides a surprising insight into the teacher's thinking and new curiosity about the content.

EXPLANATION OF HOW DIPPY BIRD WORKS

1. The fluid in Dippy's bottom bulb is methylene chloride. This fluid has a very low boiling point. Methylene chloride also requires less of a lowering in temperature for the gas to condense to a liquid.

2. The head is dipped into a glass of water. The liquid begins to evaporate. . . . This takes away heat from Dippy's head . . . causing head to cool.

3. The methylene chloride gas inside Dippy's head cools and condenses. Lower pressure is created because there is less and less gas molecules in Dippy's head.

4. The lower pressure in Dippy's head and higher pressure in the bulb draws the methylene chloride up Dippy's neck.

REFLECTION

> The Dippy Bird demonstrated to me what I don't know and needed to learn. One, importance of precise observations, and because it made me think and apply the concepts I was learning. When I first saw "Dippy," I didn't have a clue about how it worked. I thought it had to do something about capillary action and that was as scientific as I could get. I jokingly thought it was a troop of Sea Monkeys swimming back and forth. After making good observations, I began to notice some subtle features that made Dippy unique. I saw that his body was a bit off center and his head was covered with a water absorbent material. This led me to think about the science we were learning. I loved thinking about the scientific laws of gas and pressure. I thought about Dippy for 2 straight days. This activity totally stimulated my thinking.

The length to which teachers went to make careful and thoughtful entries illustrates their level of inquisitiveness about the content. Writing explanations for scientific phenomena is difficult, even for teachers. Because written explanations provide an invaluable glimpse into how well content is understood, many of the instructors prompted teachers to write explanations of phenomena in their notebooks. Those teachers with an inquisitive nature, like the Dippy Bird author, demonstrated their inquiring nature by taking pride in writing their explanations and by their eagerness for receiving feedback.

In the following reflection, a physics student laments her lack of background knowledge and anxiety over the content. She, fortunately, shows enough curiosity and tenacity about the content to come back after lunch and learn more.

> I knew my physics background was limited . . . but I didn't realize how limited. . . . I still have no clue on how to use the "b" in the formula or what it means. I'm also not really clear why I need to know slope, or how it helps me understand math or physics more

clearly. After lunch seemed a little easier—there was actually some discussion of not coming back—so I was glad it was a little easier. We used terms—force, motion, friction that were/are familiar to me, but I don't feel like I own them yet.

Although the lab notes provided the most information, reading reflections also provided evidence of teachers' subject-matter knowledge. In most cases, the readings followed hands-on lab work. In this first example, the teacher makes reference to her content knowledge, its connections to the previous lab work, and her curiosity to learn more.

Some of the information in the reading was easy and some of it was more difficult. The beginning of the article was pretty much a review of things I knew from my previous classes. The information on the basic colors was a good review of wave terminology . . . Information about electrons moving up and down in energy levels and causing waves was hard for me to wrap my brain around. I am also still trying to grasp adding and subtracting colors when we did our experiment yesterday. Our results were very different from those described in the book. Although I know the filters were not "perfect," I am excited to learn more.

Another teacher wrote the following after doing an osmosis experiment and reading two articles. Her concise summary reflects her change in thinking as well as the depth of her new understandings.

While reading on osmosis, I was surprised by the use of [the terms] osmosis and diffusion. Educational texts made explicit the difference between the two phenomena. Medical reference applied osmosis and diffusion interchangeably. . . . In my own education, diffusion and osmosis were always presented as ideas with important contrasts . . . I was surprised that applied osmolality is determined by concentrations of diffusible ions, not just the movement of solvent. Yet, the osmolality discrepancy allowed me to focus on the unifying concept: osmosis is just a special case of diffusion.

The next two entries highlight new learnings that took teachers by surprise.

Entry One: This article ["The Fossils Say Yes"] and the trip to the museum today really opened up my eyes and surprised me as to which organisms are related to whom! What is even more astonishing is how much scientists do know about the interrelationships of species, even though less than one percent of the species that have ever lived are preserved as fossils.

Entry Two: When water is added to the red blood cells, we could not see any cells under the microscope. At first, I thought that I was unable to use the microscope correctly. When Debbie couldn't find any cells and we learned that none of the other groups could find any cells under the microscope, we realized that there weren't any cells to be found—we had lysed the cells!

The entries selected, however, are but the tip of the iceberg. Hundreds of pages reflect teacher learning, including predictions, observations, data collection, results, conclusions, and new understandings. The notebooks clearly reflected teachers' amazement and surprise by their findings. Exclamations in the margins showed that they were curious, and they cared about what they learned— "WOW," "Unbelievable!" and "We were so wrong!!" were not uncommon phrases. For example, after doing a chemistry lab, one teacher wrote, "This lab [dry ice aquarium] was not formally written up, but the connection to diffusion in biology hit me like a sledge hammer."

The next remark illustrates how teachers were not only curious about the content but also about how the scientific process enhanced their curiosity.

In addition to helping me learn about the Kinetic Molecular Theory of Matter, this experiment also taught me about the inquiry process (although it is a time consuming one, it is incredibly valuable and powerful as a learning/teaching tool) and that much of science consists of finding what doesn't work and disproving hypotheses. Science is circular; every time a hypothesis is disproven, you begin again, with a new hypothesis. The inquiry process just heightens my curiosity to know more.

TEACHER CURIOSITY AND CREATIVITY

Reflective entries also provided insight into how teachers were planning to change their current classroom practices related to pedagogical content knowledge and general pedagogical understanding. In many cases, notebook entries illustrated how teachers thought about how their new understandings would impact student content learning. A number of entries reflected the teachers' intentions to enhance or change their future lessons to make content more meaningful for their students. For example, after performing a conservation of mass experiment, one student wrote the following:

I have used this laboratory experiment [magnesium chloride and baking soda reaction] to demonstrate conservation of mass. The added layers of information presented here will help me to activate students'

> knowledge of this lab at different points to enforce a concept other than conservation. I could ask them to think about exothermic and endothermic reactions as well as acids and bases, etc.

Another entry illustrates how a teacher's new understandings, acquired by using a different instructional format (Internet websites), might impact her students' learning.

> I will use the websites provided to help my students be visually aware of the different phases of mitosis. I now have a greater understanding of the phases of mitosis and the difference in cell division in mitosis and meiosis. I wonder how these websites can help show students [how cell parts move] in a controlled environment and in a more game/video like learning environment.

As labs were discussed and debriefed, teachers frequently talked about how to apply what they learned to their classrooms. Margin notes and sidebars frequently recorded comments that they wanted to remember and possibly try. In the following excerpt, the teacher both states the principle to remember and gives examples. "Know the big ideas that you want to get across . . . like solubility depends upon the amount of substance that dissolves and not the speed [the substance dissolves]."

As new teaching pedagogical strategies were presented, teachers frequently used their notebooks to write about the strategy for their future reference. For example, upon learning about a vocabulary strategy called "red light-green light," a teacher wrote the following in his notebook. "Red light—never seen the word; yellow light—heard it but can't define it; green light—heard it and can use it. Put groups together—make a mix of groupings with G. Y. R. then play concentration. [This strategy] can give feedback to teacher to vary Y and R and re-teach."

Because teachers were placed in the role of students, they had more time to reflect on the act of teaching. Frequently, pedagogical reflections addressed their desire to be more responsive to their student's needs. It gave them a better understanding about not only the struggles students have in learning the content but also how their own curiosity could be transferred to students. "This [black box] activity inspired me to always implement an engage piece when introducing scientific concepts. All of the engage activities had the same effect on me as a student & therefore I am confident my students will find inspiration. The engage activities piqued my interests & provoked me to make connections."

Here we see the use of words like "inspired" and "piqued my interests," illustrating that this teacher was curious about her learning and, again, how it could inspire student engagement or bring out the curiosity in her students.

It was interesting to find that as the teachers experienced inquiry-based instructional strategies, their comments reflected their desire to restructure their hands-on labs. They consistently wrote about their need to increase student engagement and understanding by using the creativity and curiosity generated by performing inquiry activities. For example, one teacher decided, "Have kids talk about data before writing conclusions" as she realized that discussing data helped her find new meaningful connections. Another teacher concluded, "Allow kids to change [their] claim after discussing and encourage kids to go and talk to other groups," after he found out that his teacher-to-teacher interactions enriched his understanding and provided new information. In this comment, made following a class discussion on inquiry, a further teacher noted, "I try to use inquiry a lot . . . I need to work on follow thru with labs to elaborate [and tie] the concepts together."

Changing one's teaching behavior is a creative and innovative act. It begins with recognizing the need to change and proceeds if, and only if, the teacher continues to value the change and finds support for the change. It is no surprise that our emphasis on inquiry-based learning and instruction formed the impetus for many of the pedagogical entries.

The amount of self-reflection related to the pedagogy and inquiry-based learning surprised the reviewers. Teachers openly expressed their struggles implementing inquiry-based learning. These sample reflective entries indicate that the teachers were actively wondering about how they could be more effective instructors. One teacher admitted, "I still struggle setting up class in a way that allows students to build their own knowledge." In describing his approach to inquiry, another teacher observed, "I do lead off labs with questions but most of my labs are [still] step-by-step." A further teacher wrote, "Some units and lessons—I have not used inquiry as much. I would like to improve," whereas another teacher noted in frustration, "I have tried doing inquiry labs but had to give too much freedom so students don't know what is expected . . . Then I abandon it [inquiry] for a little while to avoid frustration." And finally, "I have become better with [teaching inquiry by] taking the summer courses and seeing how to use the process with the hands-on activities first."

Another topic that garnered numerous comments related to the integration of literacy in science and math classes. Few teachers indicated that they were effective at integrating their content courses with literacy instruction; however, many were very curious about what and how they could do more. As literacy strategies were introduced, teachers commented about how they might use the strategy. After learning how to use a literacy strategy called "JOT" (just one thing), one teacher wrote the following: "JOT . . . I would use this activity because in Life Science there are many pictures which will catch the interest and expose the students' previous knowledge and make connections with other students' background when the results are shared after the activity."

And after learning about a strategy called "three-column notes," another teacher contributed: "While usually I have had students take traditional lecture and copy notes, this [three-column vocabulary] will allow students to create definitions in their own words and also create their own depiction in a drawing. By taking ownership students' retention will be strengthened."

And, finally, after writing about a strategy, one teacher said it all: "This notebook entry is helpful because it will remind me to try these things in class."

In addition, we also had teachers involved who were not math and science teachers. The following pedagogical reflections provide evidence of the importance of cross-curricular professional learning. The following entries by non-science teachers who are "out of their area" show how they are curious about both the content and how to integrate the content into their area.

> As a special education teacher, I think this [word splash reading strategy] will be a very useful tool for reading expository text and I'll be curious to see how it enhances learning. My role on my team is to provide literacy instruction strategies for all 8th graders to support the content areas. Many kids, special ed especially, have big challenges with reading and understanding textbooks. This strategy supports vocabulary development, reading for information, identifying main ideas, and summarizing.

> As a social studies teacher, I do a joint *Animal Farm*/Russian Revolution-Rise of Soviet Communism unit. To add in a DNA analysis/critical thinking piece about the Romanov family would be a great addition!

> In language arts, I would work with kids on scientific writing and writing conclusions using evidence from their experiments to support their conclusions!

CURIOSITY AND WORLD VIEW

World view takes on a life of its own, and teachers used it to show their surprise about how the world works or to reflect some personal concern. For example, after comparing a variety of antacid brands to the effect of baking soda, a student noted, "Read the label. Are you buying something that is treating what you need it to—Do you really need that fancy package and 'minty' taste to get the job done?" And, in response to a teacher who questioned the need to teach middle level students about acids, a teacher wrote, "[Because acid rain has] real life applications. Real life consequences."

For teachers, science notebooks were also used to express dissonance between science, religion, and/or philosophy. One student used a reading reflection to express her dissonance between the science content and her personal beliefs. These two entries, both from the same student, highlight the need for students to be able to express themselves when discussing potentially controversial subjects. They also illustrate how the courses enhanced teachers' curiosity about others' perspectives.

> I have a difficult time reading this article with an open mind when I am a Christian who believes in God. However, I try to have an open mind as this leads me to wonder about other perspectives.
>   I'm not sure I agree with the statement that "This is their [bacteria] planet, and we are on it only because they allow us to be." I do agree that we couldn't survive a day without them.

Although we didn't find large numbers of these examples, we believe that this is an area that is worth pursuing further, and that this type of curiosity that comes from pushing one's thinking is important and notable.

Conclusion

The role of fostering curiosity in teaching and teacher education is of utmost importance if we want to see classroom practice change in meaningful ways. Teacher educators want teachers who are lifelong learners and are continuously motivated to learn both content and pedagogical practices. In science education, notebooks as an instructional tool in science teacher professional learning can provide teacher educators and university faculty with an authentic way of discerning teachers' knowledge. However, maybe more importantly, the use of this tool can also help us to discern teachers' dispositions, especially curiosity. We see from this brief look at these science notebook entries that teachers reveal their own curiosities about content, pedagogy, and world view. We also see that after experiencing new models and tools for learning, teachers are curious about trying new classroom practices. These notebooks were more than just a record of lab experiences, a journal, or a reflective tool. They became a compendium of information for instructors to learn more about what teachers were learning and in what contexts teacher curiosity was inspired.

References

Ball, D., Thames, M., & Phelps, G. (2005). *Knowledge of mathematics for teaching: What makes it special?* Paper presented at the annual meeting of the American Educational Research Association, Montreal, Canada.

Chak, A. (2007). Teachers' and parents' conceptions of children's curiosity and exploration. *International journal of early years education, 15*(2), 141–159.

Lincoln, Y. S., & Guba, E. G. (1985). *Naturalistic inquiry.* Newbury Park, CA: Sage.

Paulson, P. (n.d.). *Developing quality through improved attitudes toward science and science teaching.* Paper presented at the annual meeting of the American Association of
Colleges for Teacher Education Online. Retrieved October 9, 2008, from http://www
.allacademic.com/meta/p35803_index.html

Ruiz-Primo, M., & Li, M. (2004). On the use of students' science notebooks as an assessment tool. *Studies in Educational Evaluation, 30,* 61–85.

Shulman, L. (1986). Those who understand: Knowledge growth in teaching. *Educational
Researcher, 15*(5), 4–14.

CHAPTER 9

Freeing the Body to Build the Creative Mind

JeongAe You
Korea Institute of Curriculum and Evaluation

JeongAe You, PhD, is a research fellow in the Department of Physical Education at the Korea Institute of Curriculum and Evaluation. Her research interests include curriculum development, teacher education, and teacher knowledge in physical education. Recently, she has served as a director for revising a national physical education curriculum in Korea.

ABSTRACT

A creative mind is an essential element in education. Our society needs well-educated humans with highly developed minds that allow each individual to creatively perform to his or her greatest potential in a variety of fields. The highly developed creative mind with limitless possibilities can result from an innovative curriculum and inspired teaching in physical education. The purpose of this chapter is to discuss the relationship between body and mind in physical education through viewing three different traditions (technocratic, critical, and postmodern physical education) and to provide two exemplary curriculum and teaching cases designed to develop the creative mind in physical education.

The development of a creative mind should be a primary concern for everyone in all fields. The field of education, which examines how learning takes place and arrives at teaching techniques that effectively meet the needs of potential learners, is no exception, and this applies to participants at every level—students, teachers, teacher candidates, teacher educators, policy makers, school administrators, and so forth. However, to date, in the educational community, very little attention has been given to developing the creative mind in educational settings around the world, despite the fact that numerous studies on creativity in education have been conducted and their results supporting creativity published. In physical education, just as in the broad field of education, little attention has been given to building creative minds, regardless of evidence that physical activity is the most appropriate modality for eliciting the creativity of children and students in general (Cleland & Gallahu, 1993; Cleland, 1994; McBride, 1991; Park & Heisler, 2001; Zachopoulou, Trevlas, Konstadinidou, & Archimedes Project Research Group, 2006).

It should be noted first that a primary reason little attention is given to developing the creative mind in the physical education community is negligence, a consequence of which is a failure to perceive the inherent essence of physical education (Armour, 1999). In general, most physical educators are quite conservative and lack a relational understanding of the complex, intersecting connections between and among physical activity, the school, culture, and society. The causes for this lack of understanding may be traced to these educators' professional perspectives that focus on reproducing the conventional curricular orientation rather than transforming it. Keeping the same ideologies and doing the same things is just like making the essence of the physical education enterprise deconstructed (Crum, 1993; Fernandez-Balboa, 1997; Sparkes, 1987; Sparkes, Templin, & Schempp, 1990). With regard to the influence of human viewpoints, Fernandez-Balboa (1997) explains the following:

> People view the world, establish goals, set and solve problems, and evaluate outcomes according to their professional knowledge. The same can be said for physical educators and their knowledge. To a great extent, who we are and what we do as physical educators depends on our knowledge and assumptions about physical education. Who we are and what we do as teachers or teacher educators is intimately related to what we believe teaching and teacher education is and ought to be. (p. 162)

Even if the title given this subject matter field, "physical education," emphasizes "physical (= body)," "the physical" has diverse meanings and "physical education" has multiple goals (Crum, 1993; Fraleigh, 1990). Depending on perspectives on body, Rintala (1991) explains that understanding, developing, and implementing physical education curricula could be totally different. She indicates that unfortunately two dominant perceptions (one involving separating mind and body in physical education and the other involving thinking in terms of "mind over body" in physical education) have existed in our schools. In her research findings, Rintala argues that both perspectives have negatively impacted the field of education in general as well as physical education specifically.

Likewise, according to Johnson (1987), outside the physical education community, the body has also been ignored and undervalued in objectivist accounts of meaning and rationality and those structures of human imagination and understanding that emerge from our embodied experiences. Both perspectives produce outcomes that are not constructive and that limit or eliminate opportunities for participants to perform well and to move in free and creative ways, whatever their educational roles.

In a sense, a full understanding of body and mind is necessary for general educators as well as for physical educators. More specifically, for physical educators, the questions that are likely to be significant include: "How is the body made and remade in physical education?" "What does the mind mean in physical education?" "In what ways is the relationship between body and mind perceived in physical education?" Further, McKay, Gore, and Kirk (1990) posit that there should be a deliberate effort to raise awareness of issues such as what physical education can contribute to student learning, how and why physical education takes on its current form and content, which groups benefit from physical education and which groups are disempowered, and how physical education can be used for emancipatory purposes.

Therefore, the purpose of this chapter is to examine how perspectives on body and mind have impacted physical education through three different traditions (technocratic, critical, and postmodern physical education) and to explore in what ways body and mind should be viewed in physical education to effectively build the creative mind. Additionally, two practical examples for cultivating the creative mind in physical education will be suggested. In the end result, this essay offers feasible implications with regard to teacher education in general and for teacher education in the field of physical education specifically.

Technocratic Physical Education: Separating Body and Mind

The concept of technocratic physical education (McKay et al., 1990) came from positivist ideology and technical rationality. The technocratic approach has been oriented toward the scientized ways of working in the educational field, such as the law-like uniformity of society and nature, the requirements for direct observation, measurability and quantification, as well as determinism and the related beliefs about causality (Lawson, 1990; Shephard, 1999; Whitson & Macintosh, 1990). For this reason, in principle and practice, technocratic physical education has focused on the dichotomous perspective, which is alive and well within the boundaries of the field itself: the idea that body must be separated from mind. That is, within the physical education field, it has sought after the singular purpose of educating only the physical body, ignoring the importance of the creative mind as well as the humanistic and social aspects of the body.

MANAGED BODY VS. INVISIBLE MIND

At the core of technocratic physical education is the image of an objective, instrumental, and mechanistic body (Kirk, 1986; Lawson, 1988; McKay et al., 1990; Rintala, 1991). On the other hand, the mind in physical education has historically been something that, though its presence is acknowledged, remains paradoxically absent. It is never considered, and facts are separated from human values because doubts are raised about the existence or importance of values (Charles, 1998; Lawson, 1990). McKay et al. (1990) explained the position of body as follows:

> The body is seldom portrayed as a pleasurable site for ecstatic, aesthetic, vertiginous, autotelic, sensuous, and holistic experiences. It is depicted as a mechanical object that must be managed, maintained, conditioned, tuned, and repaired for instrumental reasons such as improving linear performance or increasing one's physical attractiveness. (p. 60)

That is, the body has been perceived as a physical object because it is irrelevant to human understanding or the reasoning process. In addition, the body has never been involved in "meaning making" or the construction of imagination and creativity, processes that emerge from our lived experiences. For this reason, the body in physical education has always been regarded as a biological object to be systematically trained with repetitive and continuous exercise under scientific principles (Ennis, 2006; Lawson, 1988).

At the same time, there has been no awareness that the mind might perform any educational roles in technocratic physical education. There is a strong belief in something akin to dualism (Rintala, 1991) that separates body and mind. Consequently, a huge volume of knowledge and understanding about body and mind is restricted almost totally to technocratic perspectives of physical activity. Moreover, physical education approached through technocratic pedagogy is viewed as impersonal. Even if there are manifold differences in the nature of physical education at various levels, each level is forced to demonstrate the same, or fixed, movements that rarely employ a free and creative mind and thinking (Fernandez-Balboa, 1995).

SCIENCE-DOMINANT PHYSICAL EDUCATION CURRICULUM

With technocratic physical education, the school curriculum emphasizes "education of the physical" that could be characterized as the physical training to develop physical fitness and sports skills associated with the speed, strength, and power of children and students (Armour, 1999; Ennis, 2006; Whitson & Macintosh, 1990). For this reason, the curriculum in technocratic physical education tends to be a "science-based curriculum" in which the scientific phenomena and aspects of the body in human performance are dominant. That is, two of the most important goals of physical education are to acquire competent motor skills with memorized objective knowledge, like game rules and strategies, and to demonstrate well-constructed body muscles through scientific training. The well-educated human in such a physical education curriculum is described as one who possesses a strong, fast, and tall body and performs with skillful movement and scientific knowledge. In such an approach, there is no room for or appreciation of creativity.

In technocratic physical education, the contents in physical fitness and motor skills based on scientific methods and principles are dominant and visible, whereas in the humanities and social sciences, the signs of the body in human performance are often invisible (McKay et al., 1990; Ross, 1987; Whitson & Macintosh, 1990). Since the contents are mainly covered as standardized and restrictive aspects of human movement, it is difficult for socially and culturally meaningful, creative learning to take place.

Physical educators tend to adhere to two representatively conventional beliefs: (a) one is that the most important accountability of physical education is to promote body health through building physical fitness or through developing sport skills, and (b) the other is that if children actively participate in team sports, they will be good persons (Corbin, 2002; Kirk, 1992; Laker, 2003; Talbot, 1997; Theodoulides & Armour, 2001; You, 2005). Moreover, most physical educators and curriculum scholars have had the misconception that the mind cannot be developed or educated in physical education classes because the development of mind cannot be observed or measured as can the development of the body.

Ultimately, curriculum development in physical education has traditionally discredited the social and moral phenomena of human movement. It is likely that the technocratic physical education curriculum would never deal with what physical activity is, what it means to human life, and for what purposes physical activity should be used in school physical education. The curriculum in the technocratic physical education approach is likely to close off rather than to open up the mind, to tighten up rather than free the body, and to investigate one way rather than search for multiple ways in moving.

PHYSICAL EDUCATION TEACHERS AS BODY MANAGERS

A technocratic pedagogy in physical education, as it is encouraged through teacher education, seeks "one dimensional excellence that produces talented functionaries or technical educators instead of educating teachers" (McKay et al., 1990, p. 57). With this notion, the teachers are trained as body managers who are able to reproduce and transform predetermined or fixed movements of the body. Issues regarding the training and preparation of teachers as approached in teacher education programs have been raised in many studies (Bain, 1990; Fernandez-Balboa, 1993, 1995, 1997; Fraleigh, 1990; Kirk, 1986; McKay et al., 1990; Lawson, 1988, 1990; Rink, 2007; Tinning, 2002; Whitson & Macintosh, 1990).

Findings indicate that most programs are deeply relevant to the positivist canons of the natural sciences in empirical-analytical assumptions and that these assumptions are the bases of knowledge in the field. They have been oriented to look at the teaching-learning process in terms of the behavioral aspects of children or students. According to Fernandez-Balboa (1997), this approach allows the teachers to do the same things and maintain the same beliefs.

Teachers who adhere to this approach tend to view their students from a single or limited perspective in terms of the goals of the program and of how those goals are best met, too often ignoring the variety of needs and competencies of students in physical education settings. The teachers also tend to facilitate an instructional environment that forces students to master the encoded sport skills and exercise routines until their movements become automatic with repetitive practices. Thus, the creativity of students is deliberately excluded and ultimately completely forgotten or bypassed in the technocratic approach to physical education.

Critical Physical Education: Combining Body and Mind

One way of attempting the transformation from the limited possibilities of technocratic physical education is to create a more just and equal learning situation through critical physical education (Fernandez-Balboa, 1993, 1995; Giroux, 1988; Kirk, 1986; Sage, 1993; Tinning, 1991). The critical physical education approach poses questions as to why some things are valued while others are devalued or not considered in schools. In this manner, the critical approach attempts to uncover the lost or silent perspectives and to construct alternatives in physical education for making students become happier learners.

LIVED BODY AND GOOD MIND

A rejection of the dichotomous perspective permits us to start from the position of the human as a lived "experiencer" and suggests a combination of those aspects that are objectively accessible with those that are subjective experiences and, hence, intangible (Rintala, 1991). In critical physical education, the body is alive or conscious. In critical physical education, the mind is perceived as occupying a position equal to the body. The body is viewed as a socially constructed product, not a technically trained object. In particular, Gibbons and Bressan (1991) explain that the lived body experience is described as a general feeling of unity and wholeness—a sense of unification between the subjective and objective aspects of being that was felt by creative movers.

The notion of the subjective aspects of the body in physical education provides valuable insight in that it extends the breadth and depth of knowledge construction and the understanding of human movement. The subjective experiences of body could take the form of personal knowledge of students in physical education. The body in critical physical education can provide a medium, not just for the improvement of motor skills and physical fitness, but for the development of other kinds of knowledge. That is, the body can function in important ways as the social, moral, humanistic, and critical bases of knowledge production about physical education (Armour, 1999; Charles, 1998; Hollands, 1984; McKay & Pearson, 1984; McKay et al., 1990).

As the concept of mind education—for example, socio-moral education—through physical activity emerges, it becomes crucial to understand what separates this process from physical training as the goal of physical education. Simultaneously, this essential effort could capture the attention of physical educators as well as general educators because many studies (Arnold, 1999; Drewe, 2000; Figley, 1984; Gibbons & Bressan, 1991; Jones, 2001; Miller, Bredemeier, & Shields, 1997; Theodoulides & Armour, 2001; Wandzilak, Carroll, & Ansorge, 1988) claim that situations in physical education are "real life," not hypothetical. The physical education classes offer a context for practicing moral behaviors that are more conducive to this practice than the context provided by other subjects (Drewe, 2000).

Among physical educators, there is a growing sense of concern based on the interrelation of body and mind that students should be taught the use of their bodies with moral attitudes and social values. Regarding the interrelation of body and mind, Figley (1984) also pointed out that:

> Individuals do not come to physical education with just their bodies. They bring their total self—their bodies, minds, feelings, attitudes, and values. Today, the concept of "totality" prevails and physical educators are indeed concerned with developing a thinking, feeling, moving, and human being. (p. 94)

Critical physical education encompasses the overall perspective that the body is interrelated with the mind. Therefore, in order to educate the total child, physical education in schools has among other functions that of serving as a medium for practicing the lived experiences of both body and mind, including humanistic, social, moral, and political phenomena.

EQUITABLE PHYSICAL EDUCATION CURRICULUM

Critical theorists have reminded curriculum scholars in physical education that there are political, moral, and social consequences accompanying all attempts to adjust and improve the curriculum (Lawson, 1988). In a sense, an equitable physical education curriculum would emphasize humanistic and phenomeno-logical experiences in physical activities instead of purely linear measures of physical fitness and motor skills (McKay et al., 1990). A return to the relationship between body and mind illustrates the roles and accountabilities of a reflective physical education curriculum. When one determines the educational limitations of the technocratic physical education curriculum, curriculum work in reflective physical education is engaged in a significantly innovative act that improves the objectives and contents of the physical education curriculum.

First of all, in order to educate the total child, including the child's physical, personal, and social development, a variety of activity forms, such as cooperative games, rhythmic activities, and adventure sports as well as traditional sports and gymnastics, were proposed in physical education curriculum documents. These forms of activity were thought to integrate the creative mind with the physical body and give meaning to students and to the society as a whole. According to two studies (Ennis, 2006; Mechikoff & Estes, 1998), this extension of the curriculum contents in reflective physical education, which goes beyond the development of the physical body to the education of the creative mind through physical activities, was a natural step following the development of physical education within the academic school environment.

Secondly, the concept and practice of mind education in the reflective physical education curriculum has been officially introduced through the moral education in physical education. The major theme of moral education in physical education is characterized as "good mind" and provides the grounds for demonstrating socially and culturally accepted or desirable behaviors (You, 2005). Specifically, the good mind implies good moral attitudes toward self, others (teachers and classmates), human movements, schools, and societies.

Third, curriculum specialists who adhere to an approach shaped by critical pedagogy have argued that the physical education curriculum should normally be associated with the reality of students' personal lives and experiences (Ennis, 2003; Fernandez-Balboa, 1995); this would ensure that the learning process would be individualized and, hence, more meaningful. In the equitable physical education curriculum, it is necessary not only to teach students how to perform movements in effective ways but also to explain why such movements are meaningful in personal life and to make learners aware of the impact performing these movements can have on societies (Ennis, 2003, 2006).

Finally, the equitable physical education curriculum has greatly contributed to elevating technical competence to a satisfactory level and, simultaneously, to acquiring an ability to move beyond commonsense categories of thought in order to gain critical and creative insight into the learning process (Kirk, 1986). Critical physical education assumes that not all students are ready to do or to learn the same things at the same time. For this reason, the curriculum makers through the reflective process are willing to accept various needs and experiences of individual students and to enact them within the educational practices.

PHYSICAL EDUCATION TEACHERS AS REFLECTIVE INTELLECTUALS

From a critical perspective, physical activities must be regarded as socially constructed, prone to multiple meanings and manipulations depending on the complex context in which the activities are embedded. Thus, physical education teachers in critical environments or circumstances teach much more than sports skills and fitness-related activities or biological sciences related to movements. In physical education teacher education (PETE) programs, the teachers have various opportunities to explore physical activities cross-culturally and to investigate their multiple interpretations and functions historically, comparatively, creatively, and critically. Further, teachers are being educated to look at educational phenomena in terms of power, injustice, and inequality in physical activities (Fernandez-Balboa, 1995, 1997). Finally, the PETE programs also help pre-service teachers to explore ethical and moral aspects in teaching physical education (Bain, 1993).

Critical teachers in physical education are generally recognized as intellectuals with a critical literacy rather than technocrats with a utilitarian perspective because they try to look critically at their teaching practices and make constant efforts to minimize the limitations and difficulties of educating students. For example, such teachers are willing to step outside of concerns with purely technical issues in teaching physical activities and to see the educational issues from various angles, including moral, ethical, social, and political perspectives. Further, they actively move to see how and in what ways the issues are raised in a dominant educational system and to find out the solutions using just ways.

Postmodern Physical Education: Integrating Body and Mind

A postmodern physical education approach to curriculum recognizes the limitations of radical changes in education and the diverse and multiple ways of constructing our schools and societies. At the same time, it is widely perceived that there is no single right or correct method of determining which perspective is accurate or correct. Questioning of truth, certainty, objectivity, and conventional use of time and space is natural in postmodern physical education. This questioning encourages practitioners to see diversity, multiple pathways, and links inside and outside the school that assist in discovering methods of achieving meaningful teaching and learning (Bouffard, 2001; MacDonald, 2003; Tinning, 2002).

In the postmodern physical education approach, body and mind can be transcended, and this process of transcendence is emancipatory. Postmodern physical education has the potential for enlightening and broadening the functions or roles that physical education can assume as a subject taught in our schools. In particular, postmodern physical education has the effect of empowering students to experience and perform a variety of physical activities through their own creative movements in a free learning environment.

EMANCIPATORY BODY AND MIND

In the physical educational community, people do traditionally think and use dichotomous terms such as mind/body, teacher/student, physical/mental, athlete/non-athlete, work/play, masculine/feminine, and able-bodied/disabled. Unfortunately, the implications of such thinking usually prove to be detrimental and unconstructive in physical education (Fernandez-Balboa, 1995; Rintala, 1991). Regarding body and mind, Caddick (1986, p. 76, cited in Tinning, 2002, p. 236) argues, "We are our bodies and only in and only through them do we know ourselves and our relationships to others." In other words, it would not be humanly possible to develop solely through the body because the mind is necessarily implicated.

In the postmodern physical education approach, the body, in particular, is no longer only an essential object or materiality for the expression of sports skill and scientific knowledge. Bodies in physical education should be empowered bodies, not regulated bodies, because the postmodernists in physical education believe that physical education contexts could provide a variety of practices and opportunities that influence the way humans experience and evaluate their bodies (Armour, 1999; Garrett, 2004). Moreover, the postmodern physical education approach would recognize and account for our embodied subjectivities in teaching and learning physical activities. Likewise, mind in postmodern physical education is neither separated from body nor combined with body. The mind cannot be viewed as a superior reality that controls the body. The mind can no longer be perceived as functioning unconsciously in physical education. It should act consciously like a moving body.

In future physical education, both body and mind should seek to transcend the arbitrary and dichotomous distinctions between body and mind. In preparation for doing this, the body and mind together can free themselves from dominant perceptions and, thus, refuse the traditional positioning of body and mind in physical education. This freedom is needed in order to allow for the development of a new perspective on body and mind. If a human being is to be perceived as an autonomous person, body and mind should be integrated.

EMPOWERED PHYSICAL EDUCATION CURRICULUM

In the postmodern viewpoint, the central goals of the physical education curriculum are "empowerment and emancipation," which suggest fundamental human rights in democratic societies such as "freedom from oppression and freedom to pursue individual goals." The aims further connect to the needs of the society in that achieving these aims would prepare students either to become contributing members of the society or to participate in the reconstruction of a more just and happier society. In order for these aims to be achieved, the physical education curriculum should also be versatile to free students from restrictive content and regimented teaching methods (Graber & Locke, 2007; Kretchmar, 2006; Rovegno & Kirk, 1995). Kirk (1997) reinforces the point:

> Children learn about their bodies and their capabilities in both physical and social environments, in relation to objects and other people. Bodies are the practical mode of engagement with a range of external events and situations, and it is through relentless and continuous monitoring of bodies and their expressive capabilities that individuals successfully engage in social activity. (p. 54)

To date, the existing curricula in technocratic and critical physical education have provided only a few opportunities for students to create and experience new activities on their own. Needless to say, the purposes, contents, methods, and assessment in the field of physical education as they relate not only to students' needs, desires, and ambitions but also to the larger society are seldom a part of the educational experiences of students. Under these circumstances, students are unlikely to construct new forms of knowledge that would broaden their understanding of the possibilities in their own lives and the larger society that can be realized through physical activity (Fernandez-Balboa, 1995). According to Azzarito and Solmon (2005), the educational failures in physical education have resulted from curriculum development with traditional, multi-activity, sport-based approaches. In a sense, the empowered physical education curriculum seeks and recognizes unfixed, uncertain, and diverse aspects of physical activities.

The empowered physical education curriculum is central to the development of an autonomous person who is able to lead an authentic life and who is attentive to the uniqueness of his or her identity. In a sense, the empowered curriculum is significantly open to the development and cultivation of the various potentials and creative talents of students through encouraging the free expressions of students' needs and desires. That is, the empowered physical education curriculum seldom pays attention merely to the development of the body and/or mind of students. Rather, this curriculum places emphasis on individual students as emancipatory human beings. Thus, the empowered physical education curriculum consists of the competencies, capabilities, or qualities that will be needed by emancipatory or autonomous humans.

PHYSICAL EDUCATION TEACHERS AS CURRICULUM MAKERS

The emancipatory physical education curriculum provides a learning environment in which students are enabled to actively produce and reproduce their own knowledge, not to use codified knowledge. In a sense, the ability to participate and succeed in curriculum making is demanded of physical education teachers. Instead of seeing themselves as users of a particular physical education curriculum, teachers should view themselves as curriculum makers who have the responsibility of formulating creative learning environments (Craig & Ross, 2008). As they gain confidence in their abilities to make curricular and instructional decisions, they could move further forward to a more challenging and creative decision-making stance.

Teachers enacting the "teacher as curriculum maker" image (Clandinin & Connelly, 1992) have characteristics of creative, innovative, and critical thinking skills that enable them to create and realize new visions in teaching physical education (Fernandez-Balboa, 1997). They are willing to seek multiple goals that place value on both individual rights and societal needs. Additionally, they are capable of searching and designing alternative content and methods that can meet the diverse needs and the rationality of students in physical education classes (Rovegno & Kirk, 1995). For example, while teachers seem to be consistent in preferring to develop their curriculum in their own ways, they are also likely to suggest open learning tasks and allow students to solve the given problems and to explore various alternatives or engage in creative activities.

Building a Creative Mind through Physical Activity

People with creative minds tend to approach the world in fresh and original ways that are not shaped by preconceptions. Unlike less creative people, they do not follow the obviously fixed order and rule in their daily lives. They have the openness toward new experience that enables them to see things that others cannot because they seldom wear the blinders of conventionality when they look around the world. They are curious about the living world, which is filled with unanswered questions (Andreasen, 2006).

The free body as a human agent includes the creative mind that promotes novel actions and constitutes new meanings. Ultimately, it could affect the social world as well as self-identities of students (Charles, 1998; Lawson, 1988). A well-organized physical education curriculum and creative teaching methods can contribute to building a creative mind through providing physical activities that allow students to experience and explore the creative mind in combination with rhythmic and creative activities.

CASE 1: A KOREAN NATIONAL PHYSICAL EDUCATION CURRICULUM TO BUILD THE CREATIVE MIND

The values of sports are encompassed in the realization of creative human freedom of playing in sports. According to Fraleigh (1990), the values of sports are many and diverse. Unfortunately, the Korean curriculum emphasized only the limited values of sports, such as the acquisition of sports skills and the promotion of health and fitness through scientific principles. For this reason, the traditional sports that are needed for strong fitness and high skills were dominant in educational content in the past curriculum.

In 2007, a new national physical education curriculum in Korea was published and will be implemented from the year 2010 in all school levels. Unlike the previous curricula, the new curriculum aims to formally document the "various educational values" of physical activities in physical education in order to revive the essence of physical education and to systematically establish the role of physical education in the schools.

In the first place, this national curriculum document is very innovative in introducing the concept of "physical activity" rather than "sport or exercise," which would be governed by rigid rules. Zeigler (2003, p. 286) defines its concept as follows: "Physical activity implies a variety of activities such as walking, exercising, sports, and types of physical recreation." That means the concept of physical activity is much broader, more inclusive, and more culturally relevant than the concept of sports (Ennis, 2003; Kirk, 1997).

The 2007 revised national curriculum introduces the proposition that "physical education" is a subject in which a participant can seek the following things: (a) to understand oneself and the world through a variety of physical activities, (b) to develop life skills for leading a physically active lifestyle, (c) to develop personality and social skills, and (d) to cultivate the competency for creatively succeeding in a movement culture.

The first aim of the curriculum is to achieve an understanding of self through physical activity and participation in a physical-activity-induced world. That is, children and students are positioned in a creative, free learning environment that enables them to discover their potential and inherent abilities through performing physical activities. In addition, students are provided the opportunity to have lived experiences that help them to understand the scientific, artistic, and humanistic meanings constructed by physical activities.

The second aim is the development of a physically active lifestyle that focuses on life skills rather than sport skills. According to Cone (2004), life skills are a basis for leading a physically active lifestyle; thus, this curriculum could develop an understanding and awareness for changing the lifestyle habits of today's youth as well as indirectly influencing their future lives in other ways. Educating students to pursue a physically active lifestyle through experiencing and exploring a variety of physical activities can be accomplished effectively by helping children and youth understand why physical activity is essential in their lives and how being active can positively impact their individual and social lives.

The third aim of the newly revised curriculum is the promotion of personality growth and social skills. Nobody lives alone in the world. Life itself means forming relationships with other people. In the field of performing physical activities, there exist a wide variety of personalities, so that students need to acquire social skills that enable them to handle many social situations: challenge, perseverance, teamwork, fair play, competition and cooperation, etiquette, leadership and followership, self-control, caring, and so forth. Because personalities and social skills are relevant and present in our daily lives, learning how to apply them in life is a crucial part of a student's overall education.

The fourth aim of this curriculum is the development of an awareness of the significance of physical activity and the creation of the physical activities themselves and their attendant culture while functioning regularly as a participant. In accordance with this curriculum, a number of opportunities for creative expression through physical activity are given to children and students. Creative expression is based on understanding the creative principles and experiencing the creative processes. Moreover, creating physical activity culture is also one of the important objectives in the revised curriculum. This objective signifies that students will be given opportunities to acquire the existing cultural norms and behaviors demonstrated in the given physical activities and, furthermore, to create a more constructive culture through self-directed physical activity.

The core of the revised curriculum is that the five values of physical activities, including health, challenge, competition, expression, and leisure (see figure 9.1), are used as the conceptual framework for content standards. That is, the physical education contents consist of healthy activity, challenging activity, competitive activity, expressive activity, and leisure activity all of which are characterized by understanding and performing humanistic, scientific, creative, and artistic aspects in a variety of physical activities.

Healthy activity aims to acquire health-related knowledge, to promote and manage physical and mental health, and to develop the ability for decision making in solving health problems. Challenging activity enables students to discover their potential and to actively challenge their limitations while participating in physical activity. Competitive activity focuses on perceiving the competition and cooperation aspect inherent in physical activity, scientifically performing physical activities, and appreciating them on the basis of fair play and mutual understanding. Expressive activity seeks to understand the aesthetic elements of physical activities, to creatively express them, and to appreciate a variety of expressive modes and the cultural aspects of physical activities. Leisure activity emphasizes the personal and social benefits of physical recreational activity in daily life and constructing a culture of leisure through self-regulatory leisure activity (Ministry of Education, 2007).

Consequently, the new national curriculum in Korea was revised with a postmodern perspective that facilitates freeing the body and also embodies various values in physical education as a subject. In the document, the creative mind is not directly mentioned. However, the philosophy and orientation of the curriculum revision are significantly related to the characteristics of the creative mind (see figure 9.1). A variety of physical activities with the five values of health, challenge, competition, expression, and leisure could ignite and build the creative mind in students' learning experiences.

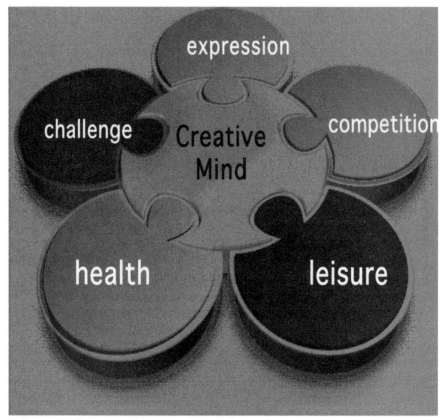

Figure 9.1   Five educational values of physical activities toward the creative mind.

CASE 2: TEACHING THE CREATIVE MIND WITH CREATIVE TEACHING

With a general teaching method, it is very hard to build the creative minds of students. Creative teaching is required to help students develop the creative mind in learning environments. Chen and Cone (2003) explain that there is a mutual relationship between how teachers design and structure learning content and what students experience within the learning environment. Specifically, it is reported that developing and promoting the creative thinking skills of students is greatly dependent on the abilities of teachers to structure the learning activities and experiences, to create an optimal learning environment, and to interact with students (McBride, 1991; Park & Heisler, 2001; Zachopoulou et al., 2006).

In general, most physical education teachers think that the only available learning content for building creativity is creative dance. Even worse, most physical education teachers in South Korea are male and have never received training through teacher education programs in how to teach creative dance. Due to their lack of training, these male teachers rarely try to introduce creative dance to students.

As a result, the boys and girls at schools have seldom had an opportunity to experience creative dance or any kind of dance form, for that matter (You & Kim, 2002; You, 2005). Instead of providing students with creative dance forms, the teachers usually ask students to acquire and practice typical, fixed, and systemized skills of team sports or fitness exercises that are critically important in real game situations. This teaching approach rarely promotes the creative minds of students because they seldom have opportunities to explore, discover, or express their own thinking, feeling, or experiencing in a variety of ways (You, 2005).

In Korea, fortunately, there are rapidly growing movements among innovative teachers to design student-centered learning environments. One of the movements is "Teaching Creative Mind with Creative Teaching." The most popular learning activities frequently used by Korean creative teachers in physical education are educational gymnastics, jump ropes, gym balls, juggling, and so forth. In fact, the highly inventive movements incorporated in these activities are far more dependent on the formulations of the students' creative minds than on a high level of motor skills of the learners (see figure 9.2).

Definitely, we need to make sure that previous contents (figure 9.2) have transformed from the noncreative activities to the creative activities by teachers with creative minds. That is, this shift can be made by creative teachers who are able to see the instructional environment with creative eyes.

The most significant characteristics in creative teaching are teaching students there are a number of creatively different human movements and then allowing students to explore and find out their own creative movements. This approach makes it possible to effectively open students' minds in a learning process, to meaningfully practice the perceived functions of the creative mind through their free bodies, and then, finally, to hold the creative mind as a learning outcome in physical education.

Implications for Teaching and Teacher Education

Education, including physical education, is not isolated from society. Both contemporary and future societies need human resources with creative minds that

Figure 9.2   Creative movements with creative minds.

enable each individual to perform to his or her greatest creative possibilities in a variety of fields. The boundless possibilities of the creative mind become accessible through a creative curriculum and creative teaching in education. In this chapter, one approach to educating the creative mind—the body in physical education—is interpreted through the lens of three different paradigms. This essay especially points out that the body should be reconceptualized as the creative self, not just the physical self. That is, the body itself is a central entity through which to understand and construct a variety of knowledge. As a result, this chapter argues that freeing our bodies in physical education is the road to endowing the body with a creative mind.

Physical education as a school subject can play a significant role in building creative minds of students through a variety of physical activities. Two studies (Graber & Locke, 2007; Kretchmar, 2006) urge that physical education professionals should emphasize the contribution of physical education as a subject not only in relation to health promotion and fitness development but also in relation to cultivation of the human freedoms: expression, discovery, invention, and creation. That is, physical education is not a subject to train or restrict students' bodies, but rather, it is a unique subject that provides student embodiment in our schools through a powerful way of knowing (Armour, 1999; Burt, 1998; Charles, 1998; Lawson, 1997). As a core of physical education, the lived experiences involved in human movement (or physical activity) can be meaningful to authentically build and display the creative minds of students.

To build the creative minds of children and students in physical education, pre-service and in-service teachers should be prepared and educated in teaching the attributes of the creative mind using physical activities. Physical education teachers without creative minds are rarely able to teach students in such a way that they develop creative minds. First of all, the teachers in pre-service and in-service teacher education need to be introduced to significantly representative paradigms in education (Fernandez-Balboa, 1997) and be made aware of how the teachers' paradigms could impact student learning in physical education.

Moreover, the teachers should themselves be challenged in implementing different teaching approaches. Through enacting these processes in teacher education, the teachers can free themselves from their own teaching limitations as well as from the environmental obstacles that surround them. Therefore, most teachers could themselves develop creative minds. As a consequence, they would produce their own curriculums alongside their students and teach in their own unique ways, rather than adhering to the approach that is expected and "taken for granted." All in all, teachers could be intellectually independent and self-motivated rather than controlled by other people and the materialistic concerns of the public at large.

References

Andreasen, N. (2006). The creative mind. *Chronicle of Higher Education, 52*(23), B2.

Armour, K. (1999). The case for a body-focus in education and physical education. *Sport, Education, and Society, 4*(1), 5–15.

Arnold, P. (1999). The virtues, moral education, and the practice of sport. *Quest, 51*(1), 39–54.

Azzarito, L., & Solmon, M. (2005). A reconceptualization of physical education: The intersection of gender/race/social class. *Sport, Education, and Society, 10*(1), 25–47.

Bain, L. (1990). Visions and voices. *Quest, 42*(1), 2–12.

Bain, L. (1993). Ethical issues in teaching. *Quest, 45*(1), 69–77.

Bouffard, M. (2001). The scientific method, modernism, and postmodernism revisited: A reaction to Shephard (1999). *Adapted Physical Activity Quarterly, 16*, 221–234.

Burt, J. (1998). The role of kinesiology in elevating modern society. *Quest, 50*(1), 80–95.

Charles, J. (1998). Technology and the body of knowledge. *Quest, 50*(4), 379–388.

Chen, W., & Cone, T. (2003). Links between children's use of critical thinking and an expert teacher's teaching in creative dance. *Journal of Teaching in Physical Education, 22*, 169–185.

Clandinin, D., & Connelly, F. (1992). Teacher as curriculum maker. In P. W. Jackson (Ed.), *Handbook of curriculum* (pp. 363–461). New York: Macmillan.

Cleland, F. (1994). Young children's divergent movement ability: Study II. *Journal of Teaching in Physical Education, 13*, 228–241.

Cleland, F., & Gallahu, D. L. (1993). Young children's divergent movement ability. *Perceptual & Motor Skills, 77*, 535–544.

Cone, S. (2004). Pay me now or pay me later: 10 years later and have we seen any change? *Journal of Teaching in Physical Education, 23*, 271–280.

Corbin, C. (2002). Physical activity for everyone: What every physical educator should know about promoting lifelong physical activity. *Journal of Teaching in Physical Education, 21*, 128–144.

Craig, C., & Ross, V. (2008). Cultivating the image of teachers as curriculum makers. In F. M. Connelly (Ed.), *The Sage handbook of curriculum and instruction* (pp. 282–305). Thousand Oaks, CA: Sage.

Crum, B. (1993). Conventional thought and practice in physical education: Problems of teaching and implication for change. *Quest, 45*(3), 339–356.

Drewe, S. (2000). The logical connection between moral education and physical education. *Journal of Curriculum Studies, 32*, 561–573.

Ennis, C. D. (2003). Using curriculum to enhance student learning. In S. J. Silverman & C. D. Ennis (Eds.), *Student learning in physical education: Applying research to enhance instruction* (pp. 109–127). Champaign, IL: Human Kinetics.

Ennis, C. D. (2006). Curriculum: Forming and reshaping the vision of physical education in a high need, low demand world of schools. *Quest, 58*(1), 41–59.

Fernandez-Balboa, J. (1993). Sociocultural characteristics of the hidden curriculum in physical education. *Quest, 45*(2), 230–234.

Fernandez-Balboa, J. (1995). Reclaiming physical education in higher education through critical pedagogy. *Quest, 47*(1), 91–114.

Fernandez-Balboa, J. (1997). Knowledge base in physical education teacher education: A proposal for a new era. *Quest, 49*(2), 161–181.

Figley, G. (1984). Moral education through physical education. *Quest, 36*(1), 89–101.

Fraleigh, W. (1990). Different educational purposes: Different sport values. *Quest, 42*(1), 77–92.

Garrett, R. (2004). Negotiating a physical identity: Girls, bodies, and physical education. *Sport, Education, and Society, 9*(2), 223–237.

Gibbons, S., & Bressan, E. (1991). The affective domain in physical education: A conceptual clarification and curricular commitment. *Quest, 43*(1), 78–97.

Giroux, H. (1988). Border pedagogy in the age of postmodernism. *Journal of Education, 170*(3), 162–181.

Graber, K., & Locke, L. (2007). Are the national standards achievable?—Conclusions and recommendations. *Journal of Teaching in Physical Education, 26,* 416–424.

Hollands, R. (1984). The role of cultural studies and social criticism in the sociological study of sport. *Quest, 36*(1), 66–79.

Johnson, M. (1987). *The body in the mind: The bodily basis of meaning, imagination, and reason.* Chicago: The University of Chicago Press.

Jones, C. (2001). Character, virtue and physical education. *European Physical Education Review, 11*(1), 139–151.

Kirk, D. (1986). A critical pedagogy for teacher education: Toward an inquiry-oriented approach. *Journal of Teaching in Physical Education, 5,* 230–246.

Kirk, D. (1992). *Defining physical education: The social construction of a school subject in postwar Britain.* London: Falmer Press.

Kirk, D. (1997). Schooling bodies in new times: The reform of school physical education in high modernity. In J. M. Fernandez-Balboa (Ed.), *Critical postmodernism in human movement, physical education, and sport* (pp. 39–64). New York: SUNY Press.

Kretchmar, R. S. (2006). Ten more reasons for quality physical education. *Journal of Physical Education, Recreation, and Dance, 77*(9), 6–9.

Laker, A. (2003). Sport in culture. In A. Laker (Ed.), *The future of physical education: Building a new pedagogy* (pp. 15–31). New York: Routledge Falmer.

Lawson, H. (1988). Occupational socialization, cultural studies, and the physical education curriculum. *Journal of Teaching in Physical Education, 7*(4), 265–288.

Lawson, H. (1990). Beyond positivism: Research, practice, and undergraduate professional education. *Quest, 42*(2), 161–183.

Lawson, H. (1997). Children in crisis, the helping professions, and the social responsibilities of universities. *Quest, 49*(1), 8–33.

MacDonald, D. (2003). Rich task implementation: Modernism meets postmodernism. *Discourse, 24*(2), 247–262.

McBride, R. E. (1991). Critical thinking: An overview with implications for physical education. *Journal of Teaching in Physical Education, 11,* 112–125.

McKay, J., Gore, J., & Kirk, D. (1990). Beyond the limits of technocratic physical education. *Quest, 42*(1), 52–75.

McKay, J., & Pearson, K. (1984). Objectives, strategies, and ethics in teaching introductory courses in sociology of sport. *Quest, 36*(2), 134–146.

Mechikoff, R. A., & Estes, S. G. (1998). *A history and philosophy of sports and physical education: From ancient civilizations to the modern world.* Boston: McGraw-Hill.

Miller, S., Bredemeier, B., & Shields, D. (1997). Sociomoral education through physical education with at-risk children. *Quest, 49*(1), 114–129.

Ministry of Education. (2007). *The 2007 revised national physical education curriculum.* Seoul, Korea: Ministry of Education.

Park, R. J., & Heisler, B. A. (2001). School programs can foster creativity through physical education. *Education, 95*(3), 225–228, 232.

Rink, J. (2007). What knowledge is of most worth? Perspectives on kinesiology from pedagogy. *Quest, 59*(1), 100–110.

Rintala, J. (1991). The mind-body revisited. *Quest, 43*(3), 260–279.

Ross, S. (1987). Humanizing the undergraduate physical education curriculum. *Journal of Teaching in Physical Education, 7,* 46–60.

Rovegno, I., & Kirk, D. (1995). Articulations and silences in socially critical work on physical education: Toward a broader agenda. *Quest, 47*(4), 447–474.

Sage, G. (1993). Sport and physical education and the new world order: Dare we be agents of social change? *Quest, 45*(2), 151–164.

Shephard, R. (1999). Postmodernism and adapted physical activity: A new gnostic heresy? *Adapted Physical Activity Quarterly, 16,* 331–343.

Sparkes, A. C. (1987). Strategic rhetoric: A constraint in changing the practice of teachers. *British Journal of Sociology of Education, 8*(1), 37–54.

Sparkes, A. C., Templin, T. J., & Schempp, P. G. (1990). The problematic nature of a career in a marginal subject. *Journal of Education for Teaching, 16*(1), 3–28.

Talbot, M. (1997). Values and aspirations for the profession. *Bulletin of Physical Education, 3*(3), 6–23.

Theodoulides, A., & Armour, K. (2001). Personal, social, and moral development through team games: Some critical questions. *European Physical Education Review, 7*(1), 5–23.

Tinning, R. (1991). Teacher education pedagogy: Dominant discourses and the process of problem setting. *Journal of Teaching in Physical Education, 11,* 1–20.

Tinning, R. (2002). Toward a "modest pedagogy": Reflections on the problematics of critical pedagogy. *Quest, 54*(3), 224–240.

Wandzilak, T., Carroll, T., & Ansorge, C. J. (1988). Values development through physical activity: Promoting sportsmanlike behaviors, perceptions, and moral reasoning. *Journal of Teaching in Physical Education, 8,* 13–22.

Whitson, D., & Macintosh, D. (1990). The scientization of physical education: Discourses of performance. *Quest, 42*(1), 40–51.

You, J. (2005). *Issues on teaching in physical education.* Seoul, Korea: Rainbow Books.

You, J. (2007). *Physical Education curriculum.* Seoul, Korea: Daehan Media.

You, J., & Kim, Y. (2002). Limitations, realities, and challenges of coeducational physical education. *Korean Journal for Sports Pedagogy, 9*(2), 1–25.

Zachopoulou, E., Trevlas, E., Konstadinidou, E., & Archimedes Project Research Group (2006). The design and implementation of a physical education program to promote children's creativity in the early years. *International Journal of Early Years Education, 14*(3), 279–294.

Zeigler, E. (2003). Guiding professional students to literacy in physical activity education. *Quest, 55*(4), 285–305.

CHAPTER 10

Teaching Creatively in-between Contested Contradictions and Complexities in the U.S. South

Ming Fang He
Georgia Southern University

Wynnetta Scott-Simmons
Mercer University

Angela McNeal Haynes
Altamaha Elementary School

Derrick M. Tennial
Georgia Perimeter College

Ming Fang He, PhD, is a professor of curriculum studies at Georgia Southern University. She has written about cross-cultural narrative inquiry of language/culture/identity in multicultural contexts, cross-cultural teacher education, curriculum studies, activist practitioner inquiry, research for social justice, exile curriculum, and narrative of curriculum in the U.S. South. She is an associate editor of the *Handbook of Curriculum and Instruction* (2008). She was an editor of *Curriculum Inquiry*, is an associate editor of *Multicultural Perspectives*, and a part editor of *Handbook of Asian Education*. Currently, she is engaged in research on the education of Asian American immigrant students in the context of school/family/community, life in Southern U.S. schools/families/communities, and the education of minority/disfranchised groups in international contexts.

Wynnetta Scott-Simmons, EdD, is an assistant professor of education at Mercer University. She has written about culturally responsive teacher education, oral history, black orality, critical and divergent literacies, cross-generational/cultural theory, black aesthetic, African

American women's literacies of silence, and theories of resistance and survival among minority communities. She is currently engaged in research focusing on African American females as keepers of the cultural code, the transition and mentorship of African American female teachers from pre-service to in-service, and extending the awareness of the rich African American educational heritage among pre-service teachers.

Angela Haynes, EdD, is a media specialist at Altamaha Elementary School and an adjunct instructor at Georgia Southern University. She has written about curriculum in the South, oral history, critical pedagogy, social justice, and critical feminist theory. She is currently engaged in using narrative to explore in-between identities and rural curriculum of place, gender, and identity with the intent to promote a curriculum of critical literacy for elementary students.

Derrick M. Tennial, EdD, is an English instructor at Georgia Perimeter College's Gateway to College Academy and an adjunct professor at Mercer University. His research interest areas include oral history, critical race theory, culture of poverty, generational and intergenerational poverty in the African American community, marginalization, culturally relevant pedagogy, African American cultures, and cultural ecology. He is currently engaged in research on the impact of culturally relevant teaching on students participating in a dropout recovery program.

ABSTRACT

In this chapter, we explore theoretical and experiential understandings of teaching creatively in-between contested contradictions and complexities in the U.S. South. We begin with a sketch of the increasingly contested contradictions and complexities in the U.S. South. We then explore theoretical and experiential understanding of teaching in-between through discussions on theoretical traditions and autobiographical reflections as we move from languages to languages, cultures to cultures, places to places. The languages we speak, the cultures we live in, and the places we work complicate our identities, multiply our sense of belonging and displacement, and demand that we teach creatively in-between. Teaching in-between is inherently personal and political. It is personal in that it begins with conscious and critical reflections to challenge assumptions, recognizes contradictions between theories, and demands complexities in practice. It is political in that every act of teaching embodies a particular stance in relation to power, freedom, and human possibility. Teaching in-between thrives on passionate involvement, strong commitment, and unfaltering advocacy for disenfranchised, underrepresented, and invisible groups and individuals. This passion, commitment, and advocacy calls for a community of teachers and educational workers with shared concerns to work passionately together as allies with schools, communities, and tribes, to take to heart the concerns of all participants, and to develop creative strategies to move beyond boundaries, transgress orthodoxies, and enact educational and social change that fosters equity, equality, freedom, and social justice. This expanded community embodies possibilities and creates hope that we can invent more in-between spaces where we might live more robustly, develop our human capacities more fully, and become humane and peaceful in inquiry and life as we teach in an increasingly changing and diversifying world.

In this chapter, we explore theoretical and experiential understanding of teaching creatively in-between contested contradictions and complexities in the U.S. South. We begin with a sketch of the increasingly contested contradictions and complexities in the U.S. South, where the four of us work with pre-service and in-service teachers. We then explore theoretical and experiential understanding of teaching in-between through discussions on theoretical traditions and autobiographical reflections as we move from languages to languages, cultures to cultures, places to places. The languages we speak, the cultures we live in, and the places we work complicate our identities, multiply our sense of belonging and displacement, and demand that we teach creatively in-between. Most of the pre-service and in-service teachers with whom we work are from an educational system constructed by what William Watkins, a black protest thinker and educator, would call "the White architects of Black education" (Watkins, 2001, 2005) in the South.

In 1998, the Southern Regional Education Board issued a report, *Education and Progress in the South*, calling the South a "place of remarkable progress and momentum." The report was released "almost 60 years to the day after President Franklin Roosevelt called for the National Emergency Council to report on conditions in the South, which he labeled 'the nation's No. 1 economic problem'" (Southern Regional Education Board, 1998). Although the U.S. South is increasingly diversified in class, race, and economic status (Duncan, 1995; Stern, 1994), the Southern school communities are still highly monoethnic (Yeo, 1999) and deeply ingrained in habits of thinking that hold fixed notions about the nature, cultures, humanity, and contexts that Vandana Shiva (1993), a physicist, environmental activist, ecofeminist, and writer, would call "monocultures of the mind." Historically, the South has often been portrayed as a region of the United

States whose inhabitants were seen "dichotomously . . . as being only Black and White, lived worlds apart—always with Black people at the bottom and White people at the top of the hierarchy" (Morris & Monroe, 2009). This black and white binary becomes an official narrative that, on the one hand, masks the hidden narrative of institutionalized and imminent racism, suppression, oppression, troubled genders (Butler, 1990), generational poverty (Tennial, 2008), and other more pressing issues (Haynes, 2008; Scott-Simmons, 2008). On the other hand, the binary ignores contested contradictions and complexities deeply embedded in the geographical, cultural, linguistic, and sociopolitical contexts of the South (He, in progress).

Georgia is ranked as the ninth-largest state and one of the fastest growing states in the South, with 8.2 million residents, including 65.1 percent white, 28.7 percent African American, and 6.2 percent of other races such as Native Americans, Asians, Hispanics and/or Latinos, and Native Hawaiian and Other Pacific Islanders (U.S. Census Bureau, 2002). In 2001, 12.6 percent of the residents in Georgia lived below the poverty level, which is close to the percentage of the United States as a whole (11.7 percent). Georgia's poverty level has dramatically dropped in the past ten years (20 percent in 1990). In 2009, there were 2,223 schools (including ten K–12 schools, 1,316 elementary, 464 middle schools, and 442 high schools). From 1990 to 2000, there were 88,578 teachers, 1,422,762 K–12 students, and 31,362 pre-K students, with 55 percent white, 38 percent African American, 4 percent Hispanic, 2 percent Asian/Pacific Islander, and smaller proportions of American Indian/Alaskan Indian (U.S. Census Bureau, 2002). In contrast, Georgia's pre-K–12 teachers were 79 percent white, 20.5 percent African American, and only 0.8 percent Hispanic and 0.3 percent Asian.

The discrepancy between the ratios of students and teachers of color further complicates contested contradictions and complexities in-between cultures, languages, places, and powers in Georgia. Some of these teachers are either blinded by the lies they have been told throughout their lives or coerced to believe the meta-narrative about the South (Loewen, 2007) without seeing contradictions and complexities in-between the good and evil of life in the South. How can we wake up these teachers, young or veteran, develop epistemological curiosity (Freire & Macedo, 1995), and cultivate critical consciousness to teach creatively in-between contested contradictions and complexities of the South?

Theoretical Traditions

Teaching in-between draws on a wide array of theoretical traditions. Our notion of teaching in-between originated from Ming Fang He's work on teaching, learning, and living in-between (He, 1998, 1999, 2003, & 2006) and her most recent work on exile pedagogy—teaching in-between (He, 2010). For He,

> [Teaching in-between] is highly contested with complicated tensions and irresolvable contradictions within diverse theoretical traditions and socio-political, cultural, and linguistic contexts. [It] is interdisciplinary, transdisciplinary, and sometimes counterdisciplinary. [It] is international, transnational, and sometimes counternational. . . . [Teaching in-between] thrives with diverse *paradigms, perspectives, and possibilities* (Schubert, 1986), and demands multiple understandings toward *commonplaces (teachers, learners, subject matters, and milieu)* (Schwab, 1969, 1971, 1973, 1983) *acting together in practical and real world environments* (Connelly, He, and Phillion, 2008). (He, 2010, p. 1029)

Many educational theorists and practitioners around the world challenge traditional ways of defining and practicing teaching, transgress nationalistic, cultural, linguistic, and epistemological boundaries, and choose radical democratic practice and intellectual exploration as a core foundation for teaching. These theorists and practitioners engage in a wide array of educational inquiries and praxis, such as critical public pedagogy, revolutionary critical pedagogy, Red pedagogy, teaching against the grain, teaching for social change, teaching for social justice, teaching to transgress, and teaching towards freedom. The radical democratic and intellectual quality of teaching creates an in-between space for educational workers to *exile voluntarily to teach creatively in-between* (He, 2009). This aspect of exile in-between is illuminated in an oral tradition of Confucianism: a good teacher should be able to remove himself/herself from the crazy materialistic world, seek a balanced human condition in-between unbalanced and contested contradictions and complexities within nature and humanity, and develop a clear vision to *cultivate beauty, integrity, justice, and humanity* (see also Schubert, 2009). Many educational workers who choose to teach in-between not only question "what is worthwhile [to teach], for whom it is worthwhile [to teach], and how we make [teaching] worthwhile" (Schubert, 2009, p. 136) but also confront issues of equity, equality, social justice, societal change, and democratic human conditions through pedagogical theory and praxis.

Henry Giroux (2004), a leading critical scholar, theorizes "the regulatory and emancipatory relationship among culture, power, and politics as expressed through the dynamics of what [he calls] public pedagogy" (p. 62), "in which learning becomes indispensable to the very process of social change, and social change becomes the precondition for a politics that moves in the direction of a less hierarchical, more radical democratic social order" (Giroux, 2000, p. 356). Educational workers engaged in such a critical public pedagogy should make "a firm commitment to intellectual rigor and a deep regard for matters of compassion and social responsibility aimed at deepening and extending the possibilities for critical agency, radical justice, economic democracy, and the just distribution of political power" (Giroux, 2004, p. 64).

Peter McLaren (2002), another leading critical scholar, theorizes the *collective, critical, systematic, participatory,* and *creative* (p. xvii) aspects of pedagogy—what he calls "revolutionary critical pedagogy"—which demands:

> mutual respect, humility, openness, trust and co-operation; a commitment to learn to "read the world" critically and expending the effort necessary to bring about social transformation; vigilance with regard to one's own process of self-transformation and adherence to the principles and aims of the group; adopting an "ethics of authenticity" as a guiding principle; internalizing social justice as passion; acquiring critical, creative, and hopeful thinking; transforming the social relations of learning and teaching; establishing democracy as a fundamental way of life; developing critical curiosity; and deepening one's solidarity and commitment to self and social transformation and the project of humanization. (p. 31)

Sandy Grande (2004), a Native American social and political thinker and scholar, employs the visions of this radical democratic orientation of pedagogy as "starting points for rethinking indigenous praxis" (p. 28). For Grande (2004),

> [What] distinguishes Red pedagogy is its basis in hope. Not the future-centered hope of the Western imagination, but rather, a hope that lives in contingency with the past—one that trusts the beliefs and understandings of our ancestors as well as the power of traditional knowledge. . . . Most of all, it is a hope that believes in the strength and resiliency of indigenous peoples and communities, recognizing that their struggles are not about inclusion and enfranchisement to "the new order" but, rather, are part of the indigenous project of sovereignty and indigenization. It reminds us that indigenous peoples have always been peoples of resistance, standing in defiance of the vapid emptiness of the bourgeois life. . . . The hope is for a Red pedagogy that not only helps sustain the life ways of indigenous peoples but also provides an explanatory framework that helps us understand the complex and intersecting vectors of powering shaping the historical-material conditions of indigenous schools and communities. (pp. 28–29)

Rooted in critical theory of the Frankfurt school associated with Walter Benjamin (a German-Jewish Marxist literary critic and philosopher), Jürgen Habermas (a German philosopher and sociologist), and Michel Foucault (a

French philosopher, historian, and sociologist), Roger Simon (1992), one of the pioneering critical theorists, crafted *Teaching Against the Grain* "to help construct a pedagogy of possibility, that works for the reconstruction of the social imagination in the service of human freedom" (p. 4). Drawing on the works of Antonio Gramsci (an Italian Marxist, political leader, and radical thinker), Marilyn Cochran-Smith (1991), a prominent teacher educator, developed her line of inquiry as *learning to teach against the grain* (1991) and *learning to teach for social change* (2004). Cochran-Smith (2001) calls for prospective teachers to "think deeply about and deliberately claim the role of educator as well as activist based on political consciousness and on ideological commitment to combating the inequalities . . . that are deeply embedded in systems of schooling and in society" (p. 4). This line of inquiry is also found in a wide array of works on *teaching for social justice* (e.g., Ayers, Hunt, & Quinn, 1998; Darling-Hammond, French, & Garcia-Lopez, 2002).

Influenced by the works of Paulo Freire and a wide array of black feminist thought, bell hooks, a writer, teacher, and insurgent intellectual, created conceptions of *Teaching to Transgress: Education as the Practice of Freedom* (1994) and *Teaching Community: A Pedagogy of Hope* (2003) to advocate for radical and liberatory pedagogy. bell hooks urges teachers to "open . . . minds and hearts . . . so that [they can] celebrate teaching that enables transgressions—a movement against and beyond boundaries . . . [a] movement which makes education the practice of freedom" (1994, p. 12). hooks also calls for teachers to imagine to "make the classroom a place that is life-sustaining and mind-expanding, a place of liberating mutuality where teacher and student together work in partnership . . . to illuminate the space of the possible where [teachers] can work to sustain . . . hope and create community with justice as the core foundation" (2003, pp. xv–xvi).

Building on the work of James Baldwin and Malcolm X, Edward Saïd (1994), one of the most distinguished cultural critics, perceived teachers as public intellectuals who "denounce corruption, defend the weak, defy imperfect or oppressive authority" (p. 6). Saïd (1994) called for public intellectuals "to raise embarrassing questions, to confront orthodoxy and dogma (rather than to produce them) . . . [which] cannot easily be co-opted by governments or corporations, and their *raison d'être* is to represent all those people and issues that are routinely forgotten or swept under the rug" (p. 11).

William Ayers (2006), a contemporary radical thinker and scholar, reaffirms that the roles of public intellectuals are to:

> draw sustenance and perspective from the humanities in order to better see the world as it is. Whatever [they] find that is out-of-balance must be challenged, the devastating taken-for-granted dissected,

exposed, illuminated. . . . The core of all [their] work must be human
knowledge and human freedom, both enlightenment and emancipation. (p. 87)

Teachers as public intellectuals "join one another to imagine and build a participatory movement for justice, a public space for the enactment of democratic
dreams" (Ayers, 2006, p. 96). Thus, "Teaching becomes ethical action, the
practice of freedom, when it is guided by an unshakable commitment to working with particular human beings to reach the full measure of their humanity, a
willingness to reach toward a future fit for all" (Ayers, 2004, p. xi). For Ayers,
teaching is a personal and political act with unfaltering commitment to human
creativity, freedom, and justice.

The radical democratic orientations—Giroux's critical public pedagogy;
McLaren's revolutionary pedagogy; Grande's Red pedagogy; Simon's teaching
against the grain; Cochran-Smith's learning to teach against the grain and teach
for social change; the teaching for social justice of Ayers, Hunt, and Quinn and
Darling-Hammond, French and Garcia-Lopez; Saïd's intellectuals as exiles; and
Ayers' teaching toward freedom—influence tremendously the developing notion
of teaching in-between (see also He, 2009). Our choice of teaching in-between
carries more of a compelling sense of being in the midst rather than being either
an excluded outcast or a triumphant architect for social justice. With equity,
equality, social justice, and human freedom as explicit goals, we choose to teach
creatively into tensions, contradictions, and complexities in-between contested
languages, cultures, individuals/groups/tribes/societies, situations, and contexts.
The politics and poetics of teaching in-between lie in educational workers'
strong advocacy on behalf of individuals, groups, families, tribes, communities,
and societies that are often at controversy, underrepresented, misrepresented, or
excluded from the official narrative. Educational workers who choose to teach
in-between connect the personal with the political, the practical with the theoretical, and the local with the global through passionate participation in and
critical reflection upon teaching, learning, inquiry, and life with an "epistemological curiosity—a curiosity that is often missing in dialogue as conversation"
(Freire & Macedo, 1995, p. 382). As Freire strongly argued:

We must not negate practice for the sake of theory. To do so would
reduce theory to a pure verbalism or intellectualism. By the same to-
ken, to negate theory for the sake of practice, as in the use of dialogue
as conversation, is to run the risk of losing oneself in the disconnectedness of practice. It is for this reason that I never advocate either a
theoretic elitism or a practice ungrounded in theory, but the unity
between theory and practice. In order to achieve this unity, one must
have an epistemological curiosity. (Freire & Macedo, 1995, p. 382)

Teachers who choose to teach in-between cultivate this *epistemological curiosity* in teaching, learning, inquiry, and life with conscious reflections on their diverse experience of living in-between, which we address in the next section, to challenge assumptions and recognize contradictions between theory and practice and to critically examine the impact of theory on practice and of practice on theory. Teaching in-between builds on long-term, heartfelt engagement and shared efforts driven by commitment to equity, equality, social justice, freedom, and human possibility. Teachers who teach in-between join one another and others to move beyond boundaries, to transgress orthodoxies, and to build a participatory intellectual movement to promote a more balanced, fair, and equitable human condition through creative acts of teaching in an increasingly diversified and contested world.

Autobiographical Roots

MING FANG

I am a woman of color, born and raised in a dramatically different culture and language, teaching and working in a university in the United States. My sense of teaching in-between is derived from my experience as a Chinese woman and a faculty member moving back and forth between constantly changing Eastern and Western theoretical traditions, languages, and cultures (He, 2009). My sense of "in-betweenness" carries more of a compelling sense of being in the midst rather than being either an excluded outcast or an assimilated triumphant. My experience is not one of being in-between public and private, black and white, the mainstream and the margin but, rather, something more complex, historically contested, culturally, and linguistically contextualized. This in-betweenness essentially comes to a question of cross-cultural movement between landscapes that are themselves in a flux of chaos, contradictions, renewals, diversities, and complexities. It also comes to a question of my life in-between contested tensions, dilemmas, contradictions, and complexities in China, in the North American academy, and in-between.

In-between Cultural Movements in China

I was born in the midst of two prominent movements in Chinese history: the Anti-Rightist Movement (1957–58) and the Great Leap Forward (1958–60). These two movements had a strong impact on the preschool years of many children in my generation. We remembered that at the beginning of the Anti-Rightist Movement in 1957, Mao Zedong [then the chairman of the Chinese

Communist Party (CCP)] proclaimed: "Let one hundred schools of thought contend; let one hundred flowers bloom." The "one hundred schools" of philosophy included the Confucianist, Daoist, and legalist schools, which clashed with one another in their attempts to reform the CCP and China. We heard that our "aunts and uncles" (intellectuals of our parents' generation) were encouraged to do self-criticism, to confess their anti-proletarian sentiments, and to express their critical views about the CCP to ameliorate socialist China. However, the hundred flowers campaign ended abruptly in a suppression of intellectuals whose intensive dissent about the CCP threatened Mao's regime. One hundred thousand "counterrevolutionaries" were "unmasked and dealt with," more than one million of our "aunts and uncles" were "subjected to police investigation," and several millions were sent to the countryside for "reeducation."

In 1958, Mao urged the simultaneous development of agriculture and industry, with a focus on heavy industry. This campaign initiated a gigantic social mobilization, which was intended to have a labor investment in industry. A new form of social organization, the people's commune, was established to enable the rural productive apparatus to function without excessive dependence on the central government. We remember hundreds upon hundreds of people working and eating together, with loudspeakers blaring all day long and people shouting slogans: "Let's leap from socialism to communism!" "Let's surpass the United States and follow Great Britain in ten years!" People were searching for pots, pans, and any other kind of metal to melt into iron and steel to make weapons to prepare to fight the wars against the Soviet Union and the U.S. and British Empires. Soon fewer and fewer people went to work together. My brothers, my sister, I, and many other children only went to school for half a day since the little food we had could not last for a whole school day. A massive starvation pervaded China.

From grade one to grade three, children of my generation learned how to read, write, and count amidst such turbulence. Our teachers were rigid with the syllabi, which focused on love for the Chinese Communist Party, Chairman Mao, and Socialist China. Our primary courses included language, math, politics, physical education, and music. In our language courses, our reading materials were mainly about Chinese fables and revolutionary heroes and heroines, such as: how Chairman Mao became the revolutionary hero and leader, how Chairman Mao's colleagues became national heroes or heroines, stories of the capitalists' and landlords' cruelty, and so forth. Most of the math questions were built upon those political topics. In politics, we were requested to memorize important events in Chinese history, especially those of the communist party. We were frequently asked to report our thoughts to our instructors, including our desire to wear colorful clothes and eat better food. In physical education, we went through rigid training. We were asked to walk like the wind, to sit like a clock, and to sleep like a bow. In music lessons, we learned to sing and dance to revolutionary songs such as "Love Our Socialist China!" "Love Our Communist Party!" "Long Live Chairman Mao!" and "Long Live the Chinese Communist Party!"

We would do whatever Chairman Mao told us to do. We felt happy and never complained about any difficulties in our lives. We were asked to think about all the hardships the Red Army had gone through when it was doing the Twenty Five Thousand Li (twelve thousand and five hundred kilometers) March, a retreat that laid the foundation for the Chinese Communist Party's success in 1949. We dressed in uniform blue. Six days a week, we went to school, listened to the teachers, and thought along the same lines as the teachers. The teachers listened to the authorities and thought along the same lines as the authorities.

My parents were teachers and, as such, were relatively privileged, being considered "engineers of human beings' brains." However, the forces in the Anti-Rightist Movement and in the Great Leap Forward led to dramatic changes in my family's status within Chinese society. These changes culminated during the Cultural Revolution (1966–76), when social values were turned upside down. Thus, for me, the in-betweenness I was born into in the Anti-Rightist Movement and the Great Leap Forward became visible in the upside-down values of the Cultural Revolution. Once my parents were highly revered, and suddenly, I witnessed my father being publicly chastised for his unfaltering advocacy for children of peasants, workers, and soldiers to have equal opportunities to learn and to thrive in life. As a child, I held onto those basic beliefs and values, meanwhile adopting the values of the Cultural Revolution without questioning. I didn't think of this as in-betweenness, nor did I understand that there were fundamental intellectual threads at work, which, I now see, are central to understanding my experience of living in-between (He, 2003).

This sense of being in-between was brought to life during the Cultural Revolution when books with inflammatory ideas were burned, libraries were closed down, lessons and textbooks were filled with revolutionary slogans but not content knowledge, schools were open with only political events, and youngsters were sent to reforming farms, factories, and military bases to receive reeducation from peasants, workers, and solders.

I remember, during hot summer nights, the children in my neighborhood would gather with constant struggling against countless mosquito bites to listen to stories of Chinese literature from an oral history storyteller in the community. Sometimes our "uncles and aunts" would risk their lives to tutor some of us in mathematics, physics, chemistry, sciences, language, and literature. Some of us even *stole* books from the banned libraries and secretly swallowed forbidden sexually implicit or explicit adult books and listened to foreign radio broadcasts.

I also remember from time to time while others played cards, went to films, or got involved in street fights, I and some other youngsters would study under oil lamps or in shabby huts after we had spent the whole day doing heavy labor or military training in reforming farms, factories, and military bases. We would memorize English words, expressions, and writings during our break time on our reforming farms or in the factories while overhearing peasants and workers flirting with one another. This is how my education and the education of my generation continued, secretly and creatively in-between.

In 1976, Den Xiao Ping took over the regime. The national standardized exams resumed. Those of us, mostly generations of intellectual groups, who were secretly and silently encouraged to learn, passed the exams and went to university. I was successful at university and became a teacher of English as a foreign language. Even then, during that comparatively stable time, my sense of being in-between, born during the earlier cultural movements, was strengthened. My students, most of whom were born during the Cultural Revolution and, therefore, had no direct experience of it, were out of sync with teachers such as myself. The China they knew and the China I knew were different. This is a difference that continues to this day, as people of different generations speak very differently of the China they know. This difference intensified my sense of living in-between within my own culture.

My years as a teacher created, I now realize, yet another thread in my sense of living in-between, this time the foreigner versus the Chinese, and the position I now find myself in as being neither the foreigner, that is, the American, nor the Chinese. The post–Cultural Revolution was a time of opening up to the West. Like many other youngsters, we valued every minute of our university time. We knew that we had to accept a very heavy course load and a rigid discipline if we were to make up for the ten years' formal schooling we had lost during the grand Cultural Revolution. We were trained to work diligently like a silkworm (making a silk cocoon with a lot of patience) and selflessly like a candle (lighting others and sacrificing ourselves). However, we creatively learned in-between mandates, displacements, and upheavals.

Meanwhile, some communication media such as TV programs, concerts, and dancing parties blew some western wind into our thinking. It was during those university years that we began to receive some western influence. Some western scholars or teachers began to come to Chinese university campuses to teach or talk with Chinese students. We met them in our classrooms, at English corners (English-speaking activity centers), in the streets, and in the libraries. We felt curious about their looks and their ways of talking and teaching. I studied with four American teachers, two Canadian teachers, and one British teacher on my Chinese campus and learned ways of teaching and learning dramatically differently from those I had learned from my parents and other Chinese teachers.

I tried to bring these ideas to my own teaching and, as always, struggled to find the balance. I was educated culturally and linguistically in-between.

This thread of being in-between became intensified during the Tiananmen Square Student Movement in 1989. Even though China's open-door policy (1978–present) was intended as an opening to the Western economic world, western values and ideas flooded into China, particularly western ideas of democracy. Tiananmen Square, the largest square in the center of Beijing, has been a national symbol of central governance for centuries (China National Tourism Administration, 2003). Tiananmen Gate, "Gate of Heavenly Peace," is the gate to the imperial city—the Forbidden City. It has functioned "as a rostrum for proclamations to the assembled masses," with the Great Hall of the People on the western side, the Museum of the Chinese Revolution and the Museum of Chinese History to its east and west, the Monument to the People's Heroes at the center of the square, and the Chairman Mao Memorial Hall and the Qianmen Gate in the south (China National Tourism Administration, 2003). Democracy-oriented students used this symbolic location to make a stand on democracy and request that the government move toward a democratic, modern China. The student movement ended with a military crackdown, political persecution, the arrest of student leaders, and the exodus of large numbers of students and intellectuals into exile.

As a university teacher, I was once again living in-between, pushed and pulled in several directions at the same time. My sympathies with my own students' desire for western democratic ideas paralleled my sympathies with Chinese situations and the country's history. I was caught between advising my students to be cautious, to respect traditional values and the current government, and to reach out to the West and exercise democratic rights. The Tiananmen Square Student Movement catapulted my thinking on my China-foreign in-betweenness, and I left China to study in Canada.

In-Betweenness: The North American Academy

My journey to North America dramatically shifted my positioning on what was foreign. Suddenly, I became the foreigner but still, perhaps even more intensely so, in-between. I brought my Chineseness, which was far more of a living presence in my new environment than was western foreignness a presence in my Chinese environment. I was living in a culture, actually cultures, that I had mostly read about and had experienced only indirectly in China. I earlier noted that the cultural in-betweenness into which I was born was, ultimately, an intellectual in-betweenness. This became strengthened on my arrival in North America. First and foremost, as in the Cultural Revolution, the experience was one commonly referred to as "cultural shock." Values that held me together and guided me were, as in the Cultural Revolution, turned topsy turvy as I landed on North American soil. But I soon found, or at least it now seems as I reflect on my experience, that landing on North American soil meant an intellectual shift. What might have been seen as cultural in-betweenness became, and was, intellectual in-betweenness.

One of the special features of in-betweenness as I experienced it in North America, and which made even more distinct my sense of in-betweenness, was constant uncertainty, unavoidable diversity, irresolvable confusion, and intensified complexity. I moved to undertake my doctoral studies in Toronto, recognized by the United Nations as the most multicultural city in the world. Diversity and multiculturalism were key words everywhere: on the radio, in the newspapers, on the streets, and, of course, in the ideologies and reference lists of the courses I was taking. Whereas I may have thought of myself as coming to North America and into something that could be more or less monocultural, I found myself wandering in the midst of uncertainties, confusions, contradictions, diversities, and complexities. The intellectual work complicated, rather than simplified, this sense of in-betweenness. In search of theoretical traditions, I found a diversity of positions in an intellectual world of multiplicity that one needed to sort through and choose ideas, theories, and ways of thinking suitable to oneself and to various topics of concern.

Some aspects of this intellectual in-betweenness were surprising from another point of view by providing unexpected connections to the intellectual roots of my upbringing. I found myself studying John Dewey and reading about John Dewey's trips to China (Clopton & Ou, 1973). I recognized, as did Hall and Ames (1999), intellectual links between Confucian thought and Deweyan thought. Indeed, my sense that Dewey shortened, rather than lengthened, the in-between bridge terrain may have, at least partially, been behind my special interest in Deweyan theory as I continued to explore education and life cross-culturally.

I found the spirit of inquiry required in intellectual life in the North American academy to be quite different from the sense of authority, certainty, and conformity that tended to accompany my ways of Chinese teaching and learning. I found myself very much in-between because I sensed a different way of thinking and reached out to it, meanwhile, being held from it by the in-betweenness I was born into and the in-betweenness I lived. I was in-between becoming an intellectually inquiry-oriented and activist self and a sustained and conformed self who thought of knowledge in formalistic ways. Bowing to the authority and conforming to orthodoxy were part of my upbringing and formal schooling in China. During many cultural and political movements in China, inflammatory ideas were perceived as anti-revolutionary, dangerously threatening, and frantically forbidden, and they were brutally punished. Finally, when I was able to internalize *inflammatory* ideas such as critical theory, critical race theory, and ecofeminism, and further develop or practice them in my learning, teaching, inquiry, writing, and ways of living, I was asked to "take away inflammatory languages" from my doctoral students' dissertation proposal writing for the purpose of obtaining the approval of my university's institutional review board. When I was able to overcome the fear of challenging orthodoxies and confronting authorities, I was accused of being disrespectful. Just as I now understand that I can never escape the in-betweenness to which I was born, I cannot escape the in-betweenness of teaching as critical or liberatory inquiry and teaching as a quest for certainty or conformity. This in-betweenness permeates my intellectual life in North America.

This in-betweenness, in another form, continues to develop as I live in the North American academy as a faculty member. Being a woman of color, who I was and will always be, I often find myself constantly entangled in-between tensions and dilemmas. This in-betweenness is compounded with multiple kinds of in-betweenness: in-betweenness within my own culture in China, in North America, and in-between. This complex in-betweenness blurs the boundaries between "colonizer and colonized, dominant and subordinate, oppressor and oppressed" (Ang, 2001, p. 2). It creates ambiguities, complexities, and contradictions.

As I encouraged my students in the United States to challenge their white privileges, I realized that as a Han, the dominant cultural group among fifty-six ethnic groups in China, I was privileged even though I was intellectually suppressed during political movements in China. I also realized that I was privileged as one of the very few Chinese women who could afford to step out of my own country to experience this complex in-betweenness, even though I kept losing my sense of belonging in North America. I became, in the mainland Chinese vernacular, an overseas Chinese woman with "longer knowledge and shorter hair" (more educated and independent and less "feminine") and a woman with a "sandwich mind" (partially Chinese and partially Western).

This in-betweenness became more complicated as I moved back and forth in-between cultures in China and North America. In May 2001, I was invited back to China as a Chinese American professor to attend an educational convention on women and minority education and give public lectures. As I flew across the North American continent back to the Asian continent, the cross-cultural, intellectual in-betweenness led to political in-betweenness. On April 19, 2001, the U.S. Department of State issued a public announcement "cautioning Americans—especially Americans of Chinese origin—that they should carefully evaluate their risk of being detained by Chinese authorities before deciding whether to travel to China" (Office of International Information Programs, U.S. Department of State, 2001). The announcement states "that individuals who have at any time engaged in activities or published writings critical of Chinese government policies . . . are particularly at risk of detention, even if they have previously visited China without incident" (Office of International Information Programs, U.S. Department of State, 2001). As a Chinese-born American, I was advised not to travel back to China.

That incident led to tensions and dilemmas. My writing on my experience of the Cultural Revolution (He, 1998) might be perceived to carry implicit criticism against the Chinese government. I was, again, exiled in-between. This time, the in-betweenness was political. I was proud of my writing but frightened by its political potential. This fearful feeling was intensified when the Chinese graduate students at the conference warned me to be careful about what I said and what I did in public, since there was a group of security officers housed just above my residence room. My sense of in-betweenness became traumatized.

This political aspect of intellectual in-betweenness became magnified as I translated my talk and my North American colleagues' talks in Chinese. I found myself stumbling through translation at the very beginning of the conference, being recognized by my Chinese colleagues as an American professor who "dressed like a Chinese and talked like a foreigner" while they themselves dressed in western ties and suits and talked about the western paradigms of research in eloquent Chinese English. To borrow a phrase from Hoffman (1989), I felt "lost in translation" since the academic language of multiculturalism and qualitative research was not mentioned in my Chinese education.

The political in-betweenness with which I approached the conference turned into linguistic in-betweenness during the conference. I found myself gaining confidence in my translation throughout the conference and, as such, while still in-between, I felt myself moving towards my Chinese self. Being "lost in translation" was for me, as it was for Hoffman, a metaphor for in-betweenness and the sense of not belonging here or there that comes with cultural movements and political upheavals. The nuanced cultural, political, and linguistic sense of in-betweenness that accompanied my attendance at the conference characterized my identity as a woman of color in the North American academy.

Living in-between cultural movements and political upheavals was the origin of my intellectual in-betweenness—a sense of restlessness, not belonging here or there, but of living creatively in-between, "constantly being unsettled, and unsettling others" (Saïd, 1994, p. 53). Living and teaching creatively to contradictions, uncertainties, displacements, and upheavals creates an in-between space for a teacher, such as myself, to teach creatively in-between.

ANGELA HAYNES

I navigate between two worlds. These worlds often run parallel, sometimes juxtapose, and occasionally collide. An uneasy truce exists between these two spheres of existence, and I operate in anxious awareness of their fragile peace. Negotiating through an existence akin to Gloria Anzaldúa's *mestiza* (Bergin, 2000, p. 139) consciousness, I traverse multiple paths with different languages, values, and mandates. As I reflect back on my life before I pursued my doctoral studies, I recognize the disquiet that flavored the daily aspects of my world. Through education, I became mindful of the sources of my discomfort—my lower-class background clashing with my advancing education. When I sit at my grandmother's table on Saturday afternoons and try to avoid another argument about politics or religion with my relatives or sit in the faculty lounge and realize that my experiences, likes, and dislikes distance me from others, I become acutely attentive to the idea that I do not exist easily in either place. bell hooks articulated the problem for me in *Where We Stand* (2000), when she states,

> I felt too much uncertainty about who I had become. . . . I finished my education with my allegiance to the working class intact. Even so, I had planted my feet on the path leading in the direction of class privilege. There would always be contradictions to face. There would always be confrontations around the issue of class. I would always have to reexamine where I stand. (p. 37)

Understanding Home—The Narrow Sphere

Recognition does not automatically lend itself to reconciliation. As Paulo Freire advocates in *Pedagogy of the Oppressed* (1970), I now have "conscientization"—an awareness of the existence of the inequalities of these two worlds—and I actively seek to establish a dialogue [again an admonishment of Freire's *Pedagogy* (1970)] that can align these worlds, but I may not be able to effectively alleviate the unrest that exists both in my mind and in the world. This innate feeling of being "at odds" exists between what I experienced through my childhood and what I learned through my education. Aoki's (cited in Pinar & Irwin, 2005) "In the Midst of Slippery Theme-Words" enables me to reflect on various identities each person brings to the drawing board when they enter the classroom.

I reflect upon my own background and begin to realize how this upbringing instilled beliefs and mannerisms that I remained oblivious to until reflection, education, and dialogue allowed me to visualize them. I was raised on a family farm. My father bounced from job to job as work became available. He often worked two or three jobs. My mother stayed at home until her youngest child, my baby brother, started school. After that, she worked in a factory for years. We spent most of my life firmly entrenched in the lower class until my father obtained a job with the local police. The stability of this job allowed us to climb to the higher rungs of the lower class.

From my parents, I obtained a strong work ethic. My father passed to me his belief in hard work, his distrust of big business, and his dislike of high society. My mother passed down her love of family. I have dealt with personal feelings of guilt because, unlike her, I choose to work instead of staying home with my kids. My parents never cast any judgment, but now I realize that some ideas are ingrained so firmly that I do not realize where the feelings of guilt or anxiety come from unless I sit down and work through the past. This line drawn in the sand wreaks havoc when I try to maintain happy familiarity with my identity. While I recognize the work ethic that both parents instilled in me, do I not also disdain the backbreaking labor that burdened their physical and mental beings while paying them a mere pittance?

Reconciling Education and Reality

But what does my family history have to do with maneuvering between my past and my current perception of myself? This reflection is more than just a catharsis for me; I begin to realize the source of my ideas and beliefs. Most of my academic career, I have bought into the idea of the "right" way to do school. Students should be in quiet, orderly rows, soaking up the knowledge that the all-knowing teacher passes out. Never in any of my studies had I seen much that convinced me otherwise—until graduate school. Now I see evidence everywhere and wonder how I could have bought into the sham for so long.

Education should be forced to acknowledge the vast background and experiences of students and find ways to weave these aspects into a bright and creative educational experience. In my personal experience, education was never bright or creative—it was formulaic and redundant. Multiculturalism as multiplicities (Aoki, cited in Pinar & Irwin, 2005) helped illuminate for me why it would matter if one said "Japanese Canadian" or "Canadian Jew" and why we need to place emphasis on this understanding into our classroom. The visual representing the multiplicities as identities allowed me to see how we must create connections between all parts of the student's self. We must find a strategy to incorporate those "ands" into our teaching repertoire. Those "ands" must validate the lived curricula of the student. We, as teachers, do have to let go of our preconceived notions of what is right and what is wrong and be open to new ideas. We have to accept students for who they are—unique and creative individuals—and not try to force them into molds into which they really do not fit.

In the Real World—Navigating the "Ands"

So many times, I hear students gripe about assignments that they feel have little relevance to them personally. I look at the assignment itself and often agree with them. Some assignments have little relevance to the student and, truthfully, look little better than busywork. These assignments are still handed out by teachers who believe that if students are quiet and if they look busy, then they must be learning. Unfortunately, as long as standardized testing occurs, this rote type of teaching will continue. As long as standardized testing is pushed, the lived curriculum can never merge with the curriculum-as-plan (Aoki, cited in Pinar & Irwin, 2005, p. 332).

Recently, my principal asked my opinion about a type of prepackaged instruction that relied completely on scripted lessons. I gave an honest answer. I told him that I was adamantly opposed to the rote memorization and teacher desk-killing that I felt this type of instruction necessitated. Well, that was the wrong answer. He proceeded to lecture me about the values of such skills and assured me that it worked because the numbers do not lie. I was thoroughly chastised, but in my mind, I wondered if those children who learned so well under such tight strictures had any chance of becoming true learners.

I do not think that it matters to the current educational system if we teach the kids. I believe our job (according to the administration) is to force-feed students the information needed for the test. Apparently, no one cares if they can think through a real problem. These children are taught a curriculum that is almost nontransferable to their real lives. The disservice goes beyond test scores; the disservice lies in the fact that these children study a curriculum that belittles their personal beliefs and values and forces them to accept a different reality in order to find acceptance and validation in society. Perhaps it was because my own early education was steeped so heavily in this type of drill-and-kill that I often felt like an imposter in graduate school.

Conversations with my colleagues in the faculty lounge, always a dangerous place, often leave me feeling alienated and confused and make me ponder the duplicitous nature of my existence. Many of these teachers are comfortably ensconced in a world that caters to their beliefs and values. In the wake of Hurricane Katrina's devastation of New Orleans, several individuals commented on the avenging wrath of God in action. Others concurred and added that certainly anyone who did not drive out of New Orleans positively deserved whatever hardships they encountered. Somehow society generates barriers that prohibit one group from recognizing the needs and desires of any other group. I wonder how educated individuals can make such biased statements; after all, hope for the erasure of inequality and injustice rests in education. Mary Aswell Doll (2000) provides an articulation of the problem when she quotes William Pinar (1993):

> Our otherness is our cultural unconscious . . . If what we know about ourselves—our history, our culture, our identity—is deformed by absences, denials, and incompleteness, then our identity—both as individuals and Americans—is fragmented. (p. 461)

These fragmented truths allow people to pass judgment over such extreme situations as Hurricane Katrina with no qualms. However, as an English teacher, I can embrace another idea espoused by Mary Aswell Doll (2000) about critical fiction, "Fiction helps us see and envision not only possibilities for more authentic selves but actualities of social practices that make us cruel" (p. 30). As a young student, I escaped to fiction to help me unravel my world. As a teacher, I use fiction to create new worlds and realities to my students.

Finding Our Voices, Spreading Our Wings

I find hope for a bright future in the classroom. I know the inequalities that exist in society for students from lower socioeconomic backgrounds. Finding a "line of flight" (Reynolds & Webber, 2004), can allow students to see the limitations of their world and avenues to creating new opportunities through positive dialogue. Using fictions, such as those by Toni Morrison and Alice Walker, allows me to start that dialogue in the classroom. In my small way, I get to turn the theoretical aspect of critical theory into a creative practical application.

From the time I was a small child, I understood that education created opportunities. Education seemed desirable because it was the antithesis of the situation in which I grew up. My parents' limited education restricted their opportunities. My home life, characterized by my parents' stress over money and my forced responsibility for my younger sister and brother due to my parents' extensive hours of work, engrained in me a steadfast determination to use education to avoid the situation that was my parents' world.

I excelled in the schoolroom that emphasized rote memorization and recitation. Most of my experience from kindergarten until twelfth grade focused on lowest-level thinking rather than creative and critical aspects of learning. This manner molded me as a learner and created a cast that confined me within the forms of limited education, which was all I knew. My public schooling, steeped in positivistic traditions (Pinar, Reynolds, Slattery, & Taubman, 1995), ensured that I passively obtained the knowledge dispensed by the teacher. On any given day, one could enter any of the classes in the school and find quiet students in razor-edged rows hard at work on worksheets or questions that scraped only the barest edge of knowledge.

This setting marked my education that the game of learning could easily be mastered through maintaining an unobtrusive manner and "reading" or analyzing the teacher to determine what important points might appear on the test. This education, so similar to the prison model described by Foucault (1977) in *Discipline and Punish*, effectively smashed imagination and creativity. The surveillance described in the Panopticon worked effectively on me. I policed my actions because I constantly considered who might be monitoring my performance. Growing up in a firmly disciplined household also contributed to the sense of surveillance that surrounded my school and home life. I never considered the classrooms at my school strict or severe. I considered them "normal" because they closely paralleled what I lived at home. I excelled because I understood how to play the game; I recognized the structure and adapted to it as necessary. I never felt at home in either world. I was and will continue to be in-between.

WYNNETTA SCOTT-SIMMONS

Points of Ruptures, Divergences, Convergence, Variations, Distinctions, and Moments of Doubt and Hope

> If black people would talk to white people, it would make us better people all around . . .
>
> —India.Aire, 2006, *Testimony:*
> *Vol. 1, Life & Relationship*

"But the problem is that those people rarely have dependable friends." This sentence comprised of simple nouns, verbs, articles, and adverbs communicated a message that was far more powerful and complicated than its separate and distinct parts. Despite its simplicity, the sentence held the power to resurrect my in-betweenness, my internalized sensitivity to and awareness of the outsider-within (Collins, 2000) position. The force of the statement, uttered by a person who was a card-carrying member of higher education and the academe, sent me reeling as I felt my academic world and my world as *other* collide. My worlds, one as public black intellectual and the other as personal theorizer seeking to conceptualize the strains of life as a minority in academe, met in a strange moment of shocked confusion. The statement was received as both a societal summary and condemning verdict. With a simple sentence, the speaker had resurrected the invisible, yet sturdy, plastic-wrapped barrier that separates my two main worlds, one as a professor and the other as a triple minority—African American, female, and intellectual.

Had my color and persona become so bleached by an education filled with dominant culture codes of behavior that I was no longer viewed as one of *those people*? If I had, in fact, lost my membership in the group of *those people*, when had that happened, and why had I not been notified? Surely, there had been signs or signals of dismemberment along my educational path. My penchant for books and philosophies rather than albums and telephone gossip led to the distance between myself and family members. I stood in-between worlds; from one world I struggled to find the correct "-ism" or "-ology" to convey my surprise and dismay. From the other world inhabited by *those people*, I struggled to contain the many "-ers" and "-tchs" that were suddenly racing through my body in search of release with the proper pitch and sisterly attitude. My outsider within and in-between enabled me to "foster new angles of vision on oppression" (Collins, 2000, p.11) and to capture points of ruptures, divergences, convergence, variations, distinctions, and moments of doubt and hope.

Literacy of Silence—Capacity to Live In-Between

My mother, a woman who would have been viewed as bereft of social capital, understood through her wealth of cultural capital the contested and complicated tensions of teaching and learning in a racialized society. She recognized the delicate nature of a storied existence as minority, as female, as a sister-outsider (Lorde, 1984). Through theories derived from her dailiness of life (Aptheker, 1989), she learned that a minority female must rely upon multiple understandings, multiple strategies, and multiple theories for success. She cautioned us to remember to look in the mirror before we left home each day. She did not suggest that we make adjustments to our clothing or makeup. Rather, she wanted us to see the face that the members of our racialized world would see. My mother believed that the socially ingrained perceptions were evoked by the tinted visage but not by our minds and hearts. She recognized that she would not be able to "protect us from the world outside the home, which constantly reminded us that black was not the color to be" (hooks, 2001, p.35). She called these life tips her *bag lady* strategies. She saved everything in some sort of bag, no doubt as a result of growing up poor and minority during the Great Depression. She saved knitting yarn, fabric swatches, plastic containers and utensils, rubber bands, empty soda cans and the pull tabs, soy sauce, ketchup, and mustard packets, and other bags. She also saved her tips for survival in an invisible bag that she used to carry with her.

Her baggage of life also contained cans of denial, packages of exclusion, and containers of marginalization and oppression. Burdened by the weight of baggage that no child should be forced to bear, my mother learned to create special places of comfort and peace from which to watch, to learn, and to read her world. She developed her own *literacy of silence* as a result of living a life as other in two worlds. She had suffered through a lifetime of in-betweeness as a multiracial child of the 30s and 40s. Not accepted outside of the family by either the dominant or minority cultures that co-wrote her shared heritage, she learned to navigate the spaces in-between worlds. In her special space, her life in-between cultures, social groups, races, and classes, she learned to listen, to watch, and to learn without drawing attention to herself. It would be in these silent spaces and places of her own creation that my mother developed literacy of life and capacity to live in-between. Much of her world lived between the covers of books about far-off places and unknown people.

My mother read both widely and broadly and learned to respect both the spoken and the written word. She learned to discuss the merits of an author's work with anyone who would listen. She used the vocabulary of books to convince and persuade. She could talk her way out of a brown paper bag when necessary and learned to listen to the stories of influential people for power words, phrases, and ideologies. Her spoken and written word prowess gained her respect by both cultures. Neighbors asked her to write letters on their behalf and to go to the school to serve as an advocate for their children. Her oral and written skills earned her high grades in school and one of the few secretarial positions available to blacks during the summer months. There, in the offices of lawyers and businessmen, she watched, listened, and learned the codes of behavior, dress, and speech of the dominant culture.

Her literacy of silence, honed after years of exclusion and omission, once again helped her to navigate and bridge her dual worlds and dual existences. She learned to watch social habits practiced by members of the dominant culture. She learned to critique, analyze, and match those practices with the ways of life experienced in her minority culture. She learned when to foreground one world and background the other. She practiced a silent pedagogy where she was constantly watching and learning and learning and watching in the silent spaces inhabited by those who find that they are both comfortable and uncomfortable in dual existences and dual worlds. A recognition of the fragility of her private in-between world helped her understand that the "transformation of silence into language and action is an act of self-revelation, and that always seems fraught with danger" (Lorde, 1984, p. 42). Stepping out of silence and moving into the light of *language and action* creates a space for divergent points of entry and capacity to live in-between.

The challenge of living a split and divided existence often inspired my mother to come up with her bag of trials and challenges in fair exchange for a bag of troubles from others. Her life as one of *those people* in both worlds weighed heavily on her broad shoulders. I am thankful that no one ever took my mother up on her offer. Despite her wish that we learn to judge people based on the content of their hearts but not the color of their skin, almost as a way of hedging our life bets, she shared many experiential strategies in the form of cautions and *bag lady* tips. She passed this method of reading the world through silent observation on to me, her oldest child.

I had been lulled into a comfortable space between cultures and had reduced my mother's cautions to an occasional whisper. As a child, I helped integrate a private all-girl school; thus, I became one of *those people*. Many of the parents at my on-the-other-side-of-the-tracks school did not want their upper-class daughters to share a classroom with those of us who had ventured beneath the veil in search of access. My mother's desire and dream for us to receive a better education than the one we would receive in our segregated "jump rope community" (Scott-Simmons, 2008) led to my personal creation of an in-between world. Education, or the pursuit of education, had fashioned a dual existence, a dual space for me to enter and exist as I traversed the space from segregation to access. The 69th Street Train Terminal became my front line, my space of demarcation, my ground zero of in-betweenness. It was here that I would change into my school uniform on the way to school and back into my street clothes on the way home. I had watched other children be chased home for the crime of wearing a school uniform, a school uniform which in the 60s and 70s had represented difference and distinction. The uniform was a symbol of my in-betweenness, of my choice that held the whispers of those left behind: "Who does she think she is?" "Let's show her what special feels like!" "I betcha can't run far and fast in those fancy shoes?!"

Like my mother, I learned to watch and listen in silence and to use the silence to listen and learn without drawing undue attention to myself. Unlike my sister, who chose to stand her ground and claim her space through the use of fists and a temper that belied her diminutive size, my literacy of silence taught me to recognize and to bear both the jealousy of and sense of betrayal felt by my fellow jump-rope community members. My line of demarcation and my education became a symbol of hope and a sign of difference to live in-between. Those who were left behind, those not chosen to receive educations of freedom and transgression, suffered the pain of educational politics designed to confine, contain, and exclude. They also stand as visible and tangible reminders of failure when teaching against the grain or teaching toward freedom are not viable options borne of hope, potential, and justice of social equality.

While I wore the uniform and learned the codes of behavior and language, I also learned to inhabit the space between cultures, literacies, and worlds. My home community, the place where I played basketball on a dirt court, chased after fireflies at night, and jumped double Dutch on the black top to the repetitive rhythms of jump rope chants, "taught me many ways to be good at the daily theorizing necessary to survive in a world that classifies me as a minority, as other" (Scott-Simmons, 2008, p. 72).

My school community taught me about the Renaissance and Reformation, the Latin and French languages, lacrosse, field hockey, and the polite speech and social responsibilities of educated women. Because the two worlds rarely met, I creatively learned to split the me that I knew to suit the worlds that I shared. As I moved through year after year at my school of privileged access, I began to represent more and more of an enigma to those in both my home and school communities. I learned to balance a love of different books, different music, different foods, and different forms of expression from different worlds. Like my mother, I learned to create and inhabit a space of personal comfort—a place between the worlds where I could watch, listen, and learn to be a me that I could live with. In the process, I became one of *those people* in two worlds—in one, unwanted, and in the other, misunderstood as a result of polite politics and ignored ignorance:

> All of us, readers and writers, are bereft when criticism remains too polite or too fearful to notice a disrupting darkness before its eyes. Educated and uneducated students alike have been playing in the darkness of polite liberalism to the detriment of their collective educations. Politeness exists on the part of the minority for not asking the questions, "Why?" or "Where am I?" Polite liberalism exists on the part of the white teacher and whiter educational system for not asking the questions, "Why not?" or "Where are they?" (Morrison, 1992, pp. 90–91)

Entry Points for Connection, Correlation, Creativity, and Communion in-between Theory and Practice

It is that space of misunderstanding that I invite my current students, graduate students of education, to occupy. For many, this is the first time they are asked to recognize and experience an in-between space. I encourage them to leave a comfortable place and space of privilege and to experience a place and space of marginalization and oppression for minority race, culture, language, gender, or religion. I invite them to hold in their hands and minds the constancy, consistency, and courage of language necessary to discuss change of minds, change of hearts, and change of attitudes. Change requires a head-on meeting of misunderstanding and discussion. Transformation requires moments of silent reflection and moments of watching, listening, and learning. Change also requires a language of connection. Language is power, and words are power in flux. They possess the ability to transmit meaning, communicate thoughts, search for connections, persuade, dissuade, and wound. They also have the power to hold a person's place in their absence. The ability to communicate, to transfer thoughts and intent, and to cultivate potential is the process that provides for the continuation and preservation of perceptions, misconceptions, and stereotypes or the ability to search for points of entry, connection, and commonality. Communication is the "social and cultural" process that connects us as humans; it makes history for future generations and sends with it the concepts of inherent power based on the forms of valued attributes.

As a community of learners, we look at film clips and read stories that focus on different cultures. We watch, read, and highlight causes of perceived difference, but we also search for common qualities and characteristics in-between traditionally held beliefs, which I refer to as points of entry, points of discussion, and points of connection. Students create their own mini-oral history projects to share with their classmates. They create audio-visual works, stories, melding vignettes of their childhood, artifacts of their education, with the educational expectations and dreams of both older and younger family members. We use the stories of life and of living, the oral narratives of our lives, and the creative art of storytelling to begin what can be a complicated and uncomfortable conversation on issues of race, religion, class, culture, and gender (see also Greene, 1995; Phillion, He, & Connelly, 2005).

It is through the telling of stories that we create entry points for connection, correlation, and communion in-between theory and practice. Geneva Gay (2000) discusses the power of stories in developing culturally responsive teaching. Individual and collective divergent stories help discover points of connection, entry points of life, multiple paths to intersections in afros and big hair, soda and pop, The Ed Sullivan Show, dancing on Daddy's feet, wooden swings, short skirts and long courtships, going steady, being pinned, and losing friends to wars overseas or wars fought at home. In-between stories we found commonalities, differences, contradictions, and disconnections.

Stories, especially those told orally, stimulate senses, invigorate engagements, and establish relationships. It is through the stimulation, engagement, and relationship that we are able to revisit, relive, and examine memories, what Morrison (1987) calls *rememory*, which provides greater opportunities for "empathetic understanding through examining hearts and minds" (Phillion & He, 2004, p. 3). Stories also evoke interplay between the speaker and the listener (Smitherman, 1977). It is a familiar method of discourse in African American communities, especially the Black churches, known as call and response: "Spontaneous verbal and non-verbal interaction between speaker and listener in which all of the speaker's statements (calls) are punctuated by expressions (responses) from the listener" (Smitherman, 1977, p. 104). It is in that in-between space that we learn to hear not only the message but also the silence. This in-between space does not become a place of darkness and confusion, rather, a place of wakening, enlightening, and understanding. It is through the silence that we find points of entry and connection and points of cultural wakening and transformation.

As an educator schooled in the incubation days of the post-Brown era, I know what it means to play in the darkness cast by the shadow of a silent education. The shadow creates something present and, yet, elusive; improbable and, yet, possible; bleak and, yet, hopeful. A shadow can also emit a feeling and a sense of ominous gloom. Where there is an intangible, ethereal, and fearful shadow, there is light of curiosity and hope in the human spirit. Our job as educators is not only to invite teachers to recognize the spaces in-between what is considered standard and customary but also to create opportunities for the silenced and neglected to create spaces of inclusion and connection through shared stories of silence, negligence, and exclusion. Our job as educators is to open and share bags of strategies to move beyond accepted and contested spaces of silence to create a balanced and just human condition in-between contradiction, complexity, and injustice.

DERRICK M. TENNIAL

Coming in-between Whitewashed Education

Martin Luther King freed the slaves. Imagine how mortified I was when I read this statement in the essay of one of the African American *high school* students. This student was not the brightest student I had at the time; however, as an African American, I expected him to know two *basic* pieces of information framed in his erroneous statement: the significance of slavery and Dr. Martin Luther King, Jr. and the chronology associated with each. I wondered: how in the world did this high school student get through elementary and middle school without acquiring a basic knowledge of African American (not to mention American) history?

Africans were brought to this country to help. Driving to work one morning in 2006 while listening to a local Atlanta radio station, an African American mother called to express her anger and disbelief at the above italicized statement that she had read in her daughter's third grade social studies book. Just like that mother, the talk show hosts, and others who called to express their opinions, I was angry that such a blatant *lie* had been printed in a state adopted textbook and potentially had been taught to hundreds of thousands of third-grade students of all ethnicities, depending on the length of time that the textbook had been in use.

My student's "misinformation" and the "misprint" in Georgia's third-grade social studies textbook are merely symptoms of a larger, even more frightening problem that I did not fully comprehend until I began teaching collegiate education courses to aspiring and practicing teachers both online and in the traditional classroom settings. These college students—current and future teachers of America—are "ignorant" of the basic stories of American history, the history of American education, and the current issues pertaining to American education as it relates to minorities in this country.

In all fairness, my college teacher education students locally and from across the country are among the best and the brightest that can be found anywhere. Their ignorance is no fault of their own; it is rooted in the very system of which they are seeking to become a part. Their ideals and knowledge simply reflect the dominant culture's ideology and version of the "truth," which has been whitewashed and watered down. Most of my students have accepted this "truth" because they are members of the dominant culture. My online and traditional classes are composed of predominantly white, middle-class females, in keeping with the current trend in the teaching force in the United States. If my predominantly white, middle-class female students are ignorant of the plight of minorities in American history and education, then it is not a far reach to assume that many of the white, middle-class females currently teaching are ignorant as well. Therefore, even more alarming is the fact they are more than likely replicating and transmitting to American public school students whitewashed versions of the truth that they have been taught and that are contained in textbooks such as Georgia's third-grade social studies book. As a result, I can perhaps understand why my high school student misconstrued or was misled to believe that Martin Luther King, Jr. freed the slaves.

Many of my students have entered my classes (online or traditional) thinking that I was simply going to teach them how to be "good little schoolmarms" who would exhibit excellent classroom discipline, submit perfect lesson plans, and continue in the same vein of "teacher excellence" that they had experienced as students in the classroom. They were mistaken and, subsequently, awakened to the fact that education has been "whitewashed" to the dominant culture's benefit and minorities' detriment.

Recently, during a discussion on culture and power in schooling and education, one of my students, a white, middle-class female whose children attend private schools, in alarm, asked the question, "Why can't we *just* teach children?" I wish the question were that simple and the answer even simpler. The truth of the matter is too much irreparable damage is being done to America's children to simply *just* teach children. However, we must reconceptualize our teaching to address the irreparable damage that is being done to America's children each time we knowingly and unknowingly perpetuate whitewashed education. According to Gloria Ladson-Billings (1995), students must be taught to "recognize, understand, and critique current social inequalities" (p. 476). In my case, these students are undergraduate and graduate students who are in teacher preparation programs that are merely teaching them how to be "good teachers" who follow the dictates and directives of the districts, who worriedly teach to the standardized test instead of being culturally relevant teachers who are quiet revolutionaries, undermining the status quo in American education by making connections to the past, exposing existing lies, and coloring the whitewashed landscape with diverse perspectives. To answer my student's question, we cannot just teach children—we must empower them with knowledge and truth, or whitewashed education will continue.

This stance places me in a precarious position. I find myself in a constant struggle, like the strong angel in the Bible who has one foot in the sea and the other one on dry land, who gives the Apostle John a book to eat and tells him it will make his stomach bitter but his mouth sweet. I find myself in an in-between space when it comes to educating my college students because I address unpleasant yet realistic "issues of power, ownership of knowledge, and political and economic contexts" (Schram, 2003, p. 4). I want them to learn all the information, policies, and procedures that are necessary for them to be successful in the classroom; however, at the same time, I want them to be quiet mercenaries whose mission is to topple the existing educational system and bring about revolutionary change to a system that needs a desperate overhaul. My teaching has awakened some of my students to the issues that plague education while others continue to sleep, accepting a romanticized view of education.

Recently, one of my students in a course evaluation accused me of being too negative. The student stated,

> Although I enjoyed the classroom discussions I felt we spent too much time focusing on the negative aspects of the education system. It's okay to discuss the problems, but we should spend more time covering the objectives outlined in the syllabus and the book. (personal communication, April 30, 2009)

The fixed, straight-by-the-book and syllabus approach is what has me in this in-between space. What this student is asking me to do is to knowingly perpetuate erroneous information found in the text we used without questioning it and to knowingly teach her lies, falsehoods, and cultural stereotypes. How am I supposed to merely be a disseminator of information when students believe that Martin Luther King freed the slaves, Africans were brought to this country to "help," and other historical misnomers? Is ignorance truly bliss? How am I supposed to *just teach* when "the history of education for African Americans [and other minorities] is not a story of liberation and prosperity but one of struggle and disappointment . . . [that] never intended to have liberatory consequences"? (Lynn, 2006, p. 116).

The situation is too dire for me to stand around and do nothing in fear that I may offend someone by exposing whitewashed education. It is in the in-between space that I continue to advocate for teacher education programs that prepare culturally responsive and creative teachers for students of color. It is in the in-between space that I continue to teach historical truths and encourage students to continually critique society to teach for social justice creatively in an unjust world. It is in the in-between space that I continue to teach against the whitewashed education, to transgress orthodoxies and dogmas, and to invent human conditions for freedom and justice.

Conceptualizing Teaching In-Between

The works of He, Haynes, Scott-Simons, and Tennial (i.e., He & Phillion, 2008; He, in progress; Tennial, 2008) exhibit particular qualities of teaching in-between. Teaching in-between is inherently personal and political. It is personal in that it begins with conscious and critical reflections to challenge assumptions, recognizes contradictions between theories, and demands complexities in practice. It is political in that every act of teaching embodies a particular stance in relation to power, freedom, and human possibility. The overt agendas of equity, equality, liberation, and social justice make teaching in-between breathe and come to life as both vulnerable and durable and always dynamic, grounded, incomplete, trembling, and real. Teachers join one another to teach to move beyond boundaries, to transgress orthodoxies, and to passionately and creatively participate in the life of schools, families, and communities to promote a more balanced, fair, equitable human condition for all.

Nevertheless, the teaching He, Haynes, Scott-Simons, and Tennial have been engaged in could be perceived as not choosing a position or taking a stance. Teaching in-between is *a creative position* where teachers and learners together experience contested contradictions and complexities in-between people, languages, cultures, emotions, and situations. This in-between position creates possibilities for teachers to teach with unfaltering commitment to the plight of the people involved in their lives and the injustice embedded in larger societies.

Teaching in-between thrives on passionate involvement, strong commitment, and unfaltering advocacy for disenfranchised, underrepresented, and invisible groups and individuals. This passion, commitment, and advocacy cannot be cultivated in isolation. Rather, it calls for a community of teachers and educational workers with shared concerns to work together as allies with schools and communities, to take to heart the concerns of all participants, and to develop creative strategies to enact educational and social change that fosters equity, equality, freedom, and social justice. This community can only flourish when the efforts of teachers join with the efforts of other educational workers such as educators, administrators, policymakers, students, parents, and community members. For us, this expanded community embodies possibilities and creates hope that we can invent more in-between spaces where we might live more robustly, develop our human capacities more fully, and become humane and peaceful in inquiry and life as we teach in an increasingly changing and diverse world.

References

Ang, I. (2001). *On not speaking Chinese: Living between Asia and the West*. New York: Routledge.

Aptheker, B. (1989). *Tapestries of life: Women's work, women's consciousness, and the meaning of daily experience*. Amherst, MA: University of Massachusetts Press.

Ayers, W. C. (2004). *Teaching toward freedom: Moral commitment and ethical action in the classroom*. Boston: Beacon.

Ayers, W. C. (2006). Trudge toward freedom: Educational research in the public interest. In G. Ladson-Billings & W. F. Tate (Eds.), *Education research in the public interest: Social justice, action and policy* (pp. 81–97). New York: Teachers College Press.

Ayers, W., Hunt, J. A., & Quinn, T. (Eds.). (1998). *Teaching for social justice: A democracy and education reader*. New York: Teachers College Press.

Bergin, L. (2000). Gloria Anzaldúa's *Borderlands/La Frontera* and René Descartes's *Discourse on Method*: Moving beyond the canon in discussion of philosophical ideas. In C. T. Tougas and S. Ebenreck (Eds.), *Presenting women philosophers* (pp. 139–146). Philadelphia: Temple University Press.

Butler, J. (1990). *Gender trouble: Feminism and the subversion of identity*. London: Routledge.

China National Tourism Administration. (2003). Tiananmen Square. *Beijing Trip*. Retrieved July 29, 2003, from http://www.beijingtrip.com/attractions/square.htm

Clopton, R. W., & Ou, T. C. (Trans. & Eds.). (1973). *John Dewey: Lectures in China, 1919–1920*. Honolulu, HI: University of Hawaii Press.

Cochran-Smith, M. (1991). Learning to teach against the grain. *Harvard Educational Review, 61*(3), 279–310.

Cochran-Smith, M. (2001). Learning to teach against the (new) grain. *Journal of Teacher Education, 52*(1), 3–4.

Cochran-Smith, M. (2004). *Walking the road: Race, diversity, and social justice in teacher education*. New York: Teachers College Press.

Collins, P. H. (2000). *Black feminist thought: Knowledge, consciousness, and the politics of empowerment*. New York: Routledge.

Connelly, F. M., He, M. F., & Phillion, J. (Eds.). (2008). *Handbook of curriculum and instruction*. Thousand Oaks, CA: Sage.

Darling-Hammond, L., French, J., & Garcia-Lopez, S. P. (2002). *Learning to teach for social justice*. New York: Teachers College Press.

Doll, M. A. (2000). *Like letters in running water: A mythopoetics of curriculum*. Mahwah, NJ: Lawrence Erlbaum.

Duncan, C. (Ed.). (1995). *Rural poverty in America*. Westport, CT: Auburn House.

Foucault, M. (1977). *Discipline and punish: The birth of the prison*. London: Penguin Books.

Freire, P. M. (1970). *Pedagogy of the oppressed*. Baltimore: Penguin Books.

Freire, P. M., & Macedo, D. (1995). A dialogue: Culture, language, and race. *Harvard Educational Review, 65*(3), 379–382.

Gay, G. (2000). *Culturally responsive teaching: Theory, research, and practice.* New York: Teachers College Press.

Giroux, H. A. (2000). Public pedagogy as cultural politics: Stuart Hall and the "crisis" of culture. *Cultural Studies, 14*(2), 341–360.

Giroux, H. A. (2004). Cultural studies, public pedagogy, and the responsibility of intellectuals. *Communication and Critical/Cultural Studies, 1*(1), 59–79.

Grande, S. (2004). *Red pedagogy: Native American social and political thought.* Lanham, MD: Rowman & Littlefield.

Greene, M. (1995). *Releasing the imagination: Essays on education, the arts, and social change.* San Francisco: Jossey-Bass.

Hall, D. L., & Ames, R. T. (1999). *The democracy of the dead: Dewey, Confucius, and the hope for democracy in China.* Chicago: Open Court.

Haynes, A. (2008). A quiet awakening: Spinning yarns from Granny's table in the new rural South. In M. F. He & J. Phillion (Eds.), *Personal, passionate, participatory inquiry into social justice in education,* (pp. 127–143). Charlotte, NC: Information Age.

He, M. F. (1998). *Professional knowledge landscapes: Three Chinese women teachers' enculturation and acculturation processes in China and Canada.* Unpublished doctoral dissertation, University of Toronto, Canada.

He, M. F. (1999). A life-long inquiry forever flowing between China and Canada: Crafting a composite auto/biographic narrative method to represent three Chinese women teachers' cultural experiences [featured article]. *Journal of Critical Inquiry into Curriculum & Instruction, 1*(2), 5–29.

He, M. F. (2003). *A river forever flowing: Cross-cultural lives and identities in the multicultural landscape.* Greenwich, CT: Information Age.

He, M. F. (2006). In-Between China and North America. In T. R. Berry & N. D. Mizelle (Eds.), *From oppression to grace: Women of color and their dilemmas within the academy* (pp. 68–76). Sterling, VA: Stylus.

He, M. F. (2009). Exile pedagogy: Teaching and living in-between. In J. A. Sandlin, B. D. Schultz, & J. Burdick (Eds.), *Handbook of public pedagogy: Education and learning beyond schooling* (pp. 1029–1062). New York: Routledge.

He, M. F. (in progress). *Narrative of curriculum in the South.* Charlotte, NC: Information Age.

He, M. F., & Phillion, J. (Eds.). (2008). *Personal-passionate-participatory inquiry into social justice in education.* Greenwich, CT: Information Age.

Hoffman, E. (1989). *Lost in translation: A life in a new language.* New York: Penguin Books.

hooks, b. (1994). *Teaching to transgress: Education as the practice of freedom.* New York: Routledge.

hooks, b. (2000). *Where we stand: Class matters.* New York: Routledge.

hooks, b. (2001). *Salvation: Black people and love.* New York: Harper Collins.

hooks, b. (2003). *Teaching community: A pedagogy of hope.* New York: Routledge.

Ladson-Billings, G. (1995). Toward a theory of culturally relevant pedagogy. *American Educational Research Journal, 32*(3), 465–491.

Loewen, J. W. (2007). *Lies my teacher told me: Everything your American history textbook got wrong.* New York: Touchstone.

Lorde, A. (1984). *Sister outsider: Essays and speeches*. Berkeley, CA: Crossing Press.

Lynn, M. (2006). Race, culture, and the education of African Americans. *Educational Theory, 56*(1), 107–119.

McLaren, P. (2002). *Life in schools: An introduction to critical pedagogy in the foundations of education* (4th ed.). Boston: Allyn & Bacon.

Morris, J. E., & Monroe, C. R. (2009). Why study the South? The nexus of race and place in investigating black student achievement. *Educational Researcher, 38*(1), 21–36.

Morrison, T. (1987). *Beloved*. New York: Penguin Books.

Morrison, T. (1992). *Playing in the dark: Whiteness and literary imagination*. Cambridge, MA: Harvard University Press.

Office of International Information Programs, U.S. Department of State. (2001, April 19). *Public announcement on detention of U.S. citizens in China* [Press release]. Retrieved October 27, 2003, from http://usinfo.org/wf-archive/2001/010419/epf403.htm

Phillion, J., & He, M. F. (2004). Using life-based literary narratives in multicultural teacher education. *Multicultural Perspectives, 6*(3), 3–9.

Phillion, J., He, M. F., & Connelly, F. M. (Eds.). (2005). *Narrative and experience in multicultural education*. Thousand Oaks, CA: Sage.

Pinar, W. F. (1993). Notes on understanding curriculum as a racial text. In C. McCarthy & W. Crichlow (Eds.), *Race, identity, and representation in education* (pp. 60–70). New York: Routledge.

Pinar, W. F., & Irwin, R. L. (2005). *Curriculum in a new key: The collected works of Ted T. Aoki*. Mahwah, NJ: Lawrence Erlbaum.

Pinar, W. F., Reynolds, W. M., Slattery, P., & Taubman, P. M. (1995). *Understanding curriculum: An introduction to the study of historical and contemporary curriculum discourses*. New York: Peter Lang.

Reynolds, W., & Webber, J. (2004). *Expanding curriculum theory: Dispositions and lines of flight*. Mahwah, NJ: Lawrence Erlbaum.

Saïd, E. W. (1994). *Representations of the intellectual*. New York: Vintage Books.

Schram, T. H. (2003). *Conceptualizing qualitative inquiry: Mindwork for fieldwork in education and the social sciences*. Upper Saddle River, NJ: Pearson Education.

Schubert, W. H. (1986). *Curriculum: Perspective, paradigm, and possibility*. New York: Macmillan.

Schubert, W. H. (2009). *Currere* and disciplinarity in curriculum studies: Possibilities for education research [Review of the book *Intellectual Advancement through Disciplinarity: Verticality and horizontality in curriculum studies*]. *Educational Researcher, 38*(2), 136–140.

Schwab, J. J. (1969). The practical: A language for curriculum. *School Review, 78*, 1–24.

Schwab, J. J. (1971). The practical: Arts of eclectic. *School Review, 79*, 493–542.

Schwab, J. J. (1973). The practical 3: Translation into curriculum. *School Review, 79*, 501–522.

Schwab, J. J. (1983). The practical 4: Something for curriculum professors to do. *Curriculum Inquiry, 13*(3), 239–265.

Scott-Simmons, W. (2008). Self, others, and jump rope community: An oral history of the triumphs of African American women. In M. F. He & J. Phillion (Eds.), *Personal, passionate, participatory inquiry into social justice in education* (pp. 71–91). Charlotte, NC: Information Age.

Shiva, V. (1993). *Monocultures of the mind: Perspectives on biodiversity and biotechnology.* Atlantic Highlands, NJ: Zed Books.

Simon, R. I. (1992). *Teaching against the grain: Texts for pedagogy of possibilities.* New York: Bergin & Garvey.

Smitherman, G. (1977). *Talkin and testifyin: The language of Black America.* Boston: Houghton Mifflin.

Southern Regional Education Board. (1998). *Roosevelt (1938): South is nation's no. 1 economic problem; "Not any longer," Southern leaders assert* [Press release]. Retrieved May 28, 2009, from http://www.sreb.org

Stern, J. (1994). *The condition of education in rural schools.* Washington, DC: U.S. Government Printing Office.

Tennial, D. (2008, November). *Unto the third & fourth generation of African-Americans: Kaleb Norris's stories of generational poverty and inequality in the South.* Unpublished doctoral dissertation, Georgia Southern University, Statesboro, GA.

United States Census Bureau. (2002). *United Census 2000.* Washington, DC: U.S. Government Printing Office.

Watkins, W. (2001). *The white architects of black education: Ideology and power in America, 1865–1954.* New York: Teachers College Press.

Watkins, W. (2005). *Black protest thought and education.* New York: Peter Lang.

Yeo, F. (1999). Multicultural education and rural schools. *Multicultural Education, 25* (1), 2–7.

CHAPTER 11

On the Need for Curious and Creative Minds in Multicultural and Cross-Cultural Educational Settings

NARRATIVE POSSIBILITIES

Shijing Xu
University of Windsor

F. Michael Connelly
Ontario Institute for Studies in Education, University of Toronto

Shijing Xu, PhD, is an assistant professor, faculty of education, University of Windsor and an affiliated research associate, National Research Centre for Foreign Language Education, Beijing Foreign Studies University. Her research focuses on narrative approaches to intergenerational, bilingual, and multicultural education issues and school/family/community connections in cross-cultural curriculum studies and teacher education.

F. Michael Connelly, PhD, is professor emeritus, University of Toronto. He discusses his pursuits in *Leaders in Curriculum Studies: Intellectual Self-Portraits*, edited by Edmund Short and Leonard Waks. He collaborates with Shijing Xu on a Sister Schools Network Project involving schools, school boards, and universities in China and Canada.

ABSTRACT

The principal public education task of our time is to provide a democratic form of education for multicultural and cross-cultural educational settings. Transnational migration of people and the

252

international flow of goods, services, and ideas increasingly lead to culturally complex communities. The need for the development of curious and creative minds applies to decidedly multicultural settings as well as mostly white settings. Curriculum programs and scholarly writings tend to focus on the recognition of cultural, linguistic, and other needs and on ways of helping minority cultures adapt to majority culture. Democratic education focused on the development of curious and creative minds requires curriculum and teaching which goes beyond adaptation to cultural reciprocity, in which all children, of whatever culture, learn about, adapt to, and create an ever-changing society. Narrative curriculum and teaching methods that stress intergenerational family cultural educational histories have the potential to contribute to this end.

Our purpose in this chapter is to explore the Teacher Education Yearbook XVIII theme of *curious and creative minds* in the context of multicultural and cross-cultural school settings. The yearbook's theme is original and thought provoking for our topic, which, historically, has been approached from the point of view of the needs and difficulties of cultural minorities and of the curriculum and teaching methods for meeting these needs and for overcoming difficulties. There is a vast literature on this cultural educational matter. One of the most recent entrée points to this literature is found in a set of chapters (Ladson-Billings & Brown; Nieto, Bode, Kang, & Raible; Erickson et al.; He, Phillion, Chan, & Xu; Ainscow; Cochran-Smith & Demers; Craig & Ross; Ayers, Quinn, Stovall, & Scheiern; Deyhle, Swisher, Stevens, & Galván; Anderson-Levitt; Farrell) in *The SAGE Handbook of Curriculum and Instruction* (Connelly, He, & Phillion, 2008). Readers will find therein several related literature summaries that provide a window into the rich literature on multicultural education, on cross-cultural education, and on the education of immigrant newcomers.

This literature reveals the immense array of teaching and curriculum matters that come under our broad topic. Some aspects of the literature are especially focused on deficits and impediments faced by cultural minorities. These matters range from language, to cultural habits, to racism, to simple cross-cultural misunderstanding. If there is one overall theme in this literature it is the attempt philosophically and through the provision of ameliorative curriculum and teaching methodologies to provide a comfortable, inviting, inclusive environment in which cultural minorities may adapt and fit into the larger majority culture. This generalization, of course, has many exceptions. Readers will find, as well, a critical literature on immigration, multiculturalism, and bilingual education policies. There are, as well, arguments and views consistent with these we present in this yearbook chapter based on the idea that cultural minorities contribute to and enrich society and the dominant culture.

The position we take in this chapter is that minority cultural adaptation to meet majority culture is only a first step towards an educationally democratic view that treats minority culture as a source of inspiration, new ideas, and enriched cultural societal possibilities. Minority cultures do, of course, need to learn the language and customs of the majority culture in order to function satisfactorily in society. Minorities do need to adapt. However, an education built solely on the idea of successful adaptation tends to result in closed minds on the part of learners and teachers—closed because the educational framework is given, and the learner's role is to acquire the cultural norms of that framework. But as John Dewey long ago argued (Dewey, 1916, 1938), democratic education in its broadest sense has both cultural transmission and cultural reconstruction qualities, that is, cultural adaptation and cultural re-creation, as its goals.

Dewey argued that all learners needed to learn the knowledge and social norms of society while, at the same time, learning to inquire into societal knowledge and norms, changing them via the process of inquiry. In a revealing exchange reported by Frankel (1977) and discussed by Eldridge (1998), Dewey, at an eightieth birthday celebration, is reported to have corrected his tribute by saying that his philosophical effort had been to *intellectualize practice*, not, as the tribute had it, to practicalize intelligence.

The significance of this correction for our purposes in this chapter is twofold. First, Dewey is saying that inquiry ultimately begins with social practice. His view runs counter to approaches to social growth and intelligence based on the application of theory. Second, Dewey saw intelligence as a social phenomenon in which knowing was socially constructed. For Dewey, then, *curious and creative minds* are minds working interactively with other minds to make meaning of social life, in effect, to *intellectualize practice*. Inquiry requires minds that are socially conditioned to challenge, inquire, solve problems, improve matters, in short, to change and reconstruct society.

This broad philosophical view applies directly and vividly to the education of minorities who must adapt to majority culture, but, and this is our argument, in a democratic form of education, they need also to be viewed as rich intellectual resources for the reconstruction and enrichment of culture. In effect, educators concerned with minority culture children need to ensure that they are educated to reach beyond what is necessarily contained in the closed mind generated by a merely socially adaptive education. To accomplish these ends, teachers and students need to be curious about and creatively inquire into the cultural diversity in our classrooms and universities.

How might cultural curiosity and creativity be encouraged in classrooms? One fundamental way of approaching this question is through generational family educational narratives (Xu, 2006). This concept is built on the idea that cultural beliefs and attitudes, like physical cultural artifacts, are more than meets the eye. They are the result of cultural creation and transmission over time through the generations. Just as Dewey set out to intellectualize practice, an intergenerational family narrative approach sets out to intellectualize cultural expression. Instead of asking "good" and "bad" adaptive questions about observed cultural behaviors and beliefs, a narrative approach asks how these behaviors and beliefs have come about, thereby exploring the history and truth that resides in cultural expressions. In this way, minority culture children are seen as exhibiting and representing a cultural tradition. Diversity in this sense is to be savored and retained. Thus, our broad answer to the question of how to counteract closed-mindedness and how to foster curious and creative minds in classrooms is through narrative.

Narratives of Experience: Countering Closed Minds

As is revealed in Xu's (2006) studies, it is common to hear statements such as: "You came to our country. It is you who should learn and adapt, not me." "We have been brought up this way. If you don't like it, you should go back to your own country." These expressions hold a view of immigration and multiculturalism that implies that it is the newcomers who should adapt and integrate. Xu (2006) suggests that while it is true that newcomers should make an effort to adapt and integrate, there is a greater truth in an inevitable process of mutual adaptation and reciprocity between newcomer and host cultures. Immigrant adaptation is not a matter of replacing the old with the new; it is not a matter of exchanging one language for another and one value system for another. It is a process of merging historically founded cultural and personal narratives of experience. These narratives can never be replaced but only altered and reshaped with much being retained and taking on new shape. Though not as obvious, the same is true for the recipient society and its cultures, which are also being influenced, modified, and reshaped in this process. While a newcomer's learning may be most obvious and most easily identified, host culture learnings, though perhaps less obvious, are, in the long run, equally important. Narratives of experience give meaning to observed cultural differences and, therefore, may counter closed-mindedness and the schism of positions for immigrant children, multiculturalism, and transnational circular migration.

The failure to develop curious and creative minds—the danger in educating for closed minds—goes beyond a missed opportunity for enriching society. Closed minds can be *dangerous minds* that lead to cross-cultural dissention, racism, and war. Our world, in small and large ways, at home and abroad, is filled with brutal instances where the presumed superiority and rightness of one cultural group over another is evident. We believe that narrative approaches that reveal the personal and cultural narrative histories of individuals and groups are important to cultivating an open-mindedness that supports curious and creative minds.

A Sketch of the Cultural Landscape: Closed Minds vs. Curious and Creative Minds

We believe that the central educational issue of our time is how to foster an enriching cross-cultural education: a democratic education that transcends cultural adaptation and opens itself to the societal contributions that might be made by cultural minorities. This broad issue has long been an educational issue in North America. Now, some believe, it may have become the central educational issue because of modern cross-cultural communication and movement (Kalantzis & Cope, 1992). We believe it has, at least in Canada. Transnational migration and shifting national power and economic relations worldwide mean that schools everywhere are becoming cultural amalgams. No one is any longer amazed to learn that the majority of school-age children of New York City (U.S. Census Bureau, 2009; Department of City Planning, New York City, 2009) or Toronto (Citizenship and Immigration Canada, 2007) come from homes where English is *not* the first language.

As is shown by Statistics Canada (2007), over the past one hundred years, more than 13 million immigrants have arrived to forge a new life, making Canada one of the world's most ethnically diverse countries. While most came from Europe during the first half of the twentieth century, non-Europeans started arriving in larger numbers as economic immigrants or refugees or as family members of previous immigrants. According to Statistics Canada projections, the racial, ethnic, linguistic, and religious diversity of the country will continue to increase. By 2017, about 20 percent of Canada's population could be visible minorities, or anywhere from 6.3 million to 8.5 million people (Statistics Canada, 2007).

In the United States, 34.2 million people were foreign born in 2004, and among them, 53 percent were born in Latin America, 25 percent in Asia, 14 percent in Europe, and 8 percent in other regions of the world (U.S. Census Bureau, 2009). In Europe, during the last decades, many newcomers arrived in E.U. countries in the context of workforce migration, family reunion, and, lately, mainly refugees from different continents (Extra & Yagmur, 2002). According to Eurostats, the population in Europe as a whole has increased by 2.9

million and is now more than 822 million with a growth rate in 2007 of 3.5 percent. Migration contributed 76 percent to the total European population increase.[1]

Besides many social, cultural, and political issues, these new groups put new demands on educational institutions. According to the United Nations Educational, Scientific and Cultural Organization (UNESCO) report, "One of the biggest challenges facing our societies is the integration of migrants in order to make them productive citizens adjusted to the conditions of their host countries" (Institute for European Studies, 2005). We provide a brief overview of this matter divided into two, admittedly somewhat arbitrary, aspects: immigrant children and multiculturalism in our discussion of the need for cultivating curious and creative minds.

IMMIGRANT CHILDREN

The increasing diversity in school has driven much curriculum policy making and local practices. Different people approach and interpret diversity with different understandings. Some emphasize *differences* and perceive cultural and linguistic differences as a challenging, complex issue for school curriculum. Some call for culturally sensitive curriculum and develop programs to accommodate diverse needs of the learners from different cultural and linguistic groups to help them adapt to and succeed in the mainstream society. Some call for redesigning and reconceptualizing curriculum to address issues and concerns that affect students of different cultural and linguistic groups.

Well intended as these efforts are, there is a social problem in our modern cross-cultural society that may lead to the possibility of inhibiting the development of curious and creative minds by educating immigrant children in "closed mind" settings. In such a setting, newcomer immigrant/visible minority groups are treated as people who have little to offer and who must adapt to and catch up with the mainstream system. Some programs are set up from a mainstream culture perspective using a deficit model in which newcomer and/or visible minority children are perceived only as being in need. Teachers in such programs are made aware of cultural and linguistic differences, and they work hard to help those children to adapt and/or catch up. These are important measures; however, we need to cultivate openness, curiosity, and creativity among our teachers and teacher candidates so that they do not see the children as having less and do not see them through the lenses of labels defined and categorized in terms of cultural deficit. Instead, they need to see the children as who they are: valuable, unique individuals, each with an enriching cultural narrative history and with as much potential as any other child.

The following is an example of how a well-intended program in a deficit model may lead to schools', teachers', and the students' undervaluing classmates and, worse yet, students undervaluing themselves. In such an environment, open-mindedness and the risk taking that often accompanies curiosity and creativity can easily be squelched. A teacher candidate who was reared by a single mom in a low-income family writes:

> From age seven to age fourteen I lived, along with my brother, in a single parent (mother) low-income home. I remember the shame and embarrassment I felt at having to collect "free lunches" every day at school while my classmates traded treats between them. Everyone knew that my lunch was free and therefore, nobody wanted to trade treats with me. I felt poor and socially disadvantaged during that time.

In our pre-service classrooms, we discussed possible ways of helping and supporting children who appear in need, for example, children from low socioeconomic backgrounds or families where English is not spoken as the first language. We discussed the importance of thinking about help and support while appreciating and seeing every child as a valuable individual and as someone with potential for a better, promising future. We discussed the problems in programs developed in a deficit model that were designed to "help" the underprivileged. There are some risks if we approach children who are socially disadvantaged in such ways that put them into categories that tend to undermine their value and treat them differently from the majority of their classmates. This could result in closed minds of children of both socially advantaged and socially disadvantaged.

In summary, we argue that it is important for both teacher candidates and practicing teachers to consider how to cultivate students' curiosity and creativity as well as among teachers themselves while reaching out with helpful programs to those who appear to be in need. Help needs to be offered sensitively and with respect for each child helped. In this way, we may empower and enrich children's living and schooling experience without seeing them as less nor making them feel less. We may "help" those in need without closing their minds or closing the minds of their peers. The same may be said for educational programs such as English as a second language and literacy development.

From a narrative point of view, simultaneously adaptive and creative educational programs are best built on the strengths students bring to their educational encounters. Many language educators (e.g., Coelho, 2003; Corson, 1999; Cummins, 1994, 2000, 2007) emphasize the importance of the integration of new learning with prior knowledge. This process involves connecting what students know in their first language to English as their second or even third language. In Ontario, Canada, educators have developed English language education programs such as *dual language* programs[2] and the *multi-literacies* project,[3] which are transforming linguistic challenges into learning opportunities and educational resources (Cummins 2007; Cummins & Davison, 2007; Cummins & Coelho, 2005; Lotherington, 2007). In practice, however, there is a long way to go.

Teachers and teacher candidates need to make use of their own curiosity and creativity to perceive and make use of linguistic and cultural differences that newcomer/visible minority children bring to school as valuable resources. Beginning with student strengths is not easy when the educational attitude is built on recognizing children in need and where well-intentioned educators spontaneously wish to address the deficits behind the needs. Yet being sensitive to the student's strengths and valuing and encouraging what the student can offer are needed first steps toward a democratic education.

MULTICULTURALISM

We may take heart in the fact that there has been increasing awareness of cultural *diversity* over the idea of cultural *differences* in school and elsewhere. This shift reflects an attempt to celebrate linguistic and cultural diversities as resources for mainstream schools rather than perceiving cultural and linguistic differences merely as challenges. Still, many teacher candidates in our teacher education program return from their school practice teaching assignments with disappointment. For example, one of our pre-service teacher education class assignments is to prepare one or more inclusive education lesson plans for use during the teacher candidates' practice teaching placements in schools. Many were unable to implement these plans. In some cases, the reason had to do with scheduling and the lack of fit between the cooperating teacher's planned curriculum and the inclusive lesson plans. But more often than not, the reason had to do with a perceived inappropriateness or perceived irrelevance of the lesson plan to the school's curriculum. In most of these cases, the teacher candidates judged that the real reason had to do with "conventional" curricula (and, perhaps, conventional teachers) in which the idea of cultural inclusivity had little place.

Some school practices are still defined in terms of mainstream culture. "Foreign" sounding and looking students are expected to adapt. Programs built on this view, hence, do not support children of diverse ethnic, cultural, and linguistic backgrounds in the way suggested. One of the more insidious practices is that of lowered academic expectations for children from low socioeconomic families and for newcomer, and other culturally diverse, children. In effect a tracking system is created, and newcomer children tend to be streamed into less rewarding educational and employment paths. The effects of lowered expectations may show up early in the curriculum. For instance, some children at grade two do not know how to write their names or how to add three to five. We may foresee what kind of future is in store for these children who are being educated in such "closed mind" settings. This matter is often the source of family–school system tension as parents recognize the detrimental effects of this form of streaming on their children (Xu, 2006).

In addition to a discussion associated with cultural diversity for visible minorities, there is an often overlooked discussion among white students. Discussions over diversifying curriculum and promoting multicultural and equitable education tend to focus mainly on addressing diverse needs of learners of visible minority groups at disadvantage or at risk in a deficit model. Diversity may not be seen to extend to white students. Whites are not seen as part of the cultural and linguistic diverse groups. There is a white "we" and a culturally diverse "them." Consequently, on this limited view, students from different white groups are seen as one dominant group. Many white students may feel that they do not have a culture. "Culture" is something that one has if underprivileged ("impoverished culture") or if one speaks another language or is "colored" ("the other culture"). White students appear to belong to a majority culture but may experience the opposite. Thus, while the curriculum may be based on the idea that minorities have a limited, somewhat defective, or even a wrong culture and, therefore, need to adapt to and take on the majority culture, children in the supposed majority culture may feel cultureless, as if in a cultural vacuum.

In our teaching, we came across situations where associate teachers and teacher candidates did not see the point of implementing multicultural education in seemingly all-white or almost all-white classrooms. One of our teacher education exercises in such situations is to explore the cultural backgrounds and experience of our white teacher education candidates. Given Canada's immigration history during the mid-twentieth century, there are a wide range of white cultural backgrounds from Central, Eastern, and Western Europe; from Africa; and from the Caribbean. According to Statistics Canada (2007), Canada's foreign-born population peaked at 22.2 percent of the population in 1931 and again in 2006 at 19.8 percent. However, whereas Europeans accounted for 16.1 percent of the immigrants in 2006, they accounted for 90.5 percent of the immigrants prior to 1961 (Human Resources and Skills Development Canada, 2009). The result of this immigration history is that the "white" situation is highly diverse culturally with various shades of whiteness and many different languages. Moreover, those with English as a first language are of several different colors, for example, English speakers from the Caribbean.

Properly done, this discussion of diversity with white students speaking English as a first language has a richness and variation that, while perhaps not quite as broad as a discussion of cultural diversity based on color and immigration status, is illuminating for teacher candidates. We ask our teacher candidates to find out what might be missing in their own education by reflecting on the fact that many grew up in European and other families in a community that was decidedly heterogeneous and multicultural yet was all, or mostly all, white and monolingual speakers of English. A class of mostly English as a first language white teacher candidates will discover among themselves a diverse tapestry of intergenerational family narratives. These narratives reveal diverse language and cultural backgrounds, parts of which may have been lost through homogenization via adaptation to white, English Canada. In addition to revealing the rich cultural diversity within the dominant white culture, individual students may learn to value, and explore, their own personal family narratives of experience.

Teaching in a school of increasing apparent diversity with newcomers of different language, culture, and color, in what way may we integrate the rich linguistic and cultural resources brought by people coming from all over the world? How may we shift our thinking from models of assimilation and/or adaptation to those of reciprocal learning? How do we move from closed to open, curious, and creative minds? In a sense, it is more important to engage white, English-speaking, mainstream children in language and cultural diversity and multicultural education than cultural minorities. These students need to see that cultural diversity is not only for others; it is part of their heritage, and it is also a privilege to be immersed in these cultural and linguistic resources. White students need to see themselves as part of "them." There is no culturally diverse, separate "them"; we are culturally diverse. There is only "us."

Our discussion so far establishes the social need for a special kind of concern in our modern society for curious and creative minds at a cultural level. We need to be curious and creative about other cultures, and we need to teach our students to respect their own and others' cultures as vital social assets. We need to teach in such a way that children feel that they have something to contribute when they find themselves in situations where they are required to adapt to someone else's culture. Mainstream children need to go beyond tolerating the cultures of others to understanding and respecting other cultures as well as their own cultural narratives.

It is true that newcomer children and visible minority children need to understand and adapt to the mainstream culture and system. But this does not mean that it is to be done in such a way that students lose their own heritage and tradition. They need to recognize and become self-aware of their cultural contribution. They need to reach inside and, by reaching inside, connect with the social by reaching into their family's and their culture's own cultural heritage. Teacher educators and teachers may contribute with this process. The opposite of the schism that may come from closed minds is the personal confidence, and the social reconstruction of society, that may come from a democratically educated population with the ability to use their curiosity to act and think creatively.

In the following section, we relate Xu's (2006) cross-cultural studies of Chinese newcomer families' educational narratives. This study shows how teacher educators may explore intergenerational family narratives. Xu, as researcher, played a role that every teacher, every day, plays out in school and community life. Every teacher has similar experiences and, with an attitude of curiosity and an open mind toward cultural diversity, may follow a similar path.

Intergenerational Chinese Family Educational Narratives: A Study of Cultural Interaction

The principal democratic educational challenge is that people with diverse language and culture need to be educated for productive cultural adaptation while, simultaneously, being educated to value and inquire into their own and others' diversity as a creative force for social reconstruction. We believe that the cultivation of curious and creative minds can lead to cross-cultural/intercultural bridges that enable our children to benefit from the cultural intersections of various ways of knowing and being as the world's cultures meet and intersect, a view developed in Xu's (2006) narrative study of Chinese newcomer families' cross-cultural schooling experience in Canadian schools.

Xu adopted narrative methodology to simultaneously study the cultural tensions and communications in the processes of newcomer Chinese cultural adaptation to Canada while appreciating the knowledge and values brought to Canada by new Chinese immigrants. She developed the concept of intergenerational family educational narratives to provide an interpretive framework for her fieldwork. Her fieldwork consisted of three to five days a week of school visits from May 2002 to December 2004 and ongoing follow-up visits and continuous participation in school events, along with new projects being developed up until the time of writing this chapter. These visits involved observing and volunteering in classrooms, in the school's parent Center, in English as a second language (ESL) programs, in the international languages program (e.g., Mandarin classes), and in a wide variety of extra-curricular programs. The fieldwork also included participant observation of teacher-parent interviews, fieldtrips, and school council meetings. In addition, she interviewed parents, grandparents, children, the school principal, teachers, settlement workers, social workers, and other community workers.

The important thing to note about this methodology is that it is designed to study the experience of newcomer Chinese families, and educators in interaction with them, and to do so with an eye to individual experience and to longstanding family cultural traditions, which, as the study revealed, went back to the teachings of Confucius. Moreover, though some aspects were pursued in more depth than might be expected of a classroom teacher, the field experience covered the ordinary range of teacher experience in school, home, and community. By sympathetically studying, in detail, family experience in their own terms, it is possible to reveal, and bring forward, the cultural strengths of these newcomer families. It is possible to see, in detail, how they view and know education, how they know children, how they know teachers, and how they know the experience of family life.

The study of these experiences, and their rendition in the form of intergenerational family educational narratives, reveals the historical richness and cultural contributions that might be made by these families as they adapt to Canadian society and to Canadian education. Teacher education candidates may explore versions of this work in their teacher education classes and during practice teaching placements in host schools and communities. Teachers, sensitive to the narrative quality of their teaching experience, may explore similar paths in their own classrooms. They may even initiate cross-cultural inquiries and discussions in their school classrooms as they engage students in discussions designed to reveal family educational narratives of experience. The discussion that may be held in pre-service teacher education classes may be repeated in their classes with children in schools, with appropriate adjustment, as these teachers take on regular classroom duties after graduation.

Through the lens of generational narratives, Xu's study reveals both hidden needs and special contributions of Chinese newcomers. Her study also shows ways that Canadian society is constantly reshaped and reconstituted by Chinese newcomers' cultural interactions with and adaptation to the host Canadian society. These insights extend beyond the Chinese newcomers in her study to other newcomers and to cultural diversity in general. This reciprocity between newcomer and host cultures can help contribute to a society that is multicultural and inclusive for all. The study calls for extended and expanded mutual *we-ness* in dialogues across civilizations in hopes of building a multidimensional bridge that connects different ways of knowing and being and, hence, harmoniously brings together ethnically, socially, culturally, and linguistically diverse people. With curious and creative minds, our children can hope to grow up in positive multicultural harmony in diversity.

Notes

1. G. Lanzieri (2008). "Population in Europe 2007: First Results." European Commission: Eurostat, Statistics in Focus (vol. 81: Population and Social Conditions).

2. See http://thornwood.peelschools.org/Dual/books/chinese/lucy/lucy.htm
3. See http://www.multiliteracies.ca

References

Ainscow, M. (2008). Teaching for diversity: The next big challenge. In F. M. Connelly (Ed.), M. F. He, & J. Phillion (Assoc. Eds.), *The SAGE handbook of curriculum and instruction* (pp. 240–260). Thousand Oaks, CA: Sage.

Anderson-Levitt, K. (2008). Globalization and curriculum. In F. M. Connelly (Ed.), M. F. He, & J. Phillion (Assoc. Eds.), *The SAGE handbook of curriculum and instruction* (pp. 349–368). Thousand Oaks, CA: Sage.

Ayers, W., Quinn, T., Stovall, D., & Scheiern, L. (2008). Teachers' experience of curriculum: Policy, pedagogy and situation. In F. M. Connelly (Ed.), M. F. He, & J. Phillion (Assoc. Eds.), *The SAGE handbook of curriculum and instruction* (pp. 306–328). Thousand Oaks, CA: Sage.

Citizenship and Immigration Canada. (2007). *Facts and figures 2007: Immigration overview —permanent and temporary residents.* Retrieved May 2, 2009, from http://www.cic.gc.ca/english/resources/statistics/menu-fact.asp

Cochran-Smith, M., & Demers, K. (2008). Teacher education as a bridge: Curriculum policy and practice. In F. M. Connelly (Ed.), M. F. He, & J. Phillion (Assoc. Eds.), *The SAGE handbook of curriculum and instruction* (pp. 261–281). Thousand Oaks, CA: Sage.

Coelho, E. (2003). *Adding English: A guide to teaching in multilingual classrooms.* Toronto, Canada: Pippin.

Connelly, F. M. (Ed.), He, M. F., & Phillion, J. (Assoc. Eds.). (2008). *The SAGE handbook of curriculum and instruction.* Thousand Oaks, CA: Sage.

Corson, D. (1999). *Language policy in schools: A resource for teachers and administrators.* Mahwah, NJ: Lawrence Erlbaum Associates.

Craig, C. J., & Ross, V. (2008). Cultivating the image of teachers as curriculum makers. In F. M. Connelly (Ed.), M. F. He, & J. Phillion (Assoc. Eds.), *The SAGE handbook of curriculum and instruction* (pp. 282–305). Thousand Oaks, CA: Sage.

Cummins, J. (1994). Knowledge, power and identity in teaching English as a second language. In F. Genesee (Ed.), *Educating second language children.* Cambridge, UK: Cambridge University Press.

Cummins, J. (2000). *Language, power and pedagogy: Bilingual children in the crossfire.* Clevedon, UK: Multilingual Matters.

Cummins, J. (2007). Promoting literacy in multilingual contexts. *What Works? Research into Practice.* Ontario, Canada: The Literacy and Numeracy Secretariat and the Ontario Association of Deans of Education.

Cummins, J., & Coelho, E. (2005). *Teaching and learning in multilingual Ontario* [Video file]. Retrieved May 1, 2009, from http://www.curriculum.org/secretariat/december7.shtml

Cummins, J., & Davison, C. (2007). *International handbook of English language teaching* (Vol. 15). New York: Springer.

Department of City Planning, New York City. (2009). *The newest New Yorkers: Overview.* Retrieved May 2, 2009, from http://www.nyc.gov/html/dcp/html/census/nny_over view.shtml

Dewey, J. (1916). *Democracy and education: An introduction to the philosophy of education.* New York: Macmillan.

Dewey, J. (1938). *Experience and education.* New York: Collier Books.

Deyhle, D., Swisher, K., Stevens, T., & Galván, R. T. (2008). Indigenous resistance and renewal: From colonizing practices to self-determination. In F. M. Connelly (Ed.), M. F. He, & J. Phillion (Assoc. Eds.), *The SAGE handbook of curriculum and instruction* (pp. 329–348). Thousand Oaks, CA: Sage.

Eldridge, M. (1998). *Transforming experience: John Dewey's cultural instrumentalism.* Nashville, TN: Vanderbilt University Press.

Erickson, F., Bagrodia, R., Cook-Sather, A., Espinoza, M., Jurow, S., Shultz, J. J., et al. (2008). Students' experience of school curriculum: The everyday circumstances of granting and withholding assent to learn. In F. M. Connelly (Ed.), M. F. He, & J. Phillion (Assoc. Eds.), *The SAGE handbook of curriculum and instruction* (pp. 198–218). Thousand Oaks, CA: Sage.

Extra, G., & Yagmur, K. (2002). Language diversity in multicultural Europe: Comparative perspectives on immigrant minority languages at home and at school. *Management of Social Transformations (MOST), Discussion Paper 63.* Paris: UNESCO.

Farrell, J. (2008). Community education in developing countries: The quiet revolution in schooling. In F. M. Connelly (Ed.), M. F. He, & J. Phillion (Assoc. Eds.), *The SAGE handbook of curriculum and instruction* (pp. 369–390). Thousand Oaks, CA: Sage.

Frankel, C. (1977). John Dewey's social philosophy. In S. M. Cahn (Ed.), *New studies in the philosophy of John Dewey* (pp. 4–5). Hanover, NH: University Press of New England.

He, M. F., Phillion, J., Chan, E., & Xu, S. J. (2008). Immigrant students' experience of curriculum. In F. M. Connelly (Ed.), M. F. He, & J. Phillion (Assoc. Eds.), *The SAGE handbook of curriculum and instruction* (pp. 219–239). Thousand Oaks, CA: Sage.

Human Resources and Skills Development Canada. (2009). *Canadians in context—immigration.* Retrieved May 11, 2009, from http://www4.hrsdc.gc.ca/.3ndic.1t.4r@-eng .jsp?iid=38

Institute for European Studies. (2005). *Multiculturalism in European Union* [Lecture series]. Retrieved May 4, 2009, from http://www.ies.be/activities/multicult/flyer-multicult -hr.pdf

Kalantzis, M., & Cope, W. (1992). Multiculturalism may prove to be the key issue of our epoch. *Chronicle of Higher Education, 39*(11), B3, B5.

Ladson-Billings, G., & Brown, K. D. (2008). Curriculum and cultural diversity. In F. M. Connelly (Ed.), M. F. He, & J. Phillion (Assoc. Eds.), *The SAGE handbook of curriculum and instruction* (pp. 153–175). Thousand Oaks, CA: Sage.

Lotherington, H. (2007). From literacy to multiliteracies in ELT. In J. Cummins & C. Davison (Eds.), *International Handbook of English Language Teaching.* Berlin, Germany: Springer.

Nieto, S., Bode, P., Kang, E., & Raible, J. (2008). Identity, community, and diversity: Retheorizing multicultural curriculum for the postmodern era. In F. M. Connelly

(Ed.), M. F. He, & J. Phillion (Assoc. Eds.), *The SAGE handbook of curriculum and instruction* (pp. 176–197). Thousand Oaks, CA: Sage.

Statistics Canada. (2007). *Immigration in Canada: A portrait of the foreign-born population, 2006 Census.* Retrieved June 5, 2008, from http://www12.statcan.ca/english/census06/analysis/immcit/pdf/97-557-XIE2006001.pdf

U.S. Census Bureau. (2009). *State and county quick facts.* Retrieved May 3, 2009, from http://quickfacts.census.gov/qfd/states/36000.html

Xu, S. J. (2006). In search of home on landscapes in transition: Narratives of newcomer families' cross-cultural schooling experience. Unpublished doctoral dissertation, University of Toronto, Canada.

Summary and Implications

Cheryl J. Craig

Louise F. Deretchin

The eleven chapters in *Cultivating Curious and Creative Minds: The Role of Teachers and Teacher Educators, Part I* (Teacher Education Yearbook XVIII) have focused readers' attention on the cultivation of curiosity and creativity within the K–12 teaching field. Each dimension offered a different perspective from which to imagine curious and creative minds being nurtured, a theme that will be followed up in *Cultivating Curious and Creative Minds: The Role of Teachers and Teacher Educators, Part II* (Teacher Education Yearbook XIX), which continues this discussion by focusing on teacher education and students/programs/schools.

Kevin Cloninger and Christina Mengert's "In Pursuit of Joy," Chapter 1, opened up the teaching discussion. Their chapter encouraged readers to see health and well-being as something infinitely more complex than the mere absence of disease. Put simply, Cloninger and Mengert connected creative activity with joy. At the same time, they underlined the fact that creative pursuits do not imply a loosening of standards or an absence of rigor in curriculum. On the contrary, creativity, pedagogy, and the science of well-being involve a high degree of rigor for those who understand that happiness, understanding, and love are possible for those who actively seek it.

"Can We Teach for Surprise?" is the provocative query that Gadi Alexander pondered in Chapter 2. The work enabled readers to walk alongside Alexander as his career progressed and he became involved in a variety of creative projects ranging from classroom instruction to educational broadcasting and from his home country of Israel to his encounter with Kieran Egan's work in Canada. In a conversational manner, Alexander invited readers inside each project to learn its strengths and challenges and the legacies of imaginative education to date.

In Chapter 3, Richard Olenchak and John Gaa addressed the topic of "Jumping to Conclusions or Jumping for Joy? Teaching as the Art of Talent

Development." Their chapter echoed the joy theme that emerged in Kevin Cloninger and Christina Mengert's Chapter 1. The Olenchak and Gaa work convincingly argued that there are similarities between the behaviors and attitudes of underachieving gifted students and the instructional underachievement of talented teachers. In both instances, hostile and/or nonresponsive working/learning environments are contributing factors.

In "Aesthetic Themes as Conduits to Creativity" (Chapter 4), authors Christy Moroye and Bruce Uhrmacher reminded readers that both teachers and learners have a degree of choice in the learning activities they pursue and in the subsequent meanings (ordinary/extraordinary) they make of them. The authors maintained that creative minds can be fueled by teachers and that creative teaching requires a safe learning environment, supports student ownership, and involves modeling the kind of creativity that is held foremost in view.

Chapter 5, "Child Study/Lesson Study: A Catalyst for Teacher Curiosity," turned readers' attention to the content areas, specifically to mathematics. Herbert Ginsburg, Joan Mast, and Merrie Snow outlined a version of teacher professional development that merged lesson study with clinical interviews undertaken with their students. The exploratory work contributed to increased teacher understanding of student learning and thinking and heightened teacher awareness of math education and pedagogy. It additionally spurred subsequent changes in teachers' classroom teaching practices and led to student growth in math learning.

In Chapter 6, "Nurturing a Creative Curiosity for K–2 Mathematics Teaching: Lessons from the Dreamkeepers," teachers' conceptual and instructional understanding of mathematics as a content area was coupled with a kind of pedagogy that not only resonated with mathematics as a school subject but also was culturally relevant to the students taught by the teachers. Authors Patricia Marshall, Allison McCulloch, and Jessica DeCuir-Gunby provided close-up views of teachers being prepared to approach mathematics classrooms as "dens of creativity" peopled by culturally diverse students who are eager to learn.

As readers, we transitioned from a discussion of mathematics education in Chapter 5 and 6 to a focus on science education in Chapters 7 and 8. Chapter 7, "The Impact of Creativity within the Inquiry Process in Science Education," contributed by Terri Hebert, challenged the traditional "sit-and-get" science instruction meted out to children in schools and to teachers in professional development settings. Her case study of a teacher involved in the Scientific Literacy Institute embodied both the challenges and the possibilities of inquiry-based teaching in science education.

Chapter 8, "Capturing Teacher Learning, Curiosity, and Creativity through Science Notebooks," also addressed teacher professional development in science education. From the outset, authors Carole Basile and Sharon Johnson reminded readers that the teaching disposition of curiosity is dependent on how teachers understand the characteristic and how they respond to how it becomes manifested in children. Through using science notebooks as professional development tools with middle school science teachers, the authors showed how teachers' curiosity can be primed. In short, how teachers viewed content, pedagogy, and world views became imaginatively opened up in ways that inspired and informed how they taught youth in science classrooms.

Next, physical education was presented as a school subject in Chapter 9 by JeongAe You from South Korea. In "Freeing the Body to Build the Creative Mind," she presented two case studies that illuminated how teachers can promote lived body experiences in youth that create unity and wholeness in their beings, which automatically implicates their minds. In JeongAe You's view, physical education teachers must be cultivated as reflective intellectuals whose pedagogical aim is to integrate body and mind—for the betterment of both—and students as whole human beings.

Having focused on the content areas of mathematics, science, and physical education in Chapters 5–9, our final two chapters addressed the topic of culture in cross-cultural settings. Chapter 10, authored by Ming Fang He, Wynnetta Scott-Simmons, Angela Haynes, and Derrick Tennial, presented each of the authors' narrative trajectories where cultural, linguistic, and socio-economic understandings were concerned. These personal stories greatly informed how they choose to teach historically underserved students in in-between fashions, squarely facing deeply engrained challenges while unswervingly pursuing possibility.

Our final chapter in *Yearbook XVIII* was authored by Shijing Xu and Michael Connelly and was titled "On the Need for Curious and Creative Minds in Multicultural and Cross-Cultural Educational Settings: Narrative Possibilities." Emanating from Canada, the work focused on the universally important topic of the transnational flow of peoples and the need for reciprocity between newcomers and host cultures. For the authors, narrative curriculum and teaching methods that stress intergenerational family cultural educational histories are vital to cultivating curious and creative minds in children. In this way, possibilities of experiencing positive multicultural harmony amid diversity are compounded.

Taken together, this volume, which focuses on teaching, presents a provocative set of essays that develop the idea of curious and creative minds from a multitude of stances and through a kaleidoscope of teaching exemplars. The collection of essays furthermore indicates that there is much work to be done and endless ways it can be approached.

Afterword

Cheryl J. Craig

Louise F. Deretchin

Given the attention paid teaching and the nature of the current educational milieu, we thought it fitting to conclude *Cultivating Curious and Creative Minds: The Role of Teachers and Teacher Educators, Part I* with teachers' poetry, specifically, a poem freely authored by Daryl Wilson (pseudonym), a middle school teacher in one of Cheryl Craig's studies. Daryl's carefully selected words keenly reflect the contested nature of the educational environment that students and teachers maneuver daily. We furthermore believe that the authors in this volume provide sorely needed ideas about *being different* Daryl alludes to through their creation of live exemplars of how to think, teach, learn, interact—indeed live—differently. As editors, we salute their efforts and those of would-be and practicing teachers like Daryl. Such educators work with a rich vision of a more productive tomorrow for the youth of today.

Among Schoolchildren

With your bowed heads this gray January morning
We set about another state test
Careful to leave no child untested, behind
The tent cubicles box you in, neat boundaries
Around your imaginations
So you will not let them run lawlessly beyond the page
We say the skills tests are the ones you will need
To master if you are to live and prosper
So for days you put up with the grueling silences,
Give it your best shot, trusting as you are,
Somewhere between failure and hope.

From the back of the classroom just about your heads
A framed dog poster is looming, the usual Dalmatian spots
Have turned into living color
With eyes that plead *dare to be different.*